184

BUSINESSES ANYONE CAN START AND MAKE A LOT OF MONEY

2ND EDITION

BANTAM BUSINESS BOOKS

Ask your bookseller for the titles you have missed

Entrepreneur®

MAGAZINE'S

184

BUSINESSES ANYONE CAN START AND MAKE A LOT OF MONEY

2ND EDITION

THE EDITORS OF
Entrepreneur®

BANTAM BOOKS
NEW YORK · TORONTO · LONDON · SYDNEY · AUCKLAND

184 BUSINESSES ANYONE CAN START AND MAKE A LOT OF MONEY
A Bantam Book / August 1990

184 BUSINESSES ANYONE CAN START AND MAKE A LOT OF MONEY was first published in March 1981

Library of Congress Cataloging-in-Publication Data

Entrepreneur magazine's 184 businesses anyone can start and make a lot
of money / the editors of Entrepreneur. — 2nd ed.
    p. cm.
    Rev. ed. of: 168 more businesses anyone can start and make a lot
of money / Chase Revel. c1984.
    ISBN 0-553-34915-5
    1. New business enterprises. 2. Small business. 3. Success in
business. I. Revel, Chase. 168 more businesses anyone can start
and make a lot of money. II. Entrepreneur. III. Title:
Entrepreneur magazines one hundred eighty-four businesses anyone can
start and make a lot of money. IV. Title: 184 businesses anyone can
start and make a lot of money.
HD62.5.R48   1990
658.1'141—dc20   90-30236
                                                          CIP

Published simultaneously in the United States and Canada

PRINTED IN THE UNITED STATES OF AMERICA

OPM   0 9 8 7 6 5 4 3 2 1

CONTENTS

1

MISCELLANEOUS SERVICES

Contents

2
PERSONAL SERVICES

3
BUSINESS SERVICES

4
FOOD

5
RETAIL

6

SPORTS AND ENTERTAINMENT

7

AUTOMOTIVE BUSINESSES

8
PUBLISHING

9
OUT OF THE ORDINARY

ACKNOWLEDGMENTS

Thousands and thousands of hours of research have gone into creating this book. For much of it, we are indebted to the staff, past and present, of *Entrepreneur*® magazine. Particular thanks go to Maria Anton, Christine Forbes, Charles Fuller, Frances Huffman, Maria Johnson, Erika Kotite, Kevin McLaughlin, Frank Mixson, and Gayle Sato.

We'd also like to express our gratitude to Barbara Alpert of Bantam, a wonderful editor, who had the vision to bring these books to life.

Rieva Lesonsky, Editor
Clare N. Thain, Publisher
Entrepreneur® magazine

INTRODUCTION

The 1990s—there has never been a better time to start and operate your own business. Even the United States Congress recognizes the entrepreneurial revolution currently under-way in America and has declared the 1990s to be "The Decade of the Entrepreneur."

Every year, over one million Americans join this entrepreneurial revolution. In fact, business ownership has become one of the nation's biggest status symbols. Why? Some say they're fed up working hard to put money in someone else's pocket. Many believe they're underpaid and unappreciated for what they do. Others seek the satisfaction that only "charting your own course" brings. Whatever the reason, these entrepreneurial "recruits" have signed into an army over 20 million strong and growing.

Wouldn't you like to be one of them? Well, you can be. It's not as difficult or as frightening as you may think. At *Entrepreneur*® magazine, we know that business ownership serves as a great equalizer. There is no discrimination against a great new product or a much needed service. There are no "glass ceilings" to bump your head against. It doesn't matter what race, religion or sex you are. Age is of no importance. Over the 17 years we've been in business, we've seen successful businesses started by 16-year-olds, as well as those over 60.

You're probably wondering, if entrepreneurship is so great, why aren't there more entrepreneurs? What keeps so many from business ownership? Fear! People are afraid they don't have enough money to start a business. Or they can't think of a good business idea. Or they mistakingly think that their job offers them security, while entrepreneurship is too risky.

But taking the risk is essential to receiving the rewards. Remember, (at the risk of sounding like a high school coach), if you don't swing the bat, you'll never get a hit.

We're not saying that starting your own business is easy. It's not! But almost every entrepreneur we've ever met says the hard work that business start-up entails is worth it. Nothing, they say, equals the satisfaction and rewards (both financially and psychologically) of business ownership.

And, believe it or not, you don't need a lot of money to get started. Many of today's most successful entrepreneurs started their now-giant corporations out of their homes (or garages) on a very limited budget.

What about the idea? That's probably the easiest part. You don't necessarily have to reinvent the wheel. There are thousands of great ideas out there waiting for you to run with them. You don't have to be the first at anything to succeed. McDonalds was not the first hamburger joint. And the Colonel certainly did not invent fried chicken.

What you do need to do is be alert. Look around your community. What's lacking? Is someone doing something you could do better? Or quicker? Or cheaper? Chances are if there's a product or service you're personally seeking, but can't find, others in your area want it too. And they'd be willing to pay for it. Question your friends, neighbors, and relatives. Find the common thread.

Simply reading this book may be the spark you've been looking for. It is just one in a series from the editors of *Entrepreneur*® magazine. In it (and the others) you'll find hundreds of ideas for businesses you can start NOW!

Most important, you need to get started. A successful business owner once told me, "The biggest obstacle to business success is the four words, 'I think I'll wait.'" Don't let this happen to you. If you dream of someday owning your own business, pursue it. Sure, you're going to encounter obstacles and setbacks along the way. But determination and persistance pay off. You can turn your dreams into reality. Only one thing can hold you back: not getting started. Remember these words, written by Goethe, an 18-century poet, "Whatever you can do or dream, begin it. Boldness has genius, power and magic in it. Begin it now!"

Rieva Lesonsky, Editor
Clare N. Thain, Publisher
Entrepreneur® magazine

184

BUSINESSES ANYONE CAN START AND MAKE A LOT OF MONEY

2ND EDITION

MISCELLANEOUS SERVICES

SENIOR DAY-CARE CENTER

High Net Profit Before Taxes:	$61,000
Average Net Profit Before Taxes:	$40,000
Minimum Start-up:	$56,000
Average Start-up:	$80,000

It's time to take a second look at America's elderly. For one thing, they aren't feeble. Thanks to medical advances and healthier life-styles, people are living independently longer. Their ranks are growing. Baby boomers aren't babies anymore. In the next decade, the oldest of the lot will start retiring. During the 1970's, the number of Americans over the age of seventy-five surged by 32 percent to over 10 million. By the year 2000, that number is expected to reach 17 million.

Though many baby boomers will remain healthy through their twilight years, some will need care. Even now, adults are struggling with the dilemma of how best to care for their aging parents. Some require twenty-four-hour attention in nursing homes, but most need only minor supervision.

Balancing Care with Independence

Senior day-care centers are stepping in to fill this need, providing a safe, supportive environment for senior adults and offering a variety of health, social, and related services, including leisure activities, exercise classes, and most of all, companionship.

Senior day-care centers benefit both the elderly and their families. Seniors enjoy socializing and remaining relatively independent. Families feel secure knowing that someone is watching their parents. And both prefer day-care to the loneliness of nursing homes or the expense of private nurses.

Other factors contribute to the growth of this industry. Dual-income couples are more and more common, leaving little time to care for elderly parents. And while most elderly people don't need constant medical attention, many do need help running errands, preparing meals, or taking medication. The skyrocketing cost of institutional care is another factor. At an average cost of $79 a day, few people can afford nursing-home care. Senior day-care, by contrast, costs about $27 to $31 a day.

Finding the Right Site

The site you choose will depend on the services you want to offer. Many operators choose buildings with large, open rooms for flexibility. Furniture can be moved around to accommodate different activities, and the open space makes watching the clients easier. Some states have certain facilities requirements for senior day-care centers: check the requirements in your state.

In addition to a good location, you'll need a qualified staff. Most centers hire full-time staffers as well as contract specialists such as exercise instructors and art teachers to lead activities. Another important service you can offer is transportation. Meals, which most senior day-care centers offer, can be catered or prepared in-house.

Get the Word Out

There's no question that the need for senior day-care services is urgent. The problem is, many people who need these services don't know they exist. Until now, senior day-care centers have relied on word of mouth and referrals to find new clients. Now they're discovering the benefits of radio, television, and print ads.

If you're a strong marketer, you can make a big impact on this industry. In addition to advertising, you can cultivate free publicity by speaking to local community groups and sending press releases to the local media. Getting the word out about senior day-care will do more than help your business: it can also help millions of older adults who want to keep their independence but need a little support.

INSTANT PRINT AND COPY SHOP

High Net Profit Before Taxes:	$93,000
Average Net Profit Before Taxes:	$70,000
Minimum Start-up:	$50,000
Average Start-up:	$97,000

Until a few years ago, the printing business was dominated exclusively by people with technical skills in printing. In these ventures, besides needing a technical background, you had to invest a huge sum of money.

With the advent of automatic plate-making cameras such as Itek, and offset duplicators designed to produce good prints with simple operations, the printing industry saw a new idea catch on: instant printing.

That idea isn't new anymore. In the past several years, instant print shops have created a new industry. Overall printing growth in the past few years has risen by more than 700 percent. Depending on location, a well-run operation can expect to be in the black two months after the doors open. In certain urban areas, instant print shops become profitable so quickly that many shop owners open more than one site.

Business clients dominate the consumer end of the market. Companies large and small have an ongoing need for specialty-printed bill forms, invoices, and promotional literature.

Copy Concept Duplicates Success

In addition to printing, simple copying has also become a profitable practice. Copier manufacturers have made huge strides in the past decade or so. Today's machines are fast, efficient (they collate, fold, staple, and sort), and produce quality reproductions. In many cases, copying can take the place of simple print jobs.

Copying is a cheap alternative for consumers—and for copy-shop owners as well. Even if you only charge $0.05 a copy, you can turn a tidy profit. And your cash outlay is not especially great. By combining copy services with simple offset printing, you can create a winning business.

Who Are the Copy Cats?

Potential customers for an instant print business are everywhere. Every nearby business office and every pedestrian that walks past your business is a potential customer for brochures, resumes, fliers, announcements, and many other kinds of short-run printing jobs. Even large printing companies occasionally send out overflow work to outside printers. Copy services are equally in demand. Just try to remember the last time you used carbon paper.

An additional market is the desktop publishing trade. By purchasing a Macintosh or IBM-compatible computer, a high-grade laser printer, related software, and a modem, you can target the cottage industry of the eighties and nineties—renting equipment to small publishing presses whose headquarters are literally 4-by-6 desktops, from which newsletters, magazines, books, and other journals are being cranked out in ever-larger numbers.

Best Locations

Although customers may seem to be everywhere, choosing the right location for your instant print/copy shop can be a major factor in its success or failure. The best locations for this type of business are strip shopping centers and single-site stores in heavily trafficked urban or suburban business districts.

Look for an area densely populated with small offices, which require occasional copying and printing but seldom have the volume to justify leasing or purchasing their own equipment. They'll be among your prime customers.

An ideal location is a business district that is also within walking distance of a college or university. Your customer mix will range from individuals off the street to students, professors, and the neighboring businesses.

Avoid areas made up primarily of medium- to large-sized businesses. Most likely, they'll have their own copiers and their printing will be handled by a larger firm. At most, you'll get their overflow work.

Making Yourself Stand Out

With all the growth in this industry of late, the biggest challenge to starting an instant print and copy shop is finding a way to make yourself stand out. Although some cities have shops like these on every corner, the existence of competition shouldn't scare you. There may yet be gaps in the market.

One way to grab your share of the market is to offer superior service. Visit print and copy shops in your area and get a feeling for their pricing, turnaround times, and attention to detail. Can you beat them on any count? Do their customers seem satisfied?

Can you offer any services that your potential competitors don't? Many copy shops now have fax machines, so that clients can send and receive faxes without buying their own equipment. Has this phenomenon hit your local copy shops yet? Consider providing pickup and delivery services to local businesses. Or think about offering a guaranteed eight-hour turnaround.

Instant print and copy services have become virtually indispensable to small businesses across the country. That people will continue to frequent them is a given. Outstanding service, marketing, and management will determine which shops will be there to capitalize on that business.

PACKAGING AND SHIPPING STORE

High Net Profit Before Taxes:	$125,000
Average Net Profit Before Taxes:	$ 61,000
Minimum Start-up:	$ 16,000
Average Start-up:	$ 29,000

Few places provoke greater despair than a post office line. The movement is slow (more like glacial) and the atmosphere isn't exactly festive. A single post office line can kill a lunch hour. And that doesn't account for the hours you spend hunting down boxes, packing tape, and labels just to get your package ready for shipping.

If you believe there should be a better way, put your money where your mouth is and open a packaging and shipping store. Alternative postal centers began popping up in the early eighties. Now they're an essential part of doing business for small companies and individual consumers around the country.

Better Than the PO

Aside from standard packaging and shipping services, many companies increase profits by adding extra services and products, including:

- Photocopying
- Greeting cards
- Gift wrapping
- Money orders
- Key duplication
- Passport photos
- Postage stamps
- Document shredding
- Facsimile communication
- Private mailboxes
- Western Union
- Secretarial duties, and
- Resume/business communications

Packaging and shipping centers are a special boon to small business owners, who can have access to the latest office equipment and support services without the equipment and staffing expenses.

Shop for the Best Location

Look for a 1,000-to-2,000-square-foot shop with good docking access for shipping companies. Since small businesses are a primary target market, try to find a location that's convenient to local businesses. If your location is less than ideal, consider offering pickup and delivery services.

In addition to steady business clients, your business may experience consumer rushes during the Christmas, Mother's Day, and Father's Day/Graduation seasons, especially if you're in a visible and accessible location. Be prepared to hire extra temporary help during these peak times to keep the customers moving. You can encourage new business at these times through aggressive advertising. One successful operator reports that coupon ads are most effective.

================ BRIGHT IDEA ================

BE KIND TO BLINDS

Now that we all went out and bought miniblinds for our living rooms, kitchens, bathrooms, and garages (not to mention the office), how do we clean them?

The answer is, we don't. And that's precisely why Stan Morantz got into the blind-cleaning business. His Philadelphia company, S. Morantz Inc., manufactures and sells blind-cleaning equipment for entrepreneurs who have it in their hearts to be kind to blinds.

Morantz's machine cleans all types of blinds, from standard venetian to mini- and wood blinds, via an ultrasonic process. By the manufacturer's account, this is the only effective way to clean dirt, grime, and grease off these slippery fixtures.

"When people clean blinds with regular soap and water, static electricity counteracts the process and merely wipes the dirt from one side to the other," Morantz maintains. "The sound-frequency method our system uses removes dirt, grime, and odor in a matter of seconds. [In addition] the machine has almost thirty other applications."

Morantz's equipment starts at about $10,000. According to Morantz, the machines are portable and fit into any station wagon or van. Thus, it's possible to clean blinds on location at office buildings or high-rise apartments. Though this business hasn't caught on the way carpet cleaning has—yet—it does show a certain promise. "It's a ground-floor business opportunity," argues Morantz, "just like buying into McDonalds in the first stages of its introduction. The possibilities are endless."

TRAVEL AGENCY

High Net Profit Before Taxes:	$125,000 plus
Average Net Profit Before Taxes:	$ 55,000
Minimum Start-up:	$ 12,500
Average Start-up:	$ 25,000

A hundred years ago, the notion of an average person traveling around the country—and indeed around the world—was nothing short of preposterous. Today, it's commonplace. For business and for pleasure, Americans jet from city to city and country to country almost at the drop of a hat. That in addition to various train, boat, bus, bike, and balloon trips. All told, U.S. travelers spend nearly $300 billion annually on travel.

Working for the Agency

Travel agencies provide an effective distribution network through which travel companies can sell their products. And they offer inexpensive consultation for leisure and business travelers. Since their inception in the early 1900's, travel agents or consultants have gained in popularity by making travel as uncomplicated as possible.

While travel agents book an enormous amount of business for airlines, cruise lines, railroads, buses, car rentals, tours, and lodging facilities, a large segment of the population still believes that agents charge fees for their services. Not so. Travel agents get their money from commissions paid by travel companies for selling their products. The average commission on a travel package is 10 percent.

A Changing Industry

In recent years, travel agencies have dealt with more than a growing market. Widespread deregulation has caused a major stir in the agency business. Today, travel agencies are still adapting to the effects of deregulation.

In the future, agencies will compete more on the basis of price and quality of service. Discount agencies will start to pop up, along with specialty agencies that charge fees for personalized business and vacation packages. Agencies may also start looking beyond normal channels to take advantage of the deregulated market. Travel agencies have much easier access to local tours and state tours with the deregulation of the motorcoach industry. And cruise lines, tours, and hotels still rely on travel agencies as a highly effective distribution network.

Starting an agency now requires creativity and vision. You must make decisions as to which markets you'll pursue. Who will you target and what products will appeal to this market? Remember that owning a travel agency is not necessarily a passport to sudden wealth. For example, a newer agency with $500,000 in gross sales volume and an average commission of 10 percent will have a gross profit of only $50,000. A new travel agency may take one to two years to reach the break-even point, although we have found operators who have gone into the black in five months under near-perfect conditions.

All this isn't meant to discourage you from the business. You should know, however, that making a new agency work will take more than just hanging out a shingle. If you have the drive to achieve the needed volume, and the management skills to keep your overhead low, you can make a good living in the travel business.

Business or Pleasure?

The two primary markets for the independent agency are small business accounts and leisure travel. While many large companies are using national chains to handle their travel arrangements, many small businesspeople prefer to work with independent agents. For many small agencies, small business accounts make up about 50 percent of overall business.

Most experts agree that the future of the small agency lies in the leisure market, where national chains have less impact, if any. Individuals traveling for pleasure, including tour groups, make up the other 50 percent of small-agency business.

Vacationing travelers are looking for individual service. They want a customized vacation and personal counseling— something they can't get at big agencies. One agency we found specializes in private yacht cruises. Though vacationers pay for the service of setting the trips up and the cruise itself is more expensive than a cruise-line package, clients receive a lot for their money, such as personal consultation and services geared to their tastes and life-styles.

Another major emphasis is budget travel. Economy fares and low-end tours have boosted airline revenues and the size of the overall market. Some travel agencies cater specifically to this market, stressing high volume and quick turnaround to keep their own revenues up. Budget travel is a category unto itself. Consumers tend to be young people or the elderly. They have a lot of questions to ask, problems with price, and changes of mind. However, if you're adept at working quickly and can attract a good volume, this business can be lucrative.

Other specialties are also being developed. Among them, incentive travel—helping corporate clients set up travel award programs. You might also wish to check into the market in your area for educational tours, unusual vacations, bed-and-breakfast rentals—use your imagination. Americans are traveling more today than ever before. With the right mix of services, you can make your business an integral part of their travel plans.

VINYL REPAIR SERVICE

High Net Profit Before Taxes:	$50,000 plus
Average Net Profit Before Taxes:	$35,000
Minimum Start-up:	$ 3,500
Average Start-up:	$10,000

We live in a plastic, vinyl, and Naugahyde world, from auto upholstery to restaurant seats, bar stools to casual furniture. Until something better comes along, automakers and furniture manufacturers will continue to churn out several million yards of plastic covering that sooner or later will be nicked, burned, cracked, or torn.

Vinyl repair services color, mend, and patch up the damage. Several manufacturers sell vinyl repair kits, and many even offer training to go along with it. When done properly, vinyl repairs are virtually undetectable.

One vinyl repairperson we spoke to left a job in the aerospace industry to start his own repair service. Although he was a successful engineer, the ups and downs of aerospace employment began to wear on his patience. His neighbor, a vinyl repairperson, suggested he give the business a try. Nine years later, our former engineer found himself with four specially equipped trucks and gross sales of $200,000 a year. His annual net income before taxes: $60,000.

This example isn't an isolated one. We encountered many vinyl repair firms that were equally successful. The trick to being competitive in this business is good management. Many people get into vinyl repair because it's a low-investment business and relatively easy to learn. But not everyone has the business savvy to make the business work. If you're a crack manager and marketer, you can take this business by storm.

Remember that vinyl repair is a service industry. If you can't approach a customer, discuss his or her problem intelligently, and gain his or her confidence, you won't be very successful.

Where's the Market?

The majority of your business will come from three sources: auto dealers, fleet owners, restaurants, furniture dealers, hotels, motels, and bars. There's a lot of business to be obtained from homes and offices as well, but people in these markets do not know about vinyl repair. Marketing to a market that doesn't know about your services will take extra time and money.

Used-car dealers are a lucrative source of income for the vinyl repairperson. Not only do cuts and nicks in the seats and upholstery need repair, but vinyl tops are also prone to weather damage and must be recolored as well as repaired. Once you have established a working relationship with a car dealership, it may require your services on a monthly basis.

Restaurants, hotels, motels, and bars also need regular servicing. Along with the regular wear and tear their upholstery receives from constant use, outright vandalism sometimes occurs, creating more business for you.

Used-office-furniture dealers are another good source of business, although few exist in some cities. These dealers buy up offices full of furniture from bankrupt, relocating, or redecorating companies, and know that the smallest nick in a secretarial chair can reduce its resale value by 50 percent.

Furniture stores are a good source of retail customers. Occasionally, they have a piece that's been damaged in their warehouse or showroom. Also, their customers are likely to call them for referrals to repairpeople.

Municipal-bus lines, taxi companies, school-bus companies, car-rental agencies, bowling alleys, theaters, schools, colleges, auditoriums, landlords of furnished apartments, boat owners, and beauty shops are other prime prospects.

CHECK-CASHING SERVICE

High Net Profit Before Taxes:	$112,000
Average Net Profit Before Taxes:	$ 78,000
Minimum Start-up:	$ 67,000
Average Start-up:	$ 80,000

Some people may remember the days after the stock market crash in 1929, when panic-stricken Americans made a run on the banks. Now something else is happening—a run from the banks.

According to some estimates, about 20 percent of Americans have no formal banking relationship. These are people who work and collect regular paychecks, but pay their bills with money orders—for everything else, they pay cash. Some of these people rely on local supermarkets or liquor stores to cash their payroll checks. Others have employers that will cash them. For the rest, there is a great need to find places where they can cash their payroll and personal checks, draw money orders, and wire money via Western Union. Enter check-cashing services.

This Is Not a Bank

Check-cashing services are privately run enterprises that have nothing to do with banks. They are not federally regulated, they do not make loans, and they do not offer checking or savings accounts. They simply provide a service to people who are unable to cash their checks easily anywhere else.

Since deregulation of financial services in the early eighties, the cost to banks for offering basic services has increased. Many banks have deemphasized their services for the smaller retail customer by increasing service charges, phasing out drive-up windows, and even closing some of their branches, especially in lower-income areas. It simply was no longer profitable to service the smaller accounts, let alone cash checks for people who had no accounts in the first place.

In response, small "no-frills" check-cashing establishments started popping up, usually in lower-income or industrial areas. They allowed people with little or no identification to cash their checks for a percentage of the face value. They also offered money orders for a small fee, postal services, national wiring services, and other conveniences. The modern-day check-cashing service was born, and today it is a thriving small business.

Making Money from Money

One Portland, Oregon, entrepreneur opened his first store in 1982 and now heads a franchise of forty operations in five states. Some of the stores average nearly $200,000 in gross annual sales, cashing an average of a hundred checks a day. Most of his stores also offer extra services such as money orders and nationwide currency wiring, at little or no profit, just to make the check-cashing service more attractive. With everything under one roof, his customers can receive cash and pay their bills all in one place. "We consider ourselves the 7-Eleven of banking," he boasts.

A Changing Image

In the beginning, check-cashing centers were established primarily in low-income areas where there was a high percentage of welfare recipients, transient workers, and illegal aliens, who could cash their payroll checks without fear of information being transferred to the authorities. Knowing their customers had little choice but to come to them, some operators unscrupulously charged as much as 20 or 25 percent of a check's face value to people who could ill afford the expense. Thus, check-cashing facilities acquired an unsavory reputation as "welfare banks" and gougers.

Now there's a broader customer base. For example, young construction workers who move frequently from town to town often find banks too slow and unsympathetic to their nomadic life-style. Also, newcomers to the community, college students, and those who are simply fed up with long lines and inconvenient hours are turning to reputable check-cashing services for their needs. As a result, such businesses are locating in better neighborhoods, paying more attention to their storefront appearance, and offering lower check-cashing rates in addition to other services like theater tickets and bus passes.

The main selling point now is convenience. Most centers are open from 9 A.M. to 9 P.M. six or seven days a week. Lines are usually short. And no holds are placed on checks—customers get their cash on the spot with the right identification.

Though contemporary check-cashing services don't adhere to the old welfare-bank image, this is still not a business for the upscale. Since many are located in tough neighborhoods, a good security system and insurance are essential.

The Future

According to the American Banking Association, many banks are reviewing their current policies regarding check cashing. In the future, banks may have to cash government checks if they want to continue to receive government deposits. Also, some consumer and community action groups are pushing for basic banking—no-interest checking accounts with reduced fees and no minimum balance for low-income customers. So far, however, banks have been reluctant to take on these policies because they are not profitable. Check-cashing businesses can provide the necessary services conveniently for their customers, and profitably for themselves.

Right now, the check-cashing industry is fragmented. Franchises do exist, but so far they do not dominate the market. This business has a strong profit potential—you can make as much as $37,000 in pretax profits your very first year. You also have a business with liquid inventory and a surprisingly small percentage of lost fees due to returned checks.

In this age of convenience, top-heavy corporations are getting stiff competition from smaller, more streamlined operations. Reduced staff, specialized services, and freedom from regulations allow check-cashing services to concentrate on what they do best—cashing checks quickly, with a minimum of identification from their customers.

One operator we talked to believes that more people are taking their business to check-cashing centers, not just because of the convenience, but because they receive more personal attention there than at the banks. "We just want to make it possible for someone with a low income to come to a check-cashing store and get money," he says. And that's good news for everyone.

DRY-CLEANING SHOP

High Net Profit Before Taxes:	$ 60,000 plus
Average Net Profit Before Taxes:	$ 40,000
Minimum Start-up:	$102,000
Average Start-up:	$150,000

According to recent estimates, over $2.5 billion a year is spent on professional fabric care. In the last fifteen years, sales of non-self-service dry cleaning have increased by almost 50 percent. About 30,000 dry-cleaning establishments currently operate nationwide. Of these, 95 percent are independently owned and operated: small businesses, not chains and franchises, dominate this industry.

Several factors contribute toward the popularity of dry cleaners. On the business side, cleaners are working faster and producing more, thereby increasing their volume. But the market has changed as well. Working women don't have time to fuss with delicate washables: it's easier to let the cleaner do it. Moreover, working women wear more dry-cleanable clothing, making trips to the cleaners a must. And with today's clothing prices, it's no wonder people want to take good care of their garments. Even supposedly washable clothes don't always stand up to repeated washings.

Be Prepared to Invest

Opening a dry-cleaning shop is not a cheap proposition. Plan to spend at least $100,000 to get your business up and running—maybe even closer to $200,000.

On the upside, though, successful dry cleaners make substantial profits. Many well-run shops net between $40,000 and $100,000 or more per year. We discovered a two-store operation grossing $456,000 and netting almost $210,000 before taxes.

Your largest up-front expense will be equipment. If your budget is limited, consider buying used equipment. It's possible to find good used goods for less than half the price you'd pay new. Be sure to shop carefully, though. Make sure the equipment is in good condition and meets all current safety standards. Check all valves and gasket casings to ensure that chemical toxins can't leak, and inspect shafts, bearings, and other metallic parts for signs of corrosion.

If you decide to buy new equipment, solicit bids from at least four distributors or manufacturers. Each will have a different concept of your equipment needs, and quotes you get will likely vary by wide margins. Sharp operators advise that you be wary of sales reps who stress the top-drawer approach to equipment buying. Having the newest and best in equipment may be desirable, but it isn't always necessary.

Think Upscale

The primary market for dry-cleaning establishments is urban and suburban residents with moderate to above-average incomes. Dual-income households are particularly desirable. Childless couples, young marrieds, and singles are the cream of the crop. They entertain more, go out more often for recreation, and most of the women work. Professional, dress-for-success types are the most likely to have dry-cleanable clothes.

Of course, this information is no secret to your competition. To attract customers, you'll have to be smarter than the average cleaner. Finding a good, convenient location is a must. But many bright operators are going one step beyond. Delivery and drive-thru services are two popular alternatives. Another is discounting. Dry cleaners that charge $1.00 per garment may not enjoy the same margins that more conventional cleaners do, but they make up for it in volume. For $1.00 people will bring almost anything in for dry cleaning—and they'll bring things in more often.

INTERIOR DESIGN

High Net Profit Before Taxes:	$113,700
Average Net Profit Before Taxes:	$ 53,500
Minimum Start-up:	$ 9,130
Average Start-up:	$ 15,500

Looking for an outlet for your creative talents—one that can bring in over $100,000 a year in net profits if you're successful? Look no further. In both the commercial and residential markets, people are turning to interior designers for help as never before. One reason is the high cost of real estate: people are more likely to make do by sprucing up a smaller space than to run out and buy or rent a more luxurious one. Another is that time—either at work or at home—is at a premium these days. Neither businesspeople nor homeowners have the leisure to map out a floor plan, pick out furniture and carpeting, and make sure everything is installed as planned.

If you have an eye for color and design and a mind for details, this could be the business you're looking for. You can start for less than $10,000 (though a larger investment in the $15,000 range is more common).

Keep the Balls Rolling

What's a typical day like for an interior designer? Routine tasks include figuring out where to place electrical outlets in a room and deciding how to alter the existing plumbing facilities to accommodate a new bathtub. In between, a designer may supervise carpet installation at one site, watch the wallpaper go up at another, and help hang artwork at yet a third.

Designers spend only about 15 to 25 percent of their time "conceptualizing"—drawing up designs. The rest of the time they're out seeking new clients, tracking down suppliers, supervising installations, and generally troubleshooting. And since designers typically work on a variety of projects at one time, just keeping track of what needs to be done—and when—can be a mind-boggling task. But keeping the balls rolling is a major part of a designer's job.

Going Commercial

Many designers choose to specialize in either commercial or residential design, while others prefer to work in both fields. Keeping your fingers in both pies has its advantages. If there's an economic downturn affecting one market, for instance, you'll still have your other accounts.

Otherwise, developing a specialty may give your new business credibility. For designers who choose to specialize, commercial design is generally the more lucrative field. Contract design (which does not include all commercial projects but only those on which a designer must bid) is a $47 billion market.

Commercial and contract designers say that the majority of their projects are offices. However, offices certainly aren't the only type of assignment in this field. Hotels, restaurants, retail stores, schools, colleges, medical facilities, and financial institutions all need the touch of an expert designer.

Prices for commercial projects vary according to the amount of work necessary—from several thousand dollars for a simple refurbishing to more than a million dollars for a large facility. Most independent designers start out working on small-scale projects and graduate to larger projects when they're established and respected. Designers who have been in business less than two years generally handle between twenty and forty small- or medium-sized projects per year, and gross between $300,000 and $500,000.

No Place Like Home

While commercial design may be lucrative, there's no shortage of interest in residential design. The average cost of a residential project is more than $35,000. Residential projects fall into three basic categories: new dwellings, remodeling, and renovations. This may include an entire home or a single room. According to a survey by Brouillard Communications, living rooms are the number-one project for residential designers.

Even though residential projects normally don't rival commercial projects in terms of size, they do present a real profit potential for the designer. One home-based designer in Texas specializes in renovating historical homes. Her projects range in price from $60,000 to $125,000 each, and by doing only three such projects a year, she brings in an impressive revenue.

Profits for Problem-Solving

Designers see problem-solving as one of their main functions, and the best of them pride themselves on patience, innovation, and resourcefulness. This is not a business for the easily flustered. Service people can skip out, furniture can arrive late, fabrics can be discontinued—the list of potential setbacks is long. Before you go into this business, make sure you have the mettle to get through these little disasters.

For people who do, the rewards can be great—not just financially but emotionally as well. Designers say that there's no greater feeling of accomplishment than seeing a finished project. These rewards can be yours. With a good background in design, a flair for harmonizing colors and styles, adaptability, and a sound marketing strategy, you could find yourself designing a profitable future.

===================== BRIGHT IDEA =====================

DESIGNING WOMAN

Employing the expertise of a home decorator used to be something that only the rich could afford. But according to Karen Fisher, president of Decorator Previews, the decorating industry has changed considerably.

"I draw most of my customers from a base that's comprised of dual-income, middle-class couples," Fisher explains.

A former interior-design editor for top magazines like *Cosmopolitan*, this New York City–based entrepreneur matches individuals and companies with qualified interior designers, architects, and landscapers for a flat fee of $100.

"I interview the client to determine exactly what they're looking for," she says. "Then I show slides of different looks to get their impressions." Fisher then shows the client portfolios of decorators who can create the looks they want.

Fisher's business has been so successful that she started licensing the concept in 1987. So far, Decorator Previews has offices in Los Angeles; San Francisco; Chicago; Westport, Connecticut; and Washington, D.C.

Fisher stresses that setting yourself apart from the competition is important. She says, "If you pay attention to what you're doing and do it differently than the rest of the world, you'll succeed."

CHILD-CARE SERVICE

High Net Profit Before Taxes:	$55,000
Average Net Profit Before Taxes:	$40,000
Minimum Start-up:	$62,000
Average Start-up:	$80,000

Thirty or forty years ago, parents didn't have to worry about child care. Wives usually stayed at home to care for their children while husbands pursued their careers. In the majority of families today, however, a single wage earner can no longer support the household. And even among those couples who can afford to live on one income, many wives are choosing careers over homemaking. Add to this trend the increasing number of single women having children and divorced parents sharing custody, and the need for child care becomes apparent.

New Alternatives Sought

Traditionally, child care has consisted of family day care, which takes place in the home of the provider; center-based care, which occurs in a freestanding facility; and in-home care, provided by a relative or hired employee. Within these parameters, a whole raft of options is open to aspiring entrepreneurs.

One of the most promising in terms of growth is the freestanding child-care center. Well-staffed facilities designed especially for day care have a special appeal for working parents who want more for their children than baby-sitting. By putting the emphasis on quality care—learning experiences, proper supervision, and safe facilities—professional day-care centers easily compete with smaller, cottage-industry home-care operations. Start-up costs for a top-flight operation aren't cheap: licensing, insurance, and facilities can run as high as $500,000. On the other hand, experts estimate that in 1990, there will be over 20 million children in need of care—an ample and growing market.

If this kind of venture sounds out of your league, consider a more innovative approach. Some of the businesses we've encountered over the years:

- Nanny training and placement
- After-school care
- Sick-child care
- Drop-in and temporary care
- Summer enrichment programs
- Nursery schools
- Day-care resource and referral
- Contracted services for employers and developers
- Supplying child-care providers
- Enrichment programs for child-care centers
- Publishing child-care directories and updates
- Seminars and workshops for providers, employers, and parents

Meeting the Requirements

If you're interested in setting up a child-care service, your first step should be contacting your state government for licensing requirements. These vary from state to state and have a significant bearing on your proposed business. In some states, tough requirements make running a profitable day-care center nearly impossible—in others, the rules are more amenable to business. Find out what you're up against before you get started. The cost of meeting state requirements will play a vital role in your business's viability.

One critical factor in setting up a successful day-care center is location. Suburban areas where there are a lot of young families are an obvious choice. Alternatively, you may want to consider locating near businesses. In some cases, a large company or business-park developer may want an on-site day-care center and may offer to help you set up.

Wherever you locate, plan to run a tight ship. Providing quality care costs money, and parents can only afford to pay so much for that care. You'll walk a thin line between expenses and income, so good management is a must.

PERSONAL SHOPPING SERVICE

High Net Profit Before Taxes:	$46,000
Average Net Profit Before Taxes:	$28,000
Minimum Start-up:	$ 3,300
Average Start-up:	$11,300

Once upon a time, there were the Cleavers—Mr. and Mrs. Cleaver, Wally, and Theodore. Mrs. Cleaver was a homemaker. She kept house, cooked, and shopped. She shopped for groceries, she shopped for her children's school clothes, and she shopped for the neighbor's fiftieth-anniversary present. Whatever happened to Mrs. Cleaver? Well, she's still around, only now she works outside the home, picks her kids up from day care, comes home, and does most of the cooking. She barely has time to go grocery shopping and puts off buying Christmas presents until December 22. Mrs. Cleaver needs help.

Who Needs Shopping Services?

Personal shopping services began to emerge about ten years ago, when women started swelling the ranks of the work force in unprecedented numbers. The one-income household was becoming the exception rather than the rule. New priorities were being placed on saving time instead of money. From there, it was a natural progression to the idea of a service of business that took the hassles of shopping off of busy people's hands—for a profit.

Another factor in the popularity of personal shopping services is that many stores today have adopted a self-service format in order to cut down on personnel and delivery costs. Customers now make their own selections, weigh their own produce, take their merchandise to the checkout counter, and transport it home, with little or no assistance from anyone in the store. And even with express lines, specialized inventories, and shopping malls, finding what you need can be a tedious and time-consuming chore that many would pay anything to escape.

Professional shoppers know the best stores, the best brands, and the best prices. They can complete errands much more quickly and efficiently than their clients ever could. Indeed, for corporate clients, sending out a professional secretary to find client gifts is much more inefficient and costly than hiring a personal shopping service.

Find a Focus

As a personal shopper, you can choose to keep your service general, or you can specialize in any number of fields. For instance, as a wardrobe shopper, you can coordinate outfits for busy working women. Some successful shopping services specialize in groceries. If you specialize in gift shopping, plan to work with a lot of male clients who don't know where to shop, as well as professional women who don't have the time.

Most personal shoppers we talked to pursue corporate accounts. In this business, it's worth the time and trouble required to attract corporate clients, because they purchase in high volume and, if satisfied, they remain long and loyal customers.

What Does It Take?

This business does not require a large start-up investment or heavy overhead costs. With careful cost-cutting, you can get into the business for as little as $3,300. You can begin with little more than a telephone, answering machine, and business cards. Good service and aggressive marketing will determine your volume of business.

Above all, you must be a good shopper. Making money shopping may sound easy, but experienced operators warn that it's not as simple as it looks. You must possess a creative flair, especially for wardrobe shopping, as well as an excellent knowledge of your area's retail outlets. You won't be able to find everything at your local mall: you'll be sourcing items at independent boutiques, thrift stores, and even auctions.

Also, you must be able to manage your time wisely. Successful personal shoppers use "preshopping" strategies such as store catalog and mail-order research, consolidating shopping trips, and good telephone detective work. The fewer hours you spend searching for an item, the more clients you can handle. Many personal shoppers have good connections with retailers and wholesalers and know where to get the best deals or the biggest selection.

If you consider yourself an expert shopper—faster than the average Beverly Hills housewife, more capable than the average secretary, able to buy cheap gifts that look like they cost a fortune—this could be the ideal business for you. When you combine something you enjoy doing with a profitable venture, the result is almost always positive.

TOOL AND EQUIPMENT RENTAL SERVICE

High Net Profit Before Taxes:	$45,000
Average Net Profit Before Taxes:	$30,000
Minimum Start-up:	$37,000
Average Start-up:	$80,000

Twenty years ago, tool and small equipment rental businesses were almost unheard of. Today, there are over 10,000 rental outlets throughout the nation and they gross over $2 billion annually.

The industry has enjoyed an average growth rate of about 15 percent and shows no sign of slowdown over the next five years. Many operators who got into tool renting during its infancy believe that the business has just begun to show its real potential. By their accounts, the predicted future growth rates are conservative. Many are enjoying a 20-percent annual increase in business and expect it to continue.

Consumers and businesses alike have shown a tremendous interest in renting. Some people in the industry envision giant rental supermarkets with all types of reusable items for rent. Delivery is expected to become increasingly important in this business, as most of the business will be conducted by phone (today, it is done in person).

A New Era—Renting Instead of Owning

What kinds of items make good rental material? The list is practically limitless. Anything from power lawn mowers to party equipment can work.

Businesspeople and consumers have acquired a new attitude toward the use of their money. Pride of ownership is giving way to a more realistic desire to get the most from each dollar. Instead of buying a complete set of camping gear, a consumer can rent the equipment and use the money saved to rent skis in the winter and a sailboat in the summer. Similarly, a new business can rent a copy machine for a fraction of what it costs to buy one, and rent a fax machine with the extra money.

Do-it-yourselfers are a prime market. Though home-owners have been doing their own home repairs for centuries, today they are also concerned about conserving their leisure time. They don't want to give up their weekends, breaking their backs to put in a new lawn or build a patio by hand. They want modern professional equipment to get the job done quickly and efficiently. But the only way they can afford that equipment is to rent it.

Businesses are also key customers—especially small firms looking for ways to expand on limited capital. Renting enables these companies to get the equipment they need without depleting their capital reserves.

This formula works for hospitals, too. Government-subsidized health-care programs, longer life spans, and the high cost of hospitalizing geriatric patients have made the rental of medical equipment a lucrative and fast-growing industry.

The concept of a rental company is simple: buy some equipment and rent it out. Of course, operating the business is a bit more complicated than that. You'll need an adequate storage facility, a good inventory and accounting system, and a marketable selection of goods. But following certain guidelines, anyone can put together a rental store and operate it successfully.

==================== BRIGHT IDEA ====================

ETIQUETTE COUNSELING

Is your climb up the corporate ladder not going as fast as you'd like? Maybe it's because you drank out of the finger bowl the last time the boss took you to lunch. If you're upwardly mobile but socially inept, Judy Kaufman & Company's Etiquette International Division, based in Beverly

Hills, California, can help. "We teach you how to succeed in business when you're really trying," says Kaufman.

For $1,500, Kaufman offers corporate clients twelve-hour courses in business etiquette and corporate savoir faire. Her students include forward-looking executives at companies like First Interstate Bancorp, Southern California Gas, and Someone's in the Kitchen.

Kaufman's various services include developing in-house publicity campaigns to boost awareness of business etiquette, or evaluating a company's existing approach to etiquette and suggesting ways to improve it, or even setting up in-house executive training programs. Upon request she will work with individual families—for instance, at the dinner table—imparting etiquette skills for more harmonious interaction among family members. Most recently, she has branched out, adding a program "to integrate principles of citizenship, confidence, and consideration into school-district curricula."

WINDOW WASHING

High Net Profit Before Taxes:	$37,500
Average Net Profit Before Taxes:	$21,540
Minimum Start-up:	$ 500
Average Start-up:	$ 570

In the window-washing business, you can think big or small. Many entrepreneurs get started with just a bucket, squeegee, some rags, and cleaning solution. That and a little elbow grease puts them in business. But larger endeavors also exist. Some window-washing firms specialize in retail stores, factories, and high-rise office buildings.

Needless to say, the equipment, manpower, and financial requirements for each type of window-washing firm vary significantly. But the demand is relatively constant. Every window in every home, apartment, office, and shop gets dirty. And often, it's professional window-cleaning services that get them clean.

Fast Growth Possible

Even if you start small, you can parlay your investment into a fairly lucrative venture. One operator we spoke to hired four employees during his first year in business. His monthly gross at the end of that first year was $6,500. His monthly net was $3,200.

The steadiest market for window-washing services is commercial buildings. Retail storefronts and small office buildings don't require much special equipment. And commercial-building managers are usually interested in keeping the place looking clean. In time, and with an additional investment, you can expand your commerical window-cleaning business to include high-rise services.

Low Investment

The minimum initial investment for a window-cleaning company is ridiculously low—$500 is not unworkable. And you don't even have to invest that until you get your first client. If you're looking for a simple business that requires a small cash outlay and offers substantial growth potential, this could be the business for you.

GIFT-BASKET SERVICE

High Net Profit Before Taxes:	$63,000
Average Net Profit Before Taxes:	$41,000
Minimum Start-up:	$11,600
Average Start-up:	$39,000

In just the past two or three years, gift-basket services have blossomed by the hundreds into part-time and full-time businesses across the United States. For new business owners, gift-basket making represents a low-investment business that's flexible (you can work from a retail shop or from home), creative, and lucrative. Gift baskets are hot sellers—a trend that promises to continue.

Making gift baskets means combining attractive wicker baskets (or any other creative container) with goodies, flowers, gifts, etc., all arranged in a special design. Most gift baskets have themes and can be custom-made for just about anybody. The best part is, everybody loves to give and receive these baskets. It's one of the most popular ways to give a gift today—and it's one of the hottest service businesses around. Although there aren't any exact statistics on the gift-basket industry, it is estimated that this is a multimillion-dollar industry. And it's still growing.

The Bottom Line

Gift-basket services can be started with just a few thousand dollars. Your biggest expense is start-up inventory such as baskets, ribbons, plastic wrap, and all the products to be put inside the baskets. Equipment needs are minimal—a telephone, typewriter, small file cabinet, and maybe a cashbox will get you started. A shrink-wrap machine and glue gun are also helpful to give the gift basket a professional look. And remember to give yourself plenty of work space to create your works of art.

After that, you're limited only by the number of baskets you can produce each day. Think about it—it isn't unusual to make and sell an average of ten baskets a day, and if each basket sells for $35 to $50, the gross intake for one day is $350 to $500. As a home-based business with part-time help and few equipment needs, a gift-basket service can bring in as much as $120,000 in gross annual sales.

Setup Options

There are several ways to set up a gift-basket service. One way is to operate out of a home or a small leased space and sell baskets by phone order only. You won't have to shoulder the cost of renting and running a retail operation. However, this method requires more marketing because it's difficult for people to remember you're there.

Another method is to start a gift-basket mail-order service. This is a little more complicated, since it involves producing a catalog and renting mailing lists. It does, on the other hand, offer the potential to make substantially more money.

The third alternative is to start a retail shop and sell gift baskets as well as other gift merchandise. If it's in a good location, such as a mall or a bustling downtown center, visibility and attractive window displays will draw in the customers. This is a more expensive venture and your start-up costs may be as much as $45,000 to $50,000.

No matter which setup you choose, your customers will probably expect you to provide packaging and shipping services as well. This is especially true at the holidays; the easier you can make it for harried holiday shoppers, the more business you will get.

Who Buys Baskets?

The two most important customer categories for a gift-basket service are women and corporations. Women in their thirties and forties, usually married with children and holding full-time jobs, are a gift-basket maker's best customers. Even though they work full-time, wives, mothers, and girlfriends still tend to be responsible for buying gifts. Gift baskets are a fast, creative alternative for women who have little time to shop.

Gift baskets have also become the gift of choice for many corporations. Sending a gift to an important client is a sensitive task—it should be personal, yet tasteful, even conservative. A gift basket easily fits the criteria, and it can fit every budget, too. Corporate clients usually represent multiple orders, not to mention additional business when corporate employees need personal gifts.

The Greatest Gift

One of the toughest parts of starting a small business is a lack of outside support. So far, gift-basket services do not have much national recognition in the form of organizations or associations. This will probably change over the next few years, however, due to the increasing popularity of this business.

Gift-basket making is shaping up into an exciting opportunity for thousands of people who have decided that it is possible to do something creative—and make money in the process.

LAUNDROMAT

High Net Profit Before Taxes:	$45,000
Average Net Profit Before Taxes:	$18,000
Minimum Start-up:	$37,000
Average Start-up:	$55,000

Let's be frank. Opening a laundromat does not require a lot of imagination. Millions of people do laundry each day—and a good percentage of them do the wash in one of the 42,000 coin-operated laundry facilities across the country. Here's a business that's straightforward and simple. You just rent space, install the equipment, and let the customers do the work. Laundromat owners of all sorts do just this, and make a nice profit while they're at it.

But other laundromat owners seem to be missing the point. In fact, they're getting downright creative. One Texas entrepreneur uses his laundromat as a kind of country-music dance hall. Customers gather for live entertainment, dancing—and, of course, a wash and rinse. Another laundromat owner installed exercise bikes on location. Customers don't have to laze about the place while they're doing their laundry: for a few extra coins, they can also work out.

Is this some kind of lunacy? Not really. Years ago, at age nineteen, Phil Akin thought of creating a laundromat with attractive decor, televisions, and refreshments. Now, his Duds 'n' Suds concept has been franchised nationally.

If you're looking for a business with solid demand and low maintenance requirements, this is it. But if you're also interested in revolutionizing an industry, beating the competition, and having some fun, all the better. Laundromats are not the dull, dingy wash houses they used to be. And that spells good news for enterprising businesspeople with a flair for fun.

Innovation Pays

What are the rewards for making laundry fun? We found one operator grossing $7,800 a month after just a few months in business. Another, whose first store will return its initial capital investment in thirty-six months, has opened four other locations in his city. Each is grossing over $5,000 monthly. With skillful operation the average store will generate from $4,000 to $6,000 per month in gross sales from washers and dryers alone. Net profits at a well-run laundry will range from 25 to 35 percent pretax.

Of course, fun isn't the only factor in a laundromat's success. Location is also key. The most profitable location is surrounded by as many people as possible—preferably apartment dwellers. The ideal place to locate is a neighborhood shopping center. You can do even better by buying out an existing location. As long as the location and machines are basically sound, you can spruce up the decor and add some interesting extras to improve business. If there are a lot of working couples and singles in your neighborhood, consider adding fluff-and-fold services or drop-off and delivery.

Next to Godliness

It is essential that your laundromat be spotless. The entire image you are trying to create with contemporary decor and equipment will be ruined if spilled detergent accumulates on the carpeting or the machines are dirty. Maintenance is vital and obviously affects profitability. Hire an attendant to keep the place picked up. In addition to cleaning up, he or she can also make note of any broken machines or mechanical problems when you aren't there.

You can also man the laundromat yourself. Find out what your customers are like and ask them for their suggestions. Is everything up to their specifications? Are there additional services they'd like to see? Would they come to a country-music night? The days of the old open-it-and-forget-it laundromat are over. But with sound management, promotion, and a little imagination, you can still clean up in this business.

SECURITY PATROL SERVICE

High Net Profit Before Taxes:	$60,000 plus
Average Net Profit Before Taxes:	$48,000
Minimum Start-up:	$17,000
Average Start-up:	$32,000

Crime does pay, and we've found the business that makes it legal! A security patrol service has extremely high profit potential, and it's a growing concern in an age of diminishing expectations. The low overhead and fast return on investment in this business make it easy to enter.

The next time you see a police officer, ask him or her how long it takes the neighborhood police to arrive at the scene of a burglary or other residential emergency. In some cities, the response time is as long as thirty to forty-five minutes—that's how long people wait to get police protection when they need it most.

Overworked and understaffed police departments in cities all over the country are unable to cope with runaway crime. Burglary has risen at an average of 38 percent a year for the past five years by some estimates. This has led to an exciting new business opportunity—private security patrols for home and business protection.

Lock Up the Market

Your security patrol service is the answer to the horrendous increase in city police calls. You can provide many services that local police can't offer. The very presence of a security patrol car in a neighborhood has been shown to reduce crime rates. Why? Because burglars don't want to risk operating in neighborhoods where private police are constantly patrolling.

Cruising the neighborhood is only one aspect of a security service. When customers are away on vacation, a security service can check doors and windows, pick up the newspaper every day, and perform other routine checks. If burglars know there's a police officer—private or city—on the beat, they'll go elsewhere for their activities. You're selling crime prevention, and security-conscious clients will seize the opportunity to buy it.

Solid Profits in Security Hardware

Patrol services are only one aspect of the security business. You can also sell and install burglar- and fire-alarm systems in conjunction with or as a sideline to your patrol services. Emphasize your professionalism and your eagerness to supplement the services of overtaxed police departments. Contact people concentrated in the area you want to patrol and sell them on your ability to save their lives before there's trouble.

What If You Have to Handle Emergencies?

Communications are the heart of the security patrol industry. Set up a precise phone system and office-client code numbers. Your relationship with the police will be of vital importance when you call in an emergency.

Judgment is important in your patrol staff. They will have to know when to call the police in on a job—and when to alert the police that the danger has passed. Run a smooth, professional organization for client safety and confidence.

Fees Vary According to Service

Contracts will vary. Will your service include drive-bys, or walking through the front gates? Client charges vary significantly from one company to the next. Emergency responses generally run about $25 per response. False alarms are a hazard a good security company has to cope with.

Residential and business clients should be on your list of sales prospects. Typically, homes of $500,000 or more in exclusive neighborhoods will want more individualized attention to protect expensive property. That doesn't mean you should ignore the more modest neighborhoods. Smaller property owners need peace of mind for their property, too. In fact, they may be in a worse position if their homes are robbed.

Exciting and Lucrative

The market is booming in security services. A neighborhood patrol service can gross as much as $100,000 in its first year of operation.

And there's room left in the market for new businesses. Once established, the security patrol business has a long-range factor of stability. Because of low overhead (no need for a high-rent office in this nuts-and-bolts operation), many three-man patrols have turned high gross sales into 25-to-31-percent net profits pretax.

Selling a broad range of services in a trustworthy fashion—then delivering on promises in emergency situations—is the main idea here. Established patrols rack up contracts in the $300,000 to $500,000 range, with as many as 4,000 homes on a single company's routes.

FURNITURE RENTAL SERVICE

High Net Profit Before Taxes:	$78,000 plus
Average Net Profit Before Taxes:	$45,000
Minimum Start-up:	$50,000
Average Start-up:	$65,000

America is going crazy for renting. Everything from roller skates to jumbo jets, bartenders to football fields, can be rented for an hour, a day, or a month.

In one month, over 350,000 Americans furnished their apartments and homes with rented furniture. Owners of furniture rental stores are making sizable profits catering to the needs of today's mobile society. Established stores gross as much as $100,000 to $350,000 a year. One store owner started out in the sixties, when the furniture rental business was virtually nonexistent, with an investment of $40,000. Ten years later, he sold his business for over $2 million.

The reason is that more and more Americans have adopted a mobile life-style. Whether for career or personal reasons, people change jobs frequently these days. They want the ability to get up and go without the hassle of moving cumbersome furniture. Young professionals, students, and the increasing singles' populations can rent furniture that reflects their life-style inexpensively. And when they move, they can change their environment with entirely new furniture.

Widespread Market

There is no typical renter of furniture. This is one of the attractions of the business—the market is so varied. Of course, there are certain characteristics common to rental customers. Some prefer not to be tied down by possessions. Others may be forced to move often because of their work. Corporate employees, athletes, and recently divorced people fit into these categories. Newlyweds, college students, and military and airline personnel are also potential renters. They usually don't want to invest heavily in permanent furnishings until they get settled.

There is a prime market in apartment dwellers. National figures show that the annual turnover rate for apartments is 30 percent. And don't forget building owners and managers: their profits are higher when they rent furnished units.

As many men as women rent furniture, and ages range from twenty to seventy-five. Widowed people often rent after liquidating an estate.

Your profitability depends on factors that include location, inventory utilization, competition, capacity for growth, and initial investment. For less than $100,000, you could put together a minimum opening inventory—no more than twenty rental packages—in an inexpensive building of about 2,000 square feet.

You don't need an expensive mall location to make money in this business. Your sales don't depend on walk-ins. People who want to rent furniture will go to the source even if it's a little out of their way. Volume doesn't depend on impulse shoppers.

===============BRIGHT IDEA===============

LOW-TECH SLEUTHING

All is not lost: it's waiting to be found. So believes Maggie Greif, owner of SLEUTH, a Columbia, Maryland, business that specializes in finding the facts—or whatever else a client wants.

After years of digging up information for family and

friends "for fun," Greif decided three years ago to turn her "natural snoopiness" into a business—locating information, products, and services for businesses and individual clients. With an initial investment of between $2,000 and $3,000, she set up an office and placed her first classified ad.

"Every project is so different," she says. "Each brings me into a whole new world of information." The number of jobs she tackles each week varies widely. A recent job she found particularly interesting was finding a source for large quantities of organic chickens "as close to Brooklyn, New York, as possible." One of her ongoing projects is helping an overseas-based importer locate novelty items that are well established in the U.S. market and might have commercial potential in Europe.

"I enjoy working with small businesses," says Greif. "They appreciate my thoroughness and attention to detail." She's also found that with her time priced at $40 an hour, businesses are better able to afford her services than are individuals. Right now, the ratio is about eighty–twenty.

Nine times out of ten, Greif is able to complete projects to the customer's satisfaction. "Sometimes the solution is not the expected one," says Greif, who claims "brainstorming" and "creative thinking" are her most valuable assets. Some projects Greif rejects on principle—missing-persons cases, recommending professional services, or anything potentially illegal.

Greif bills clients even when she can't track down what they're seeking. "My time is valuable," she asserts. "It's not a question that comes up often with business clients. They understand that if it hadn't been me spending the time, it would have been them."

While she has begun to computerize some of her projects, she emphasizes that a personal, hands-on approach sets her apart from regular information brokers. "I work with people," she says. "I talk to one person, then that person leads me to another, and so on. Personal involvement will always be the heart of my business."

CARPET-CLEANING SERVICE

High Net Profit Before Taxes:	$100,000 plus
Average Net Profit Before Taxes:	$ 29,000
Minimum Start-up:	$ 9,000
Average Start-up:	$ 16,000

In the last twenty years, carpet-cleaning sales have jumped from under $10 million to $90 million annually. The predictions are that they will grow to a projected $150 million in the next few years. While carpet cleaning may not be a particularly novel business (let's face it, thousands of operators already exist), new businesses can still make a mint with quality service, sound management, and savvy marketing.

Years ago, you could start a viable part-time carpet-cleaning business with little more than rented equipment and a Yellow Pages listing. These days, the competition is tougher. You'll have to invest some time and planning if you hope to prosper.

Filling the Gaps

One way to crack the carpet-cleaning market is to offer superior service. Simple as this sounds, a surprising number of carpet-cleaning services (not to mention a variety of other home-repair people) don't adhere to even the most basic rules of good service.

We called ten consumers who had recently hired services to clean their home carpets. Here are their comments:

"They told me we could walk on our carpets in three hours. It took four days for them to dry out enough not to feel wet to the bare foot."

"When our carpeting dried out, I could pick dirt out of it with my fingers."

"I hired my carpet cleaner this time, although I have cleaned the carpet myself in the past. I wanted to get a better, more professional job. Now that it's done, it doesn't look any better than when I did it myself."

"The man who sold me the service was very businesslike in his talk, appearance, and dress. But when the guy who did the work came, he acted like he didn't have a brain in his head. He caused more mess than he did good."

Comments like these indicate that there is a need for good on-location carpet cleaning. If you can meet these needs, you'll get as much business as you can handle.

Gross $12 to $15 an Hour

If netting $7.00 to $10 an hour on an employee's time (at $5.00 per hour) sounds attractive to you, and you have some time to spend setting the business up and training your work force, carpet cleaning may be the ideal business for you.

Why This Business Has Grown

Thirty years ago, carpets were not common. In homes, hardwood floors were the thing; in commercial settings, tile was the standard. Today, however, most homes have wall-to-wall carpeting—some even have carpets in the bath and kitchen. Business establishments carpet everything but the walls—and we've even seen exceptions to that rule.

Wall-to-wall carpeting simply can't be removed for cleaning. Even if you could do it economically, it wouldn't be the same size and fit when you went to lay it down again. That's why on-location carpet-cleaning thrives in today's market: it's the only game in town.

Can Money Be Made?

The going rate for cleaning a square foot of carpeting varies from city to city, depending on population density and whether you are serving the upper crust or just average families. Some of the big franchisors suggest $0.15 per square foot. Cleaning 300 square feet of carpet properly takes one person about an hour, and you can charge $45. The cost of materials is about $2.00, and you will pay your worker about $5.00 an hour—including travel and setup time. Thus, when the 300-square-foot job is completed, you will have netted $28. And remember, with properly trained personnel you don't even have to spend time supervising the job.

If every serviceperson you hire can be kept busy and could complete a minimum of one hour of work for every three hours of pay (allowing for travel and setup between jobs), you can make at least $84 per worker every day. The on-location cleaner who is sharp enough to keep ten people busy can, in a short time, show a gross profit of $840 per day.

The Key to Success

The average operator in this business does 5.4 jobs per week, grossing an average of $563. We did not find any absentee owners in our research, probably because this is the kind of business that's difficult to operate on a small scale with a hired manager. Most of the owners we surveyed operated from their homes and spent less than $100 per week advertising.

What makes the difference between average operators and highly successful ones? Quality workmanship, excellent customer service, and strategic promotion were the main factors. Superior service translates into more referrals (and hence more business). Moreover, advertising proved to be a wise investment. All those in the successful group were spending between 20 and 30 percent of their gross on advertising and promotion.

Obviously, increasing your ad budget will decrease your net profit. But we found that an accelerated growth rate clearly compensated for this. Some owners had reached the point where they were executives only, handling the estimates and scheduling while their employees did the actual cleaning.

MOBILE SURFACE CLEANING

High Net Profit Before Taxes:	$200,000
Average Net Profit Before Taxes:	$ 30,000
Minimum Start-up:	$ 8,000
Average Start-up:	$ 14,500

Here's a different way to clean up in the service sector: mobile surface washing. With the help of high-pressure cleaning equipment, you can blast the dirt off buildings, boats, cars, bridges, billboards—just about anything that gets dirty (and what doesn't?).

The equipment is operated out of a self-contained van unit. The fully equipped vehicle is driven to the job site for on-the-spot cleaning of anything from planes to farm equipment, swimming pools, oil refinery tanks, and sports arenas. The secret is spray and rinse: a biodegradable chemical is sprayed on to lift the dirt, then it is rinsed off with water.

From Part-Time to Full-Time

Many of the owners we spoke with went into the business part-time to start and did so well they soon decided to go full-time. It is possible for one person to operate a unit fifteen to twenty hours per week, gross $30,000 a year, and net up to 65 percent before taxes and owner's salary. Not bad for part-time work!

A full-time operator with a single van can gross as much as $70,000. We even found one owner of eight van units grossing $500,000 after only three years in business. Because his cost for chemicals and supplies is lowered through large purchases, he nets 50 percent pretax.

Easy to Get Started

With a little careful shopping, you can break into this business for less than $12,000 and begin realizing a profit within the first few months. This investment will provide you with basic equipment, chemicals, and supplies. The only limitation is that you will be doing all the work yourself.

To position yourself for long-term growth and maximum profits, plan to spend about $20,000. This will enable you to buy better equipment and to hire a part-timer to help you set up and clean up. The time you save will turn into extra jobs, and it won't be long before you can buy your second unit.

One major advantage to this business is that you can run it from your home. There is no need for a fancy office with a secretary because your customers only see your van. It is a good idea, however, to have an answering service handle calls, or at least to install an answering machine. The cost is minimal when you consider the number of sales you may miss by being away from home. Many answering services will even schedule appointments and job dates for you, but until you have the experience to predict exactly how long it will take to complete a cleaning assignment, it is best simply to have the service take messages.

A Natural for Repeat Business

As long as there's dirt, there's a demand for cleaning. The secret to long-term success in this business is as simple as that. After you've done a cleaning job, the structure will get dirty again. And once clients see how a clean exterior improves their local image, they will want to maintain their new standards. In some cases—for instance, gas stations where oil and grease stains are a constant problem—you should be able to set up contracts for regular service.

Many Options for Additional Profits

Expanding your mobile cleaning service is as easy as tracking down dirt. For example, car lots represent a profitable market. Salespeople have a hard enough time selling cars—especially used cars—under the best of circumstances. If the vehicle is covered with a layer of dust, making a sale is almost impossible. Lot owners may hire someone full-time to keep cars clean and shiny or take the cars to a local wash. But this is more expensive and time-consuming than having you stop by every few days for a quick wash-and-rinse job.

Owners of truck or car fleets will also be interested in contracting with you for periodic cleaning. This prolongs the life of a paint job, ensures that their vehicles are presenting a good image, and in snowy conditions, protects undercarriages from corrosion caused by road salt.

Real-estate brokers may also provide you with a substantial amount of business because they find it much easier to sell a clean house. Painters and architects can save a great deal of time by hiring you to prepare a surface. With the addition of a special compound to the chemical base, you can actually strip off a peeling layer of paint.

More unusual customers include cemetery managers, who realize the benefit of having stone monuments cleaned. Insurance brokers may contract with you to work on their claims: for example, smoke- and fire-damaged exteriors and interiors.

The potential for new customers is large. One owner cleaned a friend's trailer as a birthday present and left the mobile park with fourteen new customers who had wandered by while he was doing the job.

VOCATIONAL TRAINING CENTER

High Net Profit Before Taxes:	$50,000 plus
Average Net Profit Before Taxes:	$30,000
Minimum Start-up:	$11,000
Average Start-up:	$30,000

Even in the midst of an economic boom, American workers are unemployed. Why? In large measure it's because their skills don't match the demands of a changing American workplace.

The American Society of Training and Development estimates that by the year 2000, 75 percent of all adults currently employed will need retraining. And that doesn't account for the millions of young people who haven't acquired any job skills yet.

"Jobs today simply require workers to learn more over time than they did in the past," says Jim Palmer, vice-president of communications for the American Association of Community and Junior Colleges. "People are switching jobs more frequently, so formal education throughout one's lifetime is becoming a necessity for many workers. Even office work isn't as simple as it used to be."

People who hope to earn more than the minimum wage will need marketable skills in the years to come—skills that many public schools fail to teach. Even a college degree doesn't guarantee a good job if it isn't combined with skills that apply to today's workplace.

Teaching the Trades

Teaching vocational skills isn't a new idea: trade schools have been doing just that for decades. But the need for specific job skills—both for young people and displaced workers—has never been more urgent.

Vocational schools teach a staggering array of courses. Through these schools, it's possible to learn the ins and outs of being a secretary, medical technician, court reporter, contractor's license preparer, hotel manager, insurance salesperson, barber, cosmetologist, manicurist, computer programmer, data processor, PBX switchboard operator, bookkeeper, draftsperson, TV technician, auto mechanic, printer, autobody repairperson, welder, typesetter, upholsterer, real-estate agent, pilot, detective, insurance investigator, model, credit collector, auctioneer, fashion buyer, actor, dog groomer, airline ticket agent, travel agent, photographer, radio announcer, disk jockey, machinist, TV cameraperson, horticulturist, dry cleaner, truck driver, office-machine repairperson, landscaper, interior decorator, veterinary assistant, makeup artist, bartender, waiter/waitress, electrician, floral designer, watch repairperson, locksmith, polygraph operator, jewelry designer, candy maker, or chef. One school even offers instruction in horseshoeing.

Fit the Training to the Need

The common thread in all vocational training these days is marketability. Many schools work directly with local industries to find out which positions and skills are most in demand, then tailor their training to fit those needs.

What can you teach? Perhaps you have a trade or profession from which the average person can earn a steady living in your community. If so, why not promote it through classes? You already have an instructor—yourself.

Even if you don't want to teach, you needn't rule yourself out. Pick any trade or profession that is in demand—maybe one that's not being offered anywhere else. Hire someone successful in that field as your instructor, and you're in business. You can devote all of your time to building a solid and profitable business.

Look for trends in your local area. What kinds of jobs are most in demand? Which positions do local business owners have the most trouble filling? What kinds of people are looking for new job skills (recent graduates, single mothers, retirees)? The needs of the marketplace change daily. Keep your eyes open for untapped niches.

Advertising Is Critical

Of course, a variety of factors will contribute to your success or failure in this business: quality of instruction, business savvy, and simple demographics. But advertising is probably the most critical factor of all. We found a direct correlation between advertising dollars spent and gross sales at the trade schools we investigated. The ratio was approximately one to three: $1.00 of advertising returned $3.00 in gross sales. The net before taxes appeared to be a fairly uniform 30 percent.

2

PERSONAL SERVICES

ERRAND SERVICE

You never realized how many little, inconsequential errands there were in life until you had to do them yourself—and hold down a full-time job at the same time. Now you find you don't have time to pick up the dry cleaning, stand in line to register your car, take your dog in for rabies shots, and drop your kids off at piano lessons.

That is, unless you make it your business to run errands. Around the country, personal errand services are doing what working people can't. Even simple tasks like buying groceries and getting the car washed can be monumental to people who work fifty and sixty hours a week. Some would pay anything to have the details of their lives worked out for them. You can provide that service—and start a business that requires little previous experience and a minimum of capital.

Many operators start with little more than a telephone answering service, working transportation, and a few ads. Lois Barnett, who runs PS Personalized Services in Chicago, says that a reputation for efficiency, reliability, and organization are all critical to success. "Of course we're insured and bonded," she says, "but in this kind of business the key is to be personally recommended or, in the initial contact, to communicate to a potential client that we're trustworthy."

===================== BRIGHT IDEA =====================

1-800-DENTIST

Americans are always on the move. And as they settle into new communities, they're faced with the anxiety of finding new doctors and dentists.

Unlike finding a new paint store or Chinese restaurant, finding good medical and dental help can be frightening. Scanning the phone book simply doesn't cut it. How can you be sure the person you call is competent? What if you have a special problem? Are professionals who take out big ads more or less reliable than the ones who don't?

Consumers get the answers to these questions and a host of others when they call 1-800-DENTIST, a telephone referral service that takes some of the angst out of finding a new dentist. Founded in 1986 by R. D. "Bob" Goodman and Charles Eberle, this smart service fields more than 1,500 calls a day and grosses almost $300,000 a month serving ten California area codes. "We've turned seven digits into seven figures," Goodman jokes.

Callers can choose dentists in their neighborhoods and get basic information on the dentist's background and specialties. The dentists pay up to $1,000 a month to join the referral network. Goodman says it was difficult at first to convince dentists to join the program; now they are clamoring to get in.

Goodman and Eberle hold the international rights to the 1-800-DENTIST telephone number, and are negotiating with representatives to market the service to the rest of the United States. And what's worked for dentists may work for other professionals—and even totally unrelated fields. In the works: Goodman is planning an auto-insurance referral number, 1-800-AUTO-ONE.

CLOSET CUSTOMIZING

High Net Profit Before Taxes:	$150,000
Average Net Profit Before Taxes:	$ 60,000
Minimum Start-up:	$ 20,000
Average Start-up:	$ 50,000

In American homes there are 344 million closets—and most of them are a mess. This situation isn't going to repair itself, either. As housing prices continue to soar, people are less likely to buy new homes and more likely to find ways of making their current situations more livable.

The help they need is available from closet customizing services. These businesses go into disorganized, haphazard, messy closets and turn them into useful storage space. Though this industry is just a few years old, it's already made a mint for entrepreneurs with tenacity, creativity, and good marketing.

A Simple Concept

Closet customizing companies don't rebuild closets; they simply redivide the space in the existing closet so it adapts to a client's particular needs. By installing a variety of shelves, drawers, and hanging rods, the closet customizer can create a closet that exactly matches a client's needs. A salesperson inspects the existing closet, measures the critical dimensions, and inventories all the articles that need to fit. Once the customer approves the design, shelving pieces are cut to size in the company's workshop and taken to the customer's house for final assembly.

Typically, prices range from $400 to $1,200, depending on the size and complexity of the project. Fees as high as $12,000 have been reported for elaborate systems—for instance, garage storage. Closet customizers also make money from the sale of accessories: tie racks, belt racks, garment bags, stacking storage bins, wire drawers, shoe racks, and similar items.

Two Routes to Go

Because of the wide range of services a closetier can provide, there are many levels at which you can start your business. The approach with the lowest initial investment is to operate out of your garage or a shop, and concentrate solely on custom closet installations. In this way, overhead expenses are kept to a minimum and customers are attracted through word of mouth and some advertising.

Another option is to open a retail storefront operation and stock a wide range of accessory items. One successful retailer stocks over 300 different closet-related items. He makes about 50 percent of his sales from these accessories, and another 50 percent from custom closet installations. Although a storefront operation is more expensive to start and maintain, your business will be more visible and appeal to a wider range of customers. Either way, you can build a thriving business on the basis of closet design.

They've Only Just Begun

In the relatively brief history of the closet business, the public has just begun to realize the extent of its need to get organized. And they're only starting to realize that closet customizing companies exist to help them. The pioneering efforts of a few closet companies have kicked off a major trend, and along with it, a wealth of opportunities for new businesses who can meet the demand.

===== BRIGHT IDEA =====

RADON-DETECTION SERVICE

In the past few years, a colorless, odorless gas has created concern among America's homeowners—and new opportunities for service-minded entrepreneurs. Radon-detection services are springing up all over the country. And as people become increasingly aware of radon's dangers, continued growth is likely in the years to come.

What is radon? It's a colorless, odorless gas that occurs naturally as a result of the breakdown of uranium in the earth's surface. This radioactive gas, which is known to cause lung cancer, can accumulate in unhealthful levels in homes. By seeping through cracks or drains in the foundation or basement of a house, radon can build up, especially during cold months when the house is otherwise sealed tight, and pose a health problem to residents.

The EPA and the Surgeon General have both warned about the dangers of radon accumulation in homes. In many areas, radon tests are required for real-estate sales. This spells opportunity for many entrepreneurs, who can help families avoid potential health hazards and make a profit to boot.

The simplest way to get into the radon business is by setting up a testing service. You can buy radon tests wholesale from any of a number of reliable labs and use those tests to measure radon levels in people's homes. Generally, this involves leaving a charcoal-filled canister in the client's home for a few days, picking it up, and sending it in to the manufacturing lab for analysis.

You can buy the kits for about $10 each, including the lab work. By starting small from your home, you needn't invest more than $250 or so to start. You can work part-time, or make a larger investment in advertising, promotion, and equipment and operate full-time. It's also possible to link this service with an existing service like pest control or home inspection.

================= BRIGHT IDEA =================

HOME HEALTH CARE

When nurse practitioner Mary M. Baker came down with a serious ear infection, she suddenly recognized an unmet consumer need. Single and sick, she didn't know where to turn for assistance.

Baker envisioned a service that would fill the void between mother's care—of the chicken-soup variety—and hospital admission. At the time, Baker was frustrated and bored with the limitations of her traditional career. So with a $10,000 loan, she started her own business, Chicken Soup, Plus, offering home care on an hourly basis for people who are sick, but not sick enough to enter the hospital.

Today, Baker's Sacramento, California, office has a staff of thirty, and her service has expanded to include round-the-clock home health care and contractual services such as the pre-employment physical examinations she provides for two private hospitals. "We grossed over $300,000 in 1988," says Baker, "and my goal is to double that by the end of 1989."

You don't have to be a nurse to start a service like Baker's: you can hire nurses to provide the care. On the other hand, Baker believes her nursing background gave her an entrepreneurial advantage. "Nurses have the characteristics, the flexibility, to be successful in business," she contends. She says that more and more nurses are moving into the business world "because of frustration. I loved nursing, but I didn't feel it allowed me to have any control over my future. When you're a nurse, you're always an employee."

IMAGE CONSULTING

High Net Profit Before Taxes:	$140,000
Average Net Profit Before Taxes:	$ 80,000
Minimum Start-up:	$ 11,000
Average Start-up:	$ 18,000

Humans have an unlimited capacity to feel insecure about their appearance. Most of us were taught by our parents to be neat and clean, to say "please" and "thank you," but today that's not enough. The wrong appearance can cost people jobs, promotions, contracts, or club memberships. Not knowing what to say at a business gathering, or how to make introductions, can cause endless embarrassment.

Enter image consulting. Millions of people want to improve their images, but don't know how to go about it. This is where you come in. As an image consultant, you can make money teaching people how to make the best of themselves and how to make the best impression on others. Americans spend about $148 million yearly visiting the 5,000 to 8,000 image consultants currently in business.

Image makers don't work for small change. Consultants with good corporate and individual client bases are grossing $100,000 to $200,000 a year. Add to that a relatively low initial investment of $10,000 to $20,000 and you've got a business that's looking good.

More Than Color and Makeup

The image-consulting industry isn't regulated, which means there is no specific training program or test one must pass in order to become a qualified consultant. Most consultants have a background in fashion merchandising, design, public relations, or cosmetology. Among the subjects most consultants cover: wardrobe, colors, hair, etiquette, and poise.

Schools around the country offer seminars and workshops on the basics of image consulting, including the Academy of Fashion and Image Consulting in McLean, Virginia, and the Fashion Academy in Costa Mesa, California.

Building Your Image

Considering today's image-conscious society, now is the time to start an image-consulting business. But it takes more than a telephone and a few hours of training to get established as an image consultant.

Marketing your image service will take a lot of time, especially in the beginning. First, decide whom you should target as potential clients—recent college graduates, working women, corporate executives, etc. Then, decide on a format for your sessions. Should they be private three-hour consultations, or daylong seminars? How many people should attend? How much should you charge? (Typical fees run anywhere from $50 to $250 an hour. An all-day fee might run between $500 and $2,000.)

Once you have a good idea of how your business will run, there are a number of ways to get your name known. For starters, don't be afraid to contact every professional you know, or anyone else who might be interested in your services. Investing in well-designed business cards, letterhead, and a four-color brochure is a good idea.

If you have what it takes to be an image consultant, you'll be joining a new and exciting industry. Your business will be to make your clients look and feel better, which means a lot of satisfaction and visible results from your efforts.

BRIDAL FAIRS

Oakland, California, entrepreneur Elisa Fisher is bringing it all together for brides on a grand scale. Her Modern Bridal Fairs attract literally thousands of people each year, about a third of whom are brides.

"I wanted to find a way to bring brides together with bridal services so that a bride didn't have to go to nine different places," says Fisher, who was once a wedding photographer herself.

Fisher started the business in 1981. Her first fair had 30 booths. For a fee of $500, her company provides the participating merchants with everything they need, including materials for building a booth and a mailing list of all the brides who go through the fair. In addition, the merchants are included in all of the fair's advertising.

Fisher's company also publishes *Modern Bridal Images*, a full-color magazine that is distributed at the fair and through local department stores. "It started as something the brides could take with them when they left the fair, like a brochure," says Fisher.

The magazine is designed like other bridal magazines, featuring articles on how to plan a wedding as well as advertising from merchants participating in the fair. Fisher also carefully checks the background of the merchants she allows to participate in the fair—for example, they have to have been in business for at least three years. "The problem with the wedding business is that it looks very easy to people on the outside," says Fisher. "Anybody who's ever had a wedding thinks she can be a consultant, so there are a lot of people who get into the business—and then get out just as quickly."

FAMILY HAIR SALON

High Net Profit Before Taxes:	$95,000
Average Net Profit Before Taxes:	$65,000
Minimum Start-up:	$49,000
Average Start-up:	$70,000

Paying $100 for a haircut may be fine for Hollywood stars, but what about regular folks? Do real people really want to fork over a week's grocery money just to get their bangs trimmed? According to the ranks of America's growing family hair-care industry, the answer is no.

What real people need is a family hair salon. Convenient, inexpensive hair care is the order of the day at these unpretentious operations. Customers don't get glasses of weak chardonnay to sip, and they don't get fluffed by a famous designer. But they can get a haircut without an appointment—and they can bring their families along for the same treatment at a price that won't bankrupt them.

Where Have All the Barbers Gone?

Cutting hair is nothing new. However, the packaging these days is quite different. Years ago, men and women went to separate hair-care professionals. Men went to barbershops, where they enjoyed a kind of camaraderie with other customers, but got generally bland haircuts. Women visited beauticians, who washed, cut, set, dried, and teased hair into shapes that defied gravity. Children got their hair cut at home—and usually looked like it. It was a crude system, but it worked. This was the pattern for years. And then came the eighties.

The eighties brought three major revelations. First, men became style conscious. They realized that their friendly neighborhood barbers knew only one style, and it hadn't changed since Prohibition. Second, women realized there was more to life than sitting under a bonnet dryer. They wanted easy-care, natural styles that their old beauticians couldn't offer. And third, kids began rebelling. Why should they be the only ones looking ill-coiffed? And working moms, who no longer had time to fuss with their youngsters' hair, acquiesced.

Yet, as we pointed out earlier, the average full-service salon just isn't a family affair. Many don't even accept children as clients. Their focus is on the upscale. Many offer manicures, foot massage, waxing, and makeup consulting—services that basic folks don't want, at prices they can't afford.

About 60 percent of the customers at family hair salons are women aged eighteen to forty-four. About half of them are married and have children. These women are attracted to the concept because they can get their kids' hair cut while they are shampooed, cut, and blown dry. Most salons are located in middle-class suburban neighborhoods, where customers need to look good on a budget.

Finding the Right Look

Location and decor are critical to a new salon. Your shop must be centrally located with plenty of available parking. Since many family salons rely on walk-in traffic, leasing a space in a mall or strip center may be a good idea. Also look for nearby shops that cater to families: grocery stores, children's clothing stores, toy stores, and so on.

Choose your decor carefully. You don't have to spend a fortune, but you should put some thought into the way your business looks. Select bright, attractive colors and durable, contemporary furniture. Above all, don't go with a color scheme or style that looks outdated. If your shop has that seventies look, potential customers will run away in droves. Again, your decor doesn't have to be fancy, just up-to-date.

Equipment will cost you anywhere from $15,000 on up. You can shop for used equipment at auctions or through used-equipment dealers. The stylists you hire will provide many of their own implements, so you will save some money there.

Keeping Your Prices Down

Remember that this business depends on maintaining reasonable prices. Regular salon prices are exorbitant, so how can you keep yours at a low level? One strategy is to hire talented stylists right out of beauty school. Not only will they work for less money than experienced stylists, but they will also know more of the latest styles and techniques.

Another important factor is volume. You can charge less for services if you perform more of them. Be prepared to do some aggressive advertising, especially at the outset. And urge your stylists to keep the flow of customers moving. As long as the quality doesn't suffer, many customers will appreciate fast service.

===================BRIGHT IDEA===================

FINANCIAL PLANNING

With a myriad of options available to consumers these days, more and more people are turning to professional help for their personal finances. Deregulation in the banking industry has made financial planning significantly more complex. As a result, the market for financial planning services is growing by leaps and bounds.

Most financial planners come from backgrounds in accounting, finance, and risk management. However, anyone who's willing to learn these fields—and any other relevant information—can become an independent financial planner. Typical duties include calculating a client's net worth, analyzing cash flow, devising a workable budget, and formulating written plans for accumulating investments and insurance.

Although there are no set requirements for becoming a financial planner, having some background is definitely desirable. Consider enrolling in a certification program, or simply taking relevant course work, through a local college. Many even have home-study courses you can follow.

Currently, there are 150,000 financial planners in the United States, up from just a handful twenty years ago. High earning potential makes this an attractive field. Planners charge hourly fees of $80 to $175, or bring in attractive commissions.

CHIMNEY SWEEP SERVICE

High Net Profit Before Taxes:	$50,000 plus
Average Net Profit Before Taxes:	$26,000
Minimum Start-up:	$ 1,000
Average Start-up:	$ 7,500

Chimney sweeps are back and dancing on rooftops all over the country. Capitalizing on the revival of this nineteenth-century trade can easily net you profits of $30,000 a year before taxes. Even on a part-time basis, you can clear up to $10,000 annually.

Tidy Profits

The profit potential of a chimney sweep depends on the number of chimneys completed each day and the number of customers maintained during the year. The average charge for sweeping is about $50, though prices can range from $25 to $75.

Pricing depends on the market, the height of the chimney, and the complexity of the job. Some sweeps charge per flue: old-fashioned chimneys can have as many as twenty flues. Most sweeps charge a flat fee for the first chimney and a reduced rate for each additional one.

A cleaning job takes a skilled sweep a maximum of an hour and a half. At this rate, you can finish five to six jobs a day. However, faster rates were reported. With efficient equipment, a top-flight sweep can handle eight jobs a day. One Florida operator claims he can race through most jobs in forty-five minutes.

A sweep working alone should be able to gross over $40,000 annually. With several sweeps, this figure can jump to $100,000 or more. Net profits run as high as 50 to 60 percent, including the owner's salary. And investment costs and expenses are low to start—usually well under $10,000.

Dressing the Part

The main reason people get their chimneys swept is safety: chimney fires are among the most common causes of household fires. But beyond the merely practical is another more fanciful side of the business. Chimney sweeping carries with it a good measure of nostalgia and charm. In that spirit, many chimney sweeps cultivate a business image that isn't exactly out of the pages of *Dress for Success*.

In top hats and tails, modern chimney sweeps look just like the English sweeping boys who scurried down chimneys in Dickens's time. And they're as handy at recounting traditional lore (it's good luck to touch a sweep, by the way) as they are with their equipment. The entertainment value they provide is often as appealing as the services they perform.

The Market Is Everywhere

Today, there are approximately 6,000 chimney sweeps in the United States—up from about 2,000 at the beginning of the eighties. The chimney-cleaning industry was dormant for a number of years, but has enjoyed a rebirth since the energy-conscious seventies brought Americans back to their fireplaces.

Though growth has been substantial in this industry, there is still room for newcomers. Many Americans still don't realize the importance of chimney cleaning. And others who do, require regular annual maintenance.

If you think chimney sweeping is strictly a regional business, think again. There are millions of homes in the country where fireplaces and wood-burning stoves ward off the cold. Of course, in northern states where wood is burned for at least half the year, the need is greater. Several sweeps can prosper in these regions.

Start for a Song

One of the greatest attractions of becoming a chimney sweep is the low initial investment. Many chimney sweeps have started with little more than a set of brushes with extension rods and tarpaulins to protect homeowners' floors.

However, to achieve a high volume of business and minimize labor, high-pressure dust collectors are available. With upgraded equipment and an initial advertising campaign, figure on start-up costs of at least $5,000. The right tools and solid marketing should help you recoup your investment within the first few months of operations.

===================== BRIGHT IDEA =====================

MAN BEARING GIFTS

There are candy grams, cookie grams, singing telegrams, and now Teddy Bear Grams. The brainchild of Derrick Sweet, Teddy Bear Grams are twelve-inch plush teddy bears that can be sent to anyone, anywhere in the world, with an attached card bearing a message.

"A teddy bear is a good vehicle to display your emotions," says Sweet, who first thought of the idea as a gift for his girlfriend. Bored with the usual offerings, he decided to send her a bear. "Within five minutes after she received the bear, people from her office were calling me asking where I got it," he says.

Sweet soon figured out that he had the potential for a successful business on his hands. After attracting two partners, Martin Bonis and Noel Perera, Sweet started Teddy Bear Grams Corp. in Ottawa, Canada, in February 1989.

"From the moment we opened our doors, we received a lot of attention," says Sweet. "Canada is just eating these things up, and we're delivering all over the world. In fact, we expect to open offices in Los Angeles and New York later this year."

MAID SERVICE

High Net Profit Before Taxes:	$34,000 plus
Average Net Profit Before Taxes:	$28,000
Minimum Start-up:	$ 4,000
Average Start-up:	$ 9,000

The cliché "It's impossible to find good help" has never been truer than it is today—and not because good help doesn't exist. The demand for maid services in America is skyrocketing, fed by the explosion of dual-income families, busy single professionals, and affluent retirees. You can supply these much-needed services and pull in as much as $100,000 your first year in business.

Atlanta entrepreneur Leone Ackerly started her company, Mini Maid, with a mere $7.00 worth of cleaning supplies. In her first year of business, she established a neighborhood service that grossed $45,000. Today, Mini Maid has franchises around the country.

Organization Is All

Two words revolutionized residential cleaning: "team concept." Two to four maids descend on a house or apartment: each maid cleans a different room. With this method, cleaning time is cut so dramatically that up to ten apartments or homes can be covered in a single day. In other words, work time is at a minimum while profits are at a maximum.

If you're serious about making money in the maid business, there's good news for you. You shouldn't do the cleaning yourself. Start by hiring a couple of maids. They'll handle the cleanups while you handle the sales and administration. Your sales ability—not your cleaning ability—will make or break your business.

Arm your cleaning staff with practical uniforms and cleaning tools, and give then a system to work with so they don't waste time and effort planning how to tackle a job. They should be able to start working the minute they arrive at a job.

Work out a cleaning system that they can use anywhere, then figure out ways to speed up your system. One of the most successful maid services in the country requires teams to go through as many as fifty drills before they're allowed to go out on a solo mission.

Minimal Start-up Requirements

A maid service can be run from a desk out of your home. Location is not the most vital consideration in starting up. However, it's obvious that the nearer a service is to the homes or apartments it serves, the lower overhead will be.

In this business, the tools of the trade are the ones that have worked for thousands of years. Your equipment needs are simple—mops, brooms, buckets, and soap.

Yet, equipment will vary in cost if not style. As the business grows, you will be able to buy in large volume and increase your profit margin nicely. Volume buying on a regular basis—especially as your clientele becomes more established and predictable—will mean that you can take advantage of wholesale price breaks, seasonal buying, and special orders.

Make Your Customers Work for You

Startling as it sounds, that's exactly what will happen if your service business is a good one. Customer satisfaction is all you need to generate more and more business for your maid service. Referrals are the cheapest and most effective way to build a reputation for your new company. And all you have to do to get them is a good job.

Systematic teamwork, dependable service, and satisfied customers all help toward raising profits. This business requires a low investment and no experience—just some hard work and common sense. As the market for maid services continues to grow, profit potential in this business looks excellent for the future.

================ BRIGHT IDEA ================

TUTORIAL SERVICE

Are public schools adequate to teach youngsters everything they need to know in today's society? Increasingly, the answer is no. Crowded classrooms, funding cutbacks, and discipline problems have all taken their toll on the public education system. In response, more and more parents are turning to private tutors to provide the personal attention and specific instruction that isn't available in most public schools.

You don't have to teach to start a tutorial service. You can make a business simply out of bringing teachers and students together. There are several markets to consider. Grade-school and high-school students may need help in math, reading, languages, and other subjects. Credentialed teachers usually make the best tutors in these subjects, but talented college grads or even advanced students also make good instructors.

Another potential market is coaching students to take standardized exams. High-school students must take them to get into college, and college students take them to get into graduate or professional schools. Preparatory courses are available for these exams, but many students prefer private instruction in their homes.

Professional qualifying exams exist in law, medicine, accounting, and a host of federal and state civil service occupations. Foreign language study, the study of English as a second language, and studies relating to career advancement are all areas where tutors are in demand.

Setting up a tutorial service is simple. A typewriter, telephone, and other basic office equipment are all you need. A continuing small ad in the local and university papers, supplemented by a Yellow Pages listing and fliers near schools, will provide adequate promotion. As for staff, many teachers are looking for extra income. Word of mouth may be all the recruitment you need.

Be sure to monitor the qualifications and work of your tutors carefully. Students should be able to change tutors at any time, and consistently unpopular tutors should be dropped. Payment for tutorial services should be made to you. Keep a percentage (25 percent is about right) and forward the rest to your tutors.

========= BRIGHT IDEA =========

DISPOSABLE-DIAPER DELIVERY

When Tobey L. J. Cotsen's friends started having babies, she found herself listening to conversations about diapers. One question stood out in her mind: "What do you do when you run out of diapers on a Sunday night?" Cotsen's answer was a profitable business called Bundle of Convenience. Their specialty? Delivering disposable diapers—and a host of other mothering essentials.

Catering to the needs of working moms, this Los Angeles—based company delivers! Offering over 200 products, Bundle of Convenience's merchandise is rivaling pizza as the "thirty-something" generation's favorite delivery item.

For almost the same price you'd pay in the stores, Bundle of Convenience is selling convenience to moms who don't want to spend hours going from store to store to buy all those little things babies require. "We're making their lives a little less hectic," says Cotsen. And with a small delivery charge, moms are happy to call Cotsen's service.

The company's warehouse contains everything a mother could want for her baby. "We have a great variety in our warehouse," Cotsen boasts. "Moms are so particular about the products they choose for their babies that we stock a lot of items that you can't find in any supermarket."

This kind of convenience is worth a lot to today's mothers, but it's worth more to Cotsen. With 250 Los Angeles moms shopping at different times and placing orders for an average of $65—some orders topping the $300 mark—she expects to gross at least $250,000 this year from this single location. After seeing the success of her service, Cotsen hopes to launch a franchise program nationwide. "I've already received more than 1,000 franchise inquiries," she says.

Cotsen credits the current baby boomlet with much of the interest in her service. But she insists that her success doesn't necessarily depend on the boomlet. "There will always be a need for this kind of service as long as moms use disposable diapers and formula," she says.

===================== BRIGHT IDEA =====================

GIFT WRAPPING SERVICE

In this era of clever packaging, perhaps we Americans now prefer the wrapping to the gift. At least most of us can appreciate a beautifully wrapped package. But with all the demands of modern living, few of us have the time to shop for gift wrap, let alone tangle with tape, paper, ribbons, and bows. And sadly, a few of us don't even know how to wrap a gift properly.

Only a few stores offer complimentary gift wrapping these days. In some, it's an ordeal just to get a box—especially during holiday seasons. And even when stores do provide gift wrapping, it's usually not a work of art. Rather, you get an inexpensive, all-occasion, cookie-cutter job.

You can take up the slack with your own gift wrapping service. Start out from a kiosk or cart at your local shopping mall. To guarantee volume, try leasing space for just the Christmas season (or Mother's Day, Valentine's Day, Graduation, etc.) to test the waters. Eventually, you can expand to a year-round packaging and shipping shop (see previous section for details).

Offer the best wrapping paper and custom bows (a far cry from the stick-on numbers most of us are accustomed to). Look for special accessories like stickers, silk flowers, and even small toys for accents. Make wrapping odd-shaped and oversized items your specialty—for instance, try wrapping a bicycle imaginatively. You may also want to offer packaging and shipping services for customers with long-distance recipients.

As a tie-in consider starting a drop-off service for mall shoppers who tire of lugging their purchases around with them during a day's browsing. A simple "hatcheck" system is sufficient, and a reasonable charge will minimize abuses. And as salespeople check in packages they'll also have the chance to ask if any need custom wrapping.

FLAT-FEE REAL-ESTATE COMPANY

High Net Profit Before Taxes:	$70,000 plus
Average Net Profit Before Taxes:	$50,000
Minimum Start-up:	$25,000
Average Start-up:	$35,000

Traditional realtors are getting a run for their money from a handful of companies who accept a flat fee to help homeowners sell their own homes. This form of do-it-yourself realty is the answer for millions of Americans who would like to sell their own homes, but shy away from the hassle of attempting it alone.

Flat-fee real estate eliminates the necessity of paying 6

percent or more in commission fees to a broker. And because sellers are able to save on the commission fee, they can price their homes below the going rate, make a faster sale, and still turn a profit. By opening a flat-fee real-estate company, you can tap into the hot real-estate market. You'll be solving a major consumer problem while making good money.

Big Profits

Successful flat-fee firms prove that real-estate companies don't have to charge commissions to make big profits. One company in Houston with only three salespeople nets well over $100,000 a year before taxes. Another two-person office in Memphis, Tennessee, boasts a yearly gross income of $150,000. The owner told us that his gross profit margin is 54 percent after subtracting sales commissions and advertising. With careful organization, he manages a $50,000 to $55,000 net income, or about 35 percent before taxes.

One beginning salesperson who works for a large Arizona firm brought in twenty listings during her first two weeks in the field. At $400 each, she earned $8,000 for the company. With salespeople like this, the company is realizing gross annual figures of $240,000 for a five-person office. At over 30 percent net profit, the firm was in the black after only a few months.

Great Idea

These companies simply provide advice and paperwork services to homeowners selling their homes. For flat fees ranging from $175 to $1,000, several services are provided.

Basically, all the companies do is carry out the detail work of writing appraisals (telling the seller how much he should ask for his home), helping with negotiations, financing, and closing details. Some companies provide the homeowners with FOR SALE signs and an effective advertisement to place in local newspapers.

Flat-fee real-estate companies don't waste time driving prospects around or sitting at an open house. The homeowners provide these services themselves. Salespeople concentrate their efforts on getting "listings," formal authorizations to sell houses.

Lots of Referral Business

The ultimate goal of your operation is repeat business and referrals. This comes with good service and getting your name known as a respected professional. When homes sell quickly, economically, and efficiently, your flat-fee company's phones will keep ringing.

===== BRIGHT IDEA =====

BOOK DETECTIVE

There are many famous detectives in fiction, but Gertrude Toll claims to be the only detective who tracks down fiction. For a fee of $10, Toll, owner of Pro Libris in Somerville, Massachusetts, will spend up to six months searching trade magazines, garage sales, swap meets, and anywhere else she can think of for a book her client wants. Many of the long-lost loves her clients want her to find are rare or out-of-print books, while others are simply odd.

Since 1983, Toll has been tracking down books. Working out of her home, Toll conducts most of her business by mail, and has received requests from as far away as Hong Kong and India.

Only about 5 percent of Toll's customers are repeat clients. "When you set up an ice cream store, if people like the flavors, they come back for more," Toll says. "In my business, while most of my customers are satisfied, they don't usually need to come back." However, librarians turn to Pro Libris again and again for replacement copies. Corporations, hospitals, and the like are now finding that with Pro Libris they can easily keep their reference and professional libraries updated.

Toll receives requests for books that are as varied as the people who want them. Subjects on Toll's seven-page wish list include architecture, Eastern philosophy, cooking, language, math, science, and even ornate plastering.

Has she ever been stumped? "I've searched for *America's Wild Turkey* by Henry Davis for five years," she laments. "Every so often I'd see it in a catalog or an ad, and I'd call to buy it and it would already be sold. That book is so elusive."

FURNITURE-STRIPPING SERVICE

High Net Profit Before Taxes:	$57,000
Average Net Profit Before Taxes:	$22,000
Minimum Start-up:	$ 5,000
Average Start-up:	$18,000

As years pass, antiques look better and better. Compared to the mass-produced furniture available in most stores today, antiques have a quality and style all their own. So it's no wonder that buying, selling, and collecting antiques continues to be a popular hobby. Antique dealers, ranging from small shops in private homes to large commercial enterprises, enjoy an endless flow of interested, well-heeled buyers as well as new collectors with limited budgets seeking their first "piece."

Whenever a business is thriving, a related service business is usually born to feed from it. And so it is with furniture stripping. Stripping furniture is not new: people have been doing it for years whenever they wanted to prepare an old piece of furniture for refinishing. But specialty houses that strip furniture as a consumer service are relatively new.

Strippers specialize in removing the old, many-layered finishes from old furniture. The general public seeks out this service because

1. It saves hours, sometimes days, of hard work;

2. It allows do-it-yourselfers to tackle the more pleasant aspects of refinishing jobs while avoiding the hard part; and

3. It eliminates the possibility of ruining a piece by employing improper stripping methods.

Antique shop owners and others in similar businesses employ the services of furniture-stripping outfits so they won't have to maintain refinishing facilities of their own.

People are willing to pay $7.00 and up to have a straight chair stripped (a task that takes a professional fifteen minutes), or from $150 on up for an entire dining set with six chairs. These fancy fees are charged for stripping jobs that require a minimum of time for the professional.

How Is the Profit Picture?

You can start this business from your home, if you have a garage or basement in which to work. Of course, this setup will limit your volume, but it is one way to start with a limited investment.

One-person operations, using occasional part-time help for pickup and delivery, are doing amazingly well. A volume of twenty-five to thirty jobs per month is common after the first few months of operation, and grosses range from $1,500 to $3,000 a month. Older shops with one or two full-time employees reported gross figures of $5,000 to $7,000 monthly—and they had been in business less than two years.

Net profits vary, but most strippers have estimated that 50 percent is adequate to cover overhead, materials, and all operating costs. The profit margin is related to volume because overhead is virtually fixed. Owner-operators are selling a service, and have lost expenses for materials. Thus, a successful shop grossing $7,000 a month will net about $3,000 for an owner-operator with two employees.

================ BRIGHT IDEA ================

DOMESTIC-HELP AGENCY

In today's dual-income society, it's no secret that domestic help is in demand. But where can the average person find qualified maids, repairpeople, nannies, and sitters? Increasingly, they're turning to domestic-help agencies.

Working people who don't have the time to clean their own homes, fix their own plumbing, or mind their own children also don't have the time to recruit and screen potential help. Yet their expectations are high. They want only the most qualified, reliable, trustworthy workers. After all, they're inviting these people to work in their homes, often without supervision.

Domestic-help agencies handle all kinds of workers for full-time, part-time, temporary, and permanent positions. Some specialize in baby-sitters or nannies. Others focus on cleaning personnel, errand runners, or repairpeople.

DomesticAide, a Lincoln, Nebraska—based franchise, offers customers a wide range of household help. "By adding services such as handymen, window washing, and others to the standard housekeeping offerings, we've created a full domestic-service business," says DomesticAide president Wayne Chevie.

To attract top-notch workers, some services offer specialized training. For instance, many nanny placement services provide classes in child care, psychology, and CPR. Strict screening of applicants is also a must: remember that clients are counting on you to provide better-than-average workers.

PET HOTEL AND GROOMING SERVICE

High Net Profit Before Taxes:	$60,000 plus
Average Net Profit Before Taxes:	$40,000
Minimum Start-up:	$53,000
Average Start-up:	$96,000

Reservations for boarding animals can be as difficult to obtain as hotel reservations. We should know. In researching this report, we called six different establishments to get one reservation for a holiday weekend. The average charge for boarding a medium-sized dog? About $15 a day.

Getting the dog bathed and clipped ("groomed" in the trade parlance) added another $15 to the bill. A typical weekend stay, Saturday and Sunday night, with grooming, totaled $60 for a typical terrier.

How much of that was profit? The cost of feeding a dog, per day, runs about $1.00. It takes a good groomer less than an hour to bathe and clip a dog. His or her commission is usually half the grooming fee—in this case $7.50. Thus, the expenses for this dog's visit probably don't add up to more than $10. That leaves a gross profit of nearly 70 percent on the $30 bill.

$1,300 Gross Profit for the Week

In an interview with the establishment's sole employee—the dog-and-cat groomer—he disclosed that the gross for a holiday week, which started on Monday and ended on Sunday, came to $1,674. This included thirty-one dogs that were brought in for grooming only.

Just an Average Operation

The groomer pointed out that holiday weeks usually run about double the normal volume. The average gross for this shop was about $800 weekly. Since the business had only been open for eight months, they couldn't provide annual figures. However, their weekly sales figures were not out of line with other pet hotels we polled.

Many pet boarding and grooming services gross $100,000 annually, some over $200,000. The average successful operation grossed between $50,000 and $60,000.

Many Facilities Are Poor

An informal poll of pet owners revealed that most are less than enthusiastic about their boarding facilities. One frequently used adjective was "dumpy."

Maintaining a clean, well-run facility will give any owner the competitive edge. Large runs (as opposed to small cages) and climate control (yes, air-conditioning) are two factors that can make a difference. Personal attention—to pets and owners alike—is also an important criterion. If owners feel good about leaving their pets at your facilities, you're already ahead of the competition.

===================== BRIGHT IDEA =====================

PET-SITTING SERVICE

You don't have to build a fancy facility to care for pets while their owners are away. In-home pet sitting is becoming as popular as conventional boarding. For a set fee, a pet sitter visits the client's home, feeds and exercises the pets, waters the plants, brings in the mail, and runs a minimum security check of the premises.

"We meet with the owner to handle administration first—

discussing the logistics like the number of visits, feeding techniques, special medication needs, and so on," says Virginia Gordon, vice-president of Critter Care, a Baton Rouge, Louisiana–based pet-care franchise. Personalized service extends to owners as well as pets. If pipes freeze or roofs cave in, Critter Care is there to help remedy the problem. Clients leave knowing that their pets—and their homes—won't go unattended in their absence.

In-home pet care is usually cheaper than conventional boarding—especially for clients with more than one pet. The cost of boarding two medium-sized dogs would be about $30 per day. Critter Care charges $10 per visit for two animals; if the two pets require two visits a day, the daily rate drops to $18.

The pet-sitting business isn't for everyone. The hours can be long (pets must be let out first thing in the morning and brought in late in the evening), and services usually work holidays and weekends. On the other hand, animal lovers find the work enjoyable. There aren't many other ways to profit from tossing a Frisbee or wrestling with a kitty during work hours.

BUSINESS SERVICES

BUSINESS BROKERAGE

High Net Profit Before Taxes:	$76,000
Average Net Profit Before Taxes:	$50,000
Minimum Start-up:	$15,000
Average Start-up:	$30,000

Selling a business is one of the biggest decisions a person can make. Much more complex than selling a house, transfers of business ownership demand considerable time and effort. Usually, business owners are so busy with their daily operations that they can't make the effort necessary to sell their businesses for a reasonable profit. All too often, the owner who attempts to sell his own business ends up selling it for less than it's actually worth, or worse, not selling it at all.

This is where the business broker steps in. A business broker represents the seller and takes over every aspect of the sales transaction. This includes assessing the value of the business, packaging it, marketing it, qualifying buyers, negotiating deals, and closing the sale.

Huge Market

The brokering business is positively booming. In only five years, the number of firms has more than doubled from

3,000 to over 7,000. But even this increase has barely put a dent in the market. Approximately 2.5 million businesses are put on the market each year, representing sales of over $200 billion. Yet less than half of those business sales are conducted by brokers, leaving plenty of room for growth in this industry.

The Business of Brokering

Brokers view their profession as a glamorous one in which high-powered deals can reach millions of dollars. This aspect of the industry attracts scores of people who, once immersed in the business, get hooked on it. Despite long hours and crazy schedules, business brokering can be—well, fun. "It tends to be addictive because it's so interesting," says one successful broker. "You're dealing with different types of businesses every day. It's never the same thing twice."

The fun, however, is mixed with a lot of hard work. This demanding profession isn't for everyone, and it requires both sales and financial skills. And although brokers do need the skills to review financial statements and the like, the desk-loving, 9-to-5 accountant or banker is not the right type for this field. Sales ability and a go-getter attitude are more important than a financial background.

Because the ability to sell a business depends directly on presenting it accurately, brokers need to discover the real reasons that a business is for sale. That's why one broker suggests that "brokers have to have an FBI personality. They have to know what they should ask—and they need to have the nerve to ask it." Finding out if sales are down or if the owner has been cheating on his taxes is part of the broker's job. And no business owner is going to reveal this information without some serious prompting. Be prepared to exert plenty of effort to get the truth.

High Returns on a Low Investment

Business brokering can bring in sizable profits, if you're a good salesperson. But you should be aware that the amount of time involved in making a sale can be lengthy: on the average, you'll need six to nine months to complete a transaction.

This means that when you're first starting up, you may not see any income for that length of time or longer. Your equipment and overhead will be relatively low in this business, but it's critical that you have enough operating capital to keep the business (and yourself) going while your business gets established. Estimates of $50,000 to $60,000 are not unreasonable.

That initial investment can pay off, however. One operator started in a one-man office in 1978, earned $90,000 in commission revenues his first year. Now he has seven employees and pulled in $350,000 in commission revenues last year. Many brokers, after only three or four years in business, are bringing in $150,000 to $300,000 in commissions. Depending on your sales ability and the size of the business you sell, profits can really soar.

Learn All About It

Business brokering represents an exciting opportunity for would-be business owners. But this is not a field you can get into without some skills and experience. Look for classes on buying and selling businesses to get a feel for what's involved, or consider buying a franchise that will train you in the ins and outs of business brokering.

===================== BRIGHT IDEA =====================

MINUTE BY MINUTE

Got a minute? If you're like a lot of corporations in this country, you probably don't. And that spells bad news, since corporations are required to keep accurate and up-to-date minutes by law.

Minutes are a record of the meetings and resolutions of a corporation and are legally binding. Without minutes, the law ceases to recognize a corporation as an entity and places the responsibility for the business's action on the doorstep of the corporate officers. Ruth Lewis, chief financial officer and staff attorney for Corporate Records Maintenance Services Inc. of Agoura Hills, California, estimates that over 90 percent of the corporations in California alone are at risk due to neglected corporate minutes.

However, Lewis and her partner Rebecca Staples (president of the firm) are out to change all that. They formed Corporate Records Maintenance Services on a part-time basis in 1987 to do one thing and one thing only: maintain corporate minutes for small businesses.

"When we first started the business, the hardest thing that we encountered was educating these people [small business owners] about the need for corporate minutes," Lewis says. "Many times a lot of them don't even know they need minutes. It's a heck of an education process."

Corporate Records Maintenance charges customers $250 for the first year and $195 per year after that. In addition to keeping minutes for companies, they also teach people how to update their minutes themselves.

With a mixture of direct mail and print advertising, Lewis and Staples have been able to take their business full-time and build a steady clientele. The partners attribute their company's success to their reasonable rates and hardworking staff.

JANITORIAL SERVICE

High Net Profit Before Taxes:	$65,000
Average Net Profit Before Taxes:	$24,000
Minimum Start-up:	$ 3,000
Average Start-up:	$ 8,000

If you're looking for a business with reasonable initial costs and don't mind getting your hands dirty, consider janitorial services. The janitorial industry is estimated to bring in between $25 and $30 billion annually. Many experts believe that janitorial services will be the biggest growth field for jobs in the United States over the next twenty years.

Janitorial-service companies supply a wide range of services, including periodic or daily cleaning of office buildings or private residences, restroom disinfecting, window cleaning, and dusting. Competition is fierce in many areas, especially large cities, but success can be achieved by anyone who's willing to work hard. After all, there's a huge market out there.

The janitorial-service industry grosses about $10 billion in annual sales and employs over 6 million people. When the economy is strong, the janitorial-service business booms. But because offices need to be cleaned no matter how well their occupants' businesses are doing, janitorial services make almost as much money during weak economic times. Several years ago, studies conducted by the Department of Labor predicted that from 1985 to 1995 more people would be employed as janitors than in any other profession, and over 779,000 new jobs would be created in the cleaning industry.

Most large buildings have replaced their in-house maintenance staff with outside janitorial services. Contracting out allows them to get their cleaning done more quickly and cuts hidden employment costs like medical insurance.

Treat It Like a Business

While it might seem that anyone with a mop and a vacuum can succeed in this business, the fact is that it takes more than cleaning skills to run a good janitorial service. You need accounting skills, management skills, promotional ability—basically all the skills you'd need to run any other business. One reason that the janitorial industry is growing so rapidly is that low start-up costs and apparent simplicity make this an attractive opportunity for entrepreneurs with little experience. Down the road, they discover that this is a real business and the skills they lack are sorely missed.

"You can't act like a janitor if you're the owner," says one successful janitorial operator. "You're a businessman. That means you've got to act like a businessman, dress like a businessman, and talk like a businessman."

Getting Contracts

With a little common sense and hard work, starting a janitorial service can be relatively easy. And if you choose your contracts carefully, you can keep start-up expenses low. Some offices can be serviced with the same tools a contractor uses to clean his or her home.

Smart entrepreneurs secure contracts before investing a lot of money in equipment. Once you have a firm monetary commitment, you can then buy all the equipment needed. Securing contracts is considered the toughest part of running a janitorial business. Large companies can afford to hire salespeople to go out after business, but small firms generally have to handle sales themselves. Contractors use cold calls and direct mailings to set up contract bid meetings with building managers.

Usually, but not always, the contract goes to the lowest bidder. Managers may also take into account the contractor's reputation, financial stability, supervisory organization, quality of past work, management ability, and technical strength, as well as price. A start-up contractor must try to meet as many of these criteria as possible. Janitorial services should be bonded and carry insurance.

Develop a System

Efficiency will be a key factor in your service's success, so take the time to train your employees. Simply handing them a mop or broom isn't enough. Develop a system for cleaning an office most efficiently—dividing the labor so that your staff works as a team. The more productive your staff is, and the less supervision they require, the more successful your company will be.

INFORMATION BROKERING

High Net Profit Before Taxes:	$135,000 plus
Average Net Profit Before Taxes:	$ 16,500
Minimum Start-up:	$ 3,500
Average Start-up:	$ 15,000

These days, it seems we need a broker for everything: real estate, stocks, mortgages and loans, mailing lists, liquidated goods—and, of course, information. What's that? You never heard of an information broker?

Perhaps you haven't, but thousands of American businesses have. In fact, information brokering is a $1.6 billion industry in America. Information brokers are a new breed of researchers who have evolved from the automation revolution that has transformed today's business world.

Thanks to Computers

The spread of computers into every facet of American life has made information brokering a viable small business. Before the computer revolution, a small-scale research service would not have been able to retrieve, catalog, store, and sell information to clients in a cost-effective way. An information broker would have needed a large, full-time research staff to find documents in libraries nationwide and a huge storage space for the wealth of publications used as sources.

The explosion of information available in virtually every field of knowledge allows businesses to gain access to new data on general and specific subjects that affect them. To keep a competitive edge, businesses must keep abreast of the latest developments in their fields and conduct various forms of market research. However, many businesses lack either the time or the money to hire others on a full-time basis to sort through the mountains of publications that might contain the data they are seeking.

This is where the information broker steps in. Normally hired on a per-project basis, the broker finds information in published and/or electronic sources, organizes it in a form that best suits the client's needs, and sells it based on the time spent and the expertise involved.

Not a Clipping Service

In some ways, the information broker resembles the clipping service; both the information broker and clipping-service professional gather data on a specific topic from a variety of sources. But this is where the similarity ends. Clipping services search publications for articles containing key words and submit the clips in bulk to the client. These articles are neither read nor analyzed by the clipping service. The client is left to sort through the data to see if they are useful.

The information broker, however, not only obtains information from public libraries or at wholesale prices from electronic data bases, but also analyzes the material to ensure its usefulness to the client. Depending on the agreement between broker and client, the broker may even be expected to present an in-depth analysis of the information.

What Do You Know?

Starting small in the information-brokering business often means selecting a few specialized fields of knowledge. Most brokers come from library backgrounds or are specialists in certain areas of knowledge. If you're thinking about starting an information brokerage, first ask what you know best. If there's a market for this knowledge, you may have already found the right specialty.

Otherwise, bear in mind that legal offices often need research help. Businesses of almost every type need specific information on their fields. Medical information is also at a premium, since the medical industry changes almost daily.

Although roughly 80 percent of this industry's total revenues are generated by the twenty largest companies, there is room for small operators. In addition to selecting a specialty, consider ways in which you can offer exceptional service. Clients often complain that the service they get from big information services is impersonal and slow. Speed, then, and personal attention should be two major considerations in designing your business.

Equipment, Please

To become an information broker, you'll need a microcomputer, a printer, a modem, and research skills. The equipment can be obtained for about $2,500, but you may also have to pay to learn the skills of electronic research in specific data bases. Over a period of time, the cost of doing this can add up to several thousand dollars. Subscribing to the various on-line services is another expense the beginning broker must bear. However, if you have basic knowledge of how to gather information and become familiar with computer-search techniques, there is no reason you can't make a profit right from the start.

Since information brokering adapts easily to a home environment, overhead costs can be kept reasonably low. Your chief outlay of time and money will be marketing, but our research shows that one-person info brokers charging $60 per hour can (after breaking even) bill from $40,000 to over $100,000 per year.

========== BRIGHT IDEA ==========

TEMPORARY HELP WITH A TWIST

Please, don't call them Kelly Girls. Many of today's temporary workers have titles—for instance, RN, JD, and CEO. Temporary employment is one of the hottest trends of the decade. Employers are wary of hiring permanent workers to fill spots that all too often are temporary. And workers are no longer wedded to the idea of working at a single company until gold-watch time. Temporary workers enjoy the freedom of working when they want and where they want, and they give employers new flexibility in staffing.

But what does this have to do with professionals like nurses, doctors, lawyers, and executives? Judging from the businesses we've interviewed recently, the answer is plenty. If a company is immobilized when a receptionist is out, imagine the panic felt when a nurse is out sick. And what does a small company do when it wants to launch a new marketing program, but doesn't have the resources for a permanent marketing exec? Professional temps are the solution for a growing number of companies that need help fast—but not for long.

Temporary-help services need not be expensive to start—especially if you pick a specialized field like medicine or law. Marketing is probably the most critical factor in the success or failure of such a venture. If your service is well run, though, you should find a market of employers eager to put your services to work.

========== BRIGHT IDEA ==========

INSTANT SIGN STORE

Fast food. Thirty-minute oil changes. Automated bank machines. In our fast-paced society, people have come to expect things instantaneously. As entrepreneurs try to keep pace with the public's demand for immediate gratification, a variety of new businesses have cropped up that cater to the "we want it now" attitude. One area that has experienced new growth is the instant sign industry.

Years ago, signs were primarily found adorning storefronts. But today, signs are plastered almost everywhere you look: on the sides of ambulances, police cars, and fire engines; along highways and roads; promoting grand openings and special sales; at trade shows, and more.

As a result, instant sign stores have become a profitable new business-to-business service. And with 19 million existing businesses in the United States, plus an additional million starting up each year, the potential customer base for an instant sign shop is virtually unlimited.

Technological Breakthrough

A relatively new segment of the sign industry, instant signs made their debut in the early 1980's, when Gerber Scientific Products in Connecticut introduced a computer system that made vinyl letters and logos that adhered to many different surfaces. The process allowed a wide variety of signs to be created in a relatively short time. Today, Gerber is still one of the leading manufacturers of instant sign equipment.

With more advanced technology being developed all the time, the instant-sign-shop owner can offer a wider variety of services and give the traditional sign maker a run for his money. For example, new developments in photographic equipment have already helped the instant sign industry to expand from banners to more complicated projects. With optical machinery, signs can even be made out of photographs.

With this new high-tech equipment, instant sign shops occupy a whole new niche in the sign-making industry. Traditional sign makers take weeks—sometimes even months—to complete a project. Today, large projects like billboards and neon signs are still left to the slower processes of the traditional sign maker. But businesses use a variety of less formal signs—for instance, to highlight special events or to use at trade shows—and these can be produced quickly and inexpensively by the instant sign shop. Instant sign equipment can also create lighted signs, vehicle lettering, and display advertising.

The Art of Signing

For the creation of simple signs, only three pieces of equipment are needed: a computer screen, a special keyboard designed for setting type and fonts, and a plotter (a cutting device). In addition, if you want to recreate specific images like logos, a scanner and digitize tablet are also necessary.

A large portion of the instant sign company's business will be geared toward making signs for exterior use, such as banners, fleet vehicles, and storefront advertising. Because vinyl is durable and easy to replace, it makes a good material for outdoor use. Though most sign stores are full-service (doing other types of signage, including gold leafing, silk screening, sandblasted signs, electrics, illuminations, and so on), the majority of their business—at least 90 percent—is vinyl work.

Computerized equipment has made it possible for nonartistic and inexperienced sign makers to break into the business successfully. Today's computers are so advanced that they do virtually all the design and production work for you. Once the vinyl has been printed and cut, applying it to the sign surface is a simple process—usually, all you have to do is peel the adhesive backing off the sign and stick it to the desired surface. Special tools smooth the sign out to a perfect finish.

Signs of the Times

There are approximately 20,000 computerized sign-making systems in operation around the nation today. They account for about $5 billion in sales. Most instant sign operations are one-, two-, or three-person operations. Though equipment, facility, and operational costs total an average of about $54,000 in this business, profit and growth potentials are attractive. Based on our research, an established instant sign business can bring in average pretax profits of $92,000.

Moreover, the future looks bright for this industry. As the technology becomes more advanced, the instant sign makers' range of applications and flexibility in design will undoubtedly continue to expand, enabling them to provide a broader market of customers with attractive and inexpensive signs. From banners to vehicles to displays, the instant sign industry is booming, as more and more entrepreneurs see the sign of the times.

LIQUIDATOR: SELLING DISTRESSED MERCHANDISE

High Net Profit Before Taxes:	$100,000 plus
Average Net Profit Before Taxes:	$ 50,000
Minimum Start-up:	$ 24,000
Average Start-up:	$ 35,000

If you are a gambler at heart, confident in your negotiation and sales abilities, imaginative, curious, and if you enjoy day-to-day challenges, you could become a professional liquidator and make as much as $250,000 a year. Even the average operator in this business nets close to $40,000 before taxes.

The personality traits described above are essential to even modest success in the liquidation business. But start-up costs are low, overhead is light, and you can start part-time from your home. The main obstacle for most newcomers is a lack of capital and contacts, but you can overcome these obstacles with diligence and patience.

Brokering liquidated goods involves matching buyers and sellers of distressed merchandise. Starting your liquidation business could be as simple as outbidding your competition by a penny per item and turning the goods over to a buyer. Your markup can be as high at 1,000 percent, though most deals fall in the 50-to-100-percent range. High volume deals bring in a lower markup, but reap high profits by sheer quantity.

How Liquidators Operate

A fire races through the basement of a local clothing store. It is extinguished before it reaches the main floor, but not before much of the merchandise has been ruined by smoke. The liquidator, Mr. X, pays a visit to the store's owner, asking about the extent of damage to the merchandise. The owner, after a thorough inventory check, informs Mr. X that $20,000 of his uninsured stock has been smoke-damaged and he must liquidate it.

Mr. X offers $2,000 cash (or 10 cents on the dollar) for the ruined goods. The store owner initially rejects Mr. X's offer as too low, only to find himself calling back a week later to accept it after a fruitless effort to obtain a better offer.

Mr. X has not been sitting idle waiting for this call; he's been preparing for it. Immediately after making his offer to the store's owner, he placed a number of calls to sources within the clothing industry. Within two days, he located the owner of a large secondhand shop willing to pay $3,500 for the goods, delivered. As soon as Mr. X's offer was accepted, a truck was hired and the goods reached their new owner within forty-eight hours.

Transporting the goods cost $200, leaving Mr. X with a profit of $1,300 for his efforts, which consisted of his initial visit to the store and eight or nine phone calls.

This scenario illustrates the way a liquidator works. Circumstances vary, but the basic ingredients are always the same. Somebody, for whatever reason, is forced to convert tangible property into cash. Someone else (the liquidator) steps in and purchases the goods at a fraction of their original cost. The liquidator then turns around and, using his or her resources and contacts, converts the goods back into cash as quickly as possible.

The liquidator must know the value of goods in today's market—his or her profit is at stake. A high bid may get the goods, but not at a price that allows profitable resale. The liquidator is not in the business of owning goods—just buying and selling them. The longer it takes to sell the goods, the less real profit he or she makes.

Liquidators deal strictly in cash. There is no such thing as installments or time payments. You need only as much starting capital as is required to conclude your first deal. This may be as little as $1,000 or as much as $50,000, depending on the deal you're trying to strike.

An Example of Unusual Outlets

One liquidator we contacted purchased 3,600 framed, low-priced paintings from a defunct art distributor. Using a small classified ad in *The Wall Street Journal,* he sold every painting within twenty-four days.

A motel operator purchased 1,000 paintings with plans to lease them to new motel owners. A bank bought 800 as gifts for new depositors. A supermarket chain bought 1,200 to promote as a special. And a small furniture store purchased the other 600 simply to sell retail.

"I could have sold another 4,000," the liquidator told us, "if I'd had them."

BUSINESS DEVELOPMENT CENTER

High Net Profit Before Taxes:	$95,000
Average Net Profit Before Taxes:	$50,000
Minimum Start-up:	$57,000
Average Start-up:	$90,000

Question: Where would you go for help if you were interested in starting your own business, but didn't know the first thing about how to do it? Or what if you're a small business owner, at home or out of town, and you need a place to set up a big meeting, fax a report, or get a letter written and typed?

What's the answer? In many cities, business development centers fit the bill. Small businesses need operating efficiency at minimum cost. With office automation becoming more complicated and extremely expensive, only the larger companies are able to afford keeping up with the technology race.

For a long time, the only option for the little guy was to farm out his business all over town—letters to a typing service, copying to a copy center, phone answering to a phone answering service, and incoming mail to a postal box service. Along the same line, someone interested in starting a business would have to visit a lawyer's office, an accounting firm, and a business consultant, and then make numerous trips to a word processing or secretarial service to get the papers in order. Now it looks as though these one-service-only options have a serious competitor: the business development center.

How It Works

A business development center is one of the newest additions to the service industry. Basically, it is where people can find all the resources necessary to answer their business needs in one place. They can hand over a portion of their headaches—whether it's typing, phone answering, or creating a business plan—to a company that will either do it for them or guide them through it. Some offer conference rooms for small meetings; packaging and shipping services; accounting, legal, and business consultation; and little extras like delivery, drive-thru, pickup, and drop-off, even free coffee and donuts.

According to most operators, the object is to create a professional, efficient, and comfortable office setting that will become an "office away from home" for the client.

Experience Counts

While the business-development-center operators we talked to came from a variety of backgrounds, having experience either owning a business or working with business owners helps. Firsthand experience in business will tell you what services your clients are likely to need. Also, a basic working knowledge of office equipment and machines will be a boon, including familiarity with computers, electric typewriters, copiers, facsimile machines, and calculators. Preferably, you will also have a number of business contacts in your Rolodex with whom to get started.

Most of your clients will be local businesspeople or soon-to-be businesspeople who will use one, several, or all of your services at one time or another. They will look to you for up-to-date, accurate information on starting a variety of businesses, as well as professional handling of their secretarial and other related needs. Whether you decide to concentrate on the consulting or the secretarial part of this operation, you still need to offer as much of "everything" as you can in order to bill your business as a full-service center.

Just the Beginning

This is truly just the beginning of a new frontier, and while the competition will soon become pretty stiff, it's currently not very significant. Start-up costs can be substantial, especially in the equipment category, ranging from $40,000 to $70,000. You need to provide your clients with state-of-the-art computer and communications services they cannot afford in-house, and that means a large investment for you.

In the long run, though, it's worth it: average net profit before taxes in this business is $50,000 and can go as high as $100,000 to $200,000. Virtually no one involved in this business sees an end in sight.

If you have a knack for helping other businesspeople take care of business, then starting a business development center may be just right for you. It is an exciting field that integrates computer technology, consulting, and secretarial support into a full-service operation, and it's just beginning to take off.

TELEPHONE ANSWERING SERVICE

High Net Profit Before Taxes:	$50,000 plus
Average Net Profit Before Taxes:	$33,000
Minimum Start-up:	$47,000
Average Start-up:	$80,000

Imagine making $2.8 million a year just answering someone else's phones. That's just what one Michigan company is doing. They started out with two staffers and a $4,000 cash investment. Now they have fourteen offices serving 6,000 customers.

Huge Demand

There are several reasons for the popularity of answering services. One is an increasing dependence on the telephone as a communication device. More and more important decisions are being made on the phone by major corporations, small businesses, doctors, and countless others. Many businesses would be literally incapacitated without a telephone. The alternatives—lengthy meetings, letters, memoranda, and the like—are just too slow.

Even the widespread popularity of answering machines hasn't eliminated the need for answering services. The most

expensive of these machines can't guarantee that an important message will be left at the sound of the tone. Many
people are so put off by these devices that they hang up
immediately. Mechanical failures are also a problem. When
push comes to shove, an answering machine simply can't
match the intelligence and personality of a live operator. And
even one lost call can mean thousands of dollars to a businessperson.

The operator can pick up any home or office phone, answer as the customer wants, and take messages, so there's
little possibility that critical calls are missed. Messages are
held until the customer calls to collect them. At many services, operators supply a number of additional services:
order-taking, making appointments, or providing basic information.

Profits Speak for Themselves

Of course, not all answering services gross over $2 million
annually. It takes several locations to do that. But a one-office
operation can gross upward of $150,000 annually, depend-
ing on the number of switchboards in operation and the
number of calls taken. Net profits reach 35 percent in well-
run shops. The average is about 15 to 20 percent.

Easy to Launch

You can start out small, as most answering services do,
and build volume to this level—or even higher—over a period
of time. The largest one-office operation we found grossed
$450,000 yearly. And two that were started at home in a
garage and a spare room gross over $150,000 yearly. Each of
these was launched by a sole operator using a ten-position,
call-director phone system, and each is now housed in a
fancy office with four switchboards each.

Starting small is definitely an option, but if you can swing
it financially, it's preferable to plan for expansion from the
beginning. Moving offices and equipment can be both costly
and time-consuming. And some utility companies charge
penalty fees when answering services relocate. If possible, try
to find a permanent location from the start.

By keeping costs to a minimum, you can start a modest answering service for less than $25,000. This covers the cost of installing one switchboard and the trunk-line cable from the telephone company, as well as "bare bones" office furniture and supplies. But remember that with this amount of start-up capital, you limit expansion and long-term profitability.

Prospects by the Thousands

Anyone with a telephone and a busy schedule is a good prospect for your services, but small businesses are an especially good target market. Small firms often lack the resources to hire telephone personnel. Yet being able to answer every phone call is critical to success. Best of all, the ranks of small businesses are growing every day.

Your best prospects are businesspeople, doctors, salespeople, and other professionals, as well as repair-service-business owners like plumbers, electricians, and anyone else who relies heavily on the telephone to conduct business. Put special emphasis on contacting people who are "on call" twenty-four hours: they need your services most.

SECRETARIAL SERVICE

High Net Profit Before Taxes:	$100,000
Average Net Profit Before Taxes:	$ 30,000
Minimum Start-up:	$ 3,000
Average Start-up:	$ 10,000

American businesses are drowning in a sea of paperwork. The cost of getting a letter out rises dramatically each year. It's not surprising that many secretarial-service firms are netting as much as $100,000 from the overflow of work available.

Secretarial services reduce costly overhead. The average secretarial service can produce and mail a letter for a fraction of what it costs in-house. For small businesses that can't afford full-time help and big organizations that have occasional overflow, secretarial services are lifesavers.

Big corporations, local government, and hospitals have enormous monthly dictation and transcription needs. They can cut payroll costs by contracting with outside services on a regular or "as needed" basis.

One bright operator now has eight branch offices with more than 200 employees and grosses more than $1.2 million a year. The firm has contracts with large hospitals for all their transcription work, and the owner nets more than $300,000 from his automated setup.

You Can Start Small

Most secretarial services start out with a single owner-operator. Typical services include typing, general bookkeeping, dictation, transcription, and copying. We found many services netting as much as $30,000 per year with a simple one-room office, desk, typewriter, word processor, and file space. You can work out of a spare room, garage, or basement in your home or apartment. Be warned, however, that small-scale home-based operations have limited profit potential. If you're ambitious, try to think big right from the start.

The Market Needs Personal Service

Large corporations can afford typing pools and private secretaries, but most smaller businesses can't keep a full-time secretary busy enough to justify the added payroll costs. That's the market for a service like this. A good location and personal service will make you competitive in most markets.

Many one-person secretarial firms net over $12,000 in their first year with little more than a Yellow Pages ad to attract customers. However, aggressive personal promotion, a speedy word processor, and two or three part-timers can build gross revenue up to $100,000.

Profits in this business depend on location, efficiency, and hustle. Some of the most profitable services we've seen offer dictation pickup and delivery, using part-time help.

Services You Should Offer

Small operators begin by offering a variety of word-processing services: correspondence, manuscripts, editing, proofreading, reports, financial statements, dictation, transcription, file organization, and statistical typing. Some services also offer to do research or special services for clients, but this time must be priced carefully so that it is profitable. Many owners offer résumé typing and preparation as well.

If you or one of your employees has a special skill, like the ability to do medical or legal typing, you can charge more for it. Be sure potential clients know the variety of services you offer. Some successful extras are translation services, bookkeeping and record keeping, file organizing and preparation, and engineering or scientific typing. Another excellent service is notary-public work.

===================== BRIGHT IDEA =====================

CONVENTIONAL SERVICES

Attending a convention has its good points: learning the latest about your industry, networking with fellow businesspeople, and getting away from the daily grind. But conventions also have their drawbacks. Between activities, you're often left with nothing to do. While you're out of town, your regular exercise routine is interrupted. And if you've brought the kids with you, you'll probably have a hard time finding a reliable sitter or making do without one.

Realizing the pitfalls of the average convention, entrepreneurs around the country are filling the void. All kinds of convention-oriented services are springing up in the form of tour groups, hotel-based exercise classes, and child-care programs.

Elsie Neely started the Children's Center in Washington, D.C., after experiencing firsthand the inadequacies of conventional child care. In 1980, Neely's attorney husband had just died. To relive old times, she decided to take her son to a Bar Association convention in Houston. "For the big banquet, I engaged a sitter for my son," Neely recalls. Midway through the evening, Neely felt a tug at her skirt. It was six-year-old Frank. "Where is your sitter?" she gasped.

"He walked out," answered the youngster.

At that moment Neely realized that out-of-town parents

have special needs. So she's tailored her Children's Center to fit those requirements. The Center offers fun outings to as many as 125 children, from infancy to age eighteen, whose parents are attending conventions or conferences, or are simply visiting the nation's capital and want to be child-free for a couple of days. Organized according to age groups, the children tour Washington's great museums and monuments and enjoy amusement parks, boat rides, roller and ice skating, movies, plays, concerts, and sporting events.

Neely works about fifteen conventions every summer. In addition to contacting convention planners herself, Neely promotes her business through the Washington Convention and Visitors Association.

SEMINAR PROMOTION

High Net Profit Before Taxes:	$1,000,000
Average Net Profit Before Taxes:	$ 25,000
Minimum Start-up:	$ 13,000
Average Start-up:	$ 25,000

Seminars have become one of the most profitable methods of selling information. With an investment as low as $3,000, a two-day seminar can bring in net profits as high as $20,000. Some promoters put on only three or four seminars each year and take home net profits before taxes of $50,000 to $100,000.

Why Are Seminars So Successful?

Seminars are a fast route to the latest information. Attendees have the opportunity to find out, straight from the mouths of experts, everything they need to know about a given subject. They can ask questions of presenters and discuss common problems with fellow participants. For people who don't have time to wade through books and magazines, seminars are a quick and concentrated way to learn what's new in their fields.

The rate for one-day seminars ranges from about $50 to $150. Weeklong seminars cost upward of $2,500. Seminars are often conducted under the headings "workshop," "conference," "course," and "meeting." Though these are often just synonyms for "seminar," there are sometimes variations in the way the material is presented.

Subject Matter Is Unlimited

The range of subjects covered in seminars is extensive, from "Selling to Nigeria" to "How to Play the Stock Market." Most subjects are geared toward people who wish to increase their education, technical skills, or ability to invest wisely.

Large corporations are the biggest subscribers to workshops. The well educated seem to be the most attuned to this service. They are often the best able to afford the seminars—either for themselves or their employees—and are usually better aware of the benefits of continuing education.

The seminar business isn't limited to corporate executives and college graduates, however. All sorts of people need new job skills, financial information, help in starting a business, or advice on everyday living. As long as the information is useful, you can probably find a viable market for your seminar.

Recruit Free Speakers

But you say you aren't an expert on any subject? You don't have to be to start your own seminar business.

Suppose you see a need in your community for a desktop publishing seminar. Desktop publishing systems are selling like hotcakes at local computer stores, but most buyers can't figure out how to use them. Even if you don't know the first thing about desktop publishing, you can sponsor a seminar on that subject by finding a speaker who does. Best of all, you can probably find a speaker who'll do the seminar for free.

Why would an expert want to conduct a seminar for free? For one thing, it's great publicity. Your seminar will give the speaker a chance to plug his or her book, extol the virtues of a particular software program, make contacts for future computer consulting work—all to a roomful of people who have already indicated an interest in the subject. Local experts may be willing to speak at your seminar for free. If a speaker must travel a long distance to attend your seminar, offer to pay expenses. Either way, you'll get a bargain.

Setting It Up

Hold your seminar at a suburban hotel or motel with meeting facilities that will hold 100 (your maximum expected attendance). These usually have a public-address system already installed.

Present each attendee with a workbook at the beginning of the class. This can be as simple as a loose-leaf notebook with an outline of the course and blank pages for notes. A typical expenditure for a low-investment seminar is about $13,000, but that excludes preopening operating expenses. Some successful promoters begin planning five to six months in advance.

Profit Projection and Break-even

If you charge $295 per person and fill the house with 100 attendees, you will gross $29,500 (less any discounts for cash and advance reservations). At these rates and with average expenses, your break-even point is twenty-two or twenty-three attendees.

Direct mail is probably the most effective marketing tool for seminars. Choosing the right mailing list is especially critical. If you choose your list carefully (we suggest hiring a list broker to help: since they work on commission from list owners, you pay them nothing), have a salable subject, and the price is right, you can expect a return of more than 1/10 of 1 percent on your list alone. A few promoters with small lists have gotten returns as high as 5 percent, but 1 percent is considered good. This is only realistic if the names on the list have been prequalified as interested in the subject and if the price is right. Experienced promoters usually make more than one mailing to their prospect lists. Saturation-type marketing pays high dividends.

EMPLOYMENT AGENCY

High Net Profit Before Taxes:	$50,000 plus
Average Net Profit Before Taxes:	$35,000
Minimum Start-up:	$22,000
Average Start-up:	$30,000

Though the concept of employment is as old as civilization, the hiring process continues to be primitive at best. And ironically, no matter which side you're on, finding the perfect match is no picnic. Job seekers end up convinced that no good jobs exist. Employers complain that qualified candidates are impossible to find. Both parties spend hours upon hours following the wrong leads and interviewing the wrong candidates.

Part of the problem is that the average person—whether potential employee or employer—isn't an expert on employment. A job seeker may know how to write computer programs or run a marketing department, but chances are he or she doesn't know the first thing about finding a job. Conversely, many department heads are great at supervising jobs and balancing budgets, but flustered by the prospect of hiring the right person.

You can provide a happy alternative. For years, employment agencies have been bringing job seekers and employers together—all for a tidy profit. A successful employment agency can bring in a six-figure gross during its first year of business. The profits are high, the cost of entering the field is relatively low, and the demand for such services is consistent.

An Alternative to the Cattle Call

For many job seekers, a job search entails little more than scanning the newspaper want ads. But want ads aren't the answer. A help-wanted ad in a metropolitan newspaper brings in an enormous response—as many as 300 or 400 résumés. With that kind of competition, job seekers have little or no chance of landing an interview, let alone an actual position.

The situation is even worse for the employer. Sifting through a bag of résumés is tedious, mind-numbing work. Many companies report that the caliber of applicants is not up to their expectations. In some cases, 85 percent of the people who applied did not meet the job qualifications. Often, want ads act as a cattle call for potential employers: they get quantity, not quality. They waste time and money dealing with unqualified candidates—time they should be spending on their regular work.

For these reasons, a good employment agency is a boon to both parties. Applicants don't have to investigate every colorfully worded newspaper ad, saving them time and transportation costs. And employers don't have to screen hundreds of applicants to find one good employee.

Investment

The investment required to open a brand-new employment agency, as opposed to buying an existing one, is relatively low. The most important goal is to create a good public image through the quality and location of the offices. Applicants coming in to register may be doubtful of the agency's abilities and professional standards if they find dreary offices in an old building, furnished with odd pieces of worn equipment. A professional environment is essential in this business. Attractive offices with a well-furnished waiting room and counseling rooms that are at least 10-by-12 feet and private is a good investment in the long run.

While many private employment agencies are located in the midst of questionable business surroundings—some prefer the high-traffic areas around shopping centers—the most successful are located in a professional atmosphere. Buildings that house doctors, lawyers, investment counselors, and insurance agents are good choices. This gives an agency the image of professionalism, which can go a long way in establishing your credibility.

Profit Potential

The success of your operation will depend on the caliber of the placement counselors you hire, the experience and abilities of your manager, and other factors such as local and national economic and employment conditions. Thus it is difficult to project a gross-income figure for a new private agency. But many established agencies top $100,000 in sales during their first year.

PARKING-LOT STRIPING SERVICE

High Net Profit Before Taxes:	$42,000
Average Net Profit Before Taxes:	$28,000
Minimum Start-up:	$ 6,700
Average Start-up:	$10,500

Here's a legitimate, stable business you can start with little cash and no special talents. Parking-lot maintenance is simple to set up on a full-time or part-time basis. You can enter the business as a parking-lot striper, and eventually add paving and other maintenance to your list of services.

Most businesses—whether in office parks or shopping malls, industrial zones or high rises—have parking lots. Depending on climate and usage, these lots must be restriped regularly; some once every five years, others annually. The average interval is eighteen months.

The average restriping contract exceeds $200, with a gross-profit margin of over 65 percent. The price for striping alone would be about one half as much, but other things usually need attention, such as resealing asphalt and filling holes. Also, numbers, names, and parking instructions often need touch-ups.

Unlimited Market

Remember that your market isn't limited to retail-business parking lots. Factories, schools, apartment buildings, motels, airports, churches—anywhere cars are parked off-street—may require your services. Some small towns, for example, do not own striping equipment of their own, but contract out the painting of traffic safety lines on streets.

Large shopping centers may have parking spaces for 2,000 to 5,000 small cars. Their striping and repair contracts can run as high as $10,000. Usually the job goes to the lowest bidder—and that could easily be you.

The aisles of factories and warehouses are often striped. In fact, OSHA safety laws require striping around machines, conveyors, and the like. Tennis courts are another potential source of business, as are fields for baseball, basketball, handball, and so on.

Room for Small Operators

In many cities, the number of parking-lot contractors doesn't seem to match the number of parking lots. In towns of 200,000 to 300,000 people, we often found no more than one or two contractors listed in the Yellow Pages. Many of these were paving contractors who also happened to do parking lots.

When we called to price restriping for a fifty-car lot, we were quoted some outrageously high prices. Obviously, most contractors weren't interested in such a small job.

After talking to over a dozen contractors, we found out why. Most contractors were interested in obtaining new parking-lot contracts, including engineering, paving, striping, bumpers, and marking. Their overhead was so high that small jobs were not worthwhile.

The market is wide open for newcomers who are willing to make personal calls on prospective customers. Chances are you will find little or no competition for small jobs. And because of your low overhead, you may also be the lowest bidder on many large striping jobs.

Case History Number One

We found a man who started his business in the winter, removing snow from merchants' parking lots. At the end of the winter, he realized he could stay in business year-round by repairing and restriping the lots.

For starting equipment, he bought a small, eight-horsepower tractor with a snow-thrower attachment for $1,250, making a $300 down payment. He used the money from contracts made during the summer repairing and restriping lots to build up an equipment inventory of three large tractors for use in the winter. His income was $23,500 the following year.

First Job—His Employer

Another operator began by obtaining his first restriping contract from the factory that employed him. He bought the striping machine on a Friday, completed the job on Saturday, and earned enough to pay for the machine before his down payment had time to clear the bank.

Every evening after work, he drove around the city looking for lots in need of repair and estimated the cost of the work to be done. The next day, during his lunch hour and coffee breaks, he phoned the owners of the lots. The work he obtained was done on weekends and evenings when the lots were not in use. On the first job he taught a teenage neighbor how to handle the striper, and eventually instructed him in all other phases of application and surface repair.

Within thirty days, the owner was averaging two or three jobs per week, which gave him the confidence to quit his job and go into business full-time. After two years, he employs four people full-time and operates two trucks a day.

PLANT RENTAL SERVICE

High Net Profit Before Taxes:	$50,000 plus
Average Net Profit Before Taxes:	$20,000
Minimum Start-up:	$16,000
Average Start-up:	$28,000

Indoor plants are here to stay. What began as a fad in the seventies is now the accepted way of decorating. Plants add life to homes and offices alike—and don't forget businesses like restaurants and banks. Experts who study buying trends expect plant sales to continue strong for years to come.

Yet surprisingly few people know how to care for plants properly. One reason is that every plant is different. A diffenbachia has different requirements for light and water than, say, a barrel cactus. The average homeowner (or office employee, waiter, or hotel clerk) doesn't know the nuances of horticulture. Every day, people buy plants that are doomed to wilt, droop, or rot because of simple ignorance.

Plant-care ignorance can be expensive. Some exotic trees cost as much as $500—simply placing that tree in the wrong spot can kill it. For people who invest a lot in greenery—business owners in particular—poor plant care can translate into financial disaster.

What's the Answer?

Plant owners are waking up to the fact that their plants are a valuable investment. No sensible restaurant owner would let the headwaiter install the plumbing or the hostess repair the cash registers. So why should these people be put in charge of plant care? A restaurant may have as many as forty or fifty expensive plants. A bank may have as many as twelve or fifteen.

When the employees or owners of a business care for the plants, the results are predictably poor. They rely on advice from the shop where the plants were purchased, advice that is usually insufficient because it is difficult for the plant-shop owner to prescribe at a distance. Many businesses conclude that the nuisance (and cost!) is not worth the decorative value.

Some large plant shops have realized that extra income can be generated with plant-service departments. We interviewed eight shop owners who offer this service; two of them have two full-time service people each.

Across the country, we found dozens of "plant doctors" and service people who did not own or have any association with plant shops, although several did have small greenhouses next to their homes. One establishment, only a year old, was netting over $3,000 per month, before taxes.

Ideal Setups

One operator we talked to concentrated her efforts in a high-income community, charging a monthly service fee to wealthy homeowners and apartment dwellers for weekly plant maintenance.

On the outskirts of this community were many dinner restaurants to which she leased or rented plants on a service-contract basis. Also, nearby were several office complexes. Many of the companies in these complexes leased plants from her. Three banks and four savings and loan companies either leased plants or contracted for weekly service.

Another entrepreneur did none of the plant maintenance himself, but employed two people who worked a few hours a day servicing his clients. These employees were homemakers who raised plants as a hobby. They had gained a wealth of experience and knowledge by caring for their large collections of plants and reading most of the books available on the subject.

He was a full-time salesman for a building-products man-ufacturer. By spending an hour or so each day selling his plant service instead of building products, in eleven months he built his gross to $2,800 per month from service con-tracts, plus additional profits from leasing plants.

Plants for Lease?

Leasing is the most profitable area of the plant business. If you grow the plants yourself, you should get your money back on a plant in two to three months. If you buy from a wholesaler, your costs will be covered in five to seven months. The 100-percent return on your investment in less than a year is excellent—and you still own the plants.

Some plants draw an even higher return if they are sus-ceptible to illness in the environment in which they are placed. A Boston fern, for example, becomes sick quickly under dry, low-light conditions. Even if returned to an op-timum environment, it is difficult to revive. Plant leasers usually request a 50-percent premium over their regular rates under these conditions.

Rates

Most plant-leasing companies structure their rates ac-cording to wholesale price. The average monthly rate is 15 to 20 percent of the wholesale price, which is usually a little over one third the retail price. In other words, a plant that retails for $25 will wholesale for $10 and rent for $1.50 to $2.00 per month.

The rental fee is based on a plant with a standard clay or plastic pot. If the renter wants a more decorative container or hanging fixture, he must pay for it (at retail) at the time of installation (more profit for you, at a 50-percent margin).

Servicing

Free weekly service is included as part of the rental fee unless there are only a few plants. Then the rental fee is raised to cover the cost of the weekly visit. Plant lessors also guarantee that each plant will remain healthy and attractive.

In a dark restaurant, most of the plants will be exchanged

each week or two for new plants. The original plants are taken back to the greenhouse for recuperation and returned when the replacement plants begin to suffer. A higher rental fee is usually charged to offset the extra handling cost.

Obviously, the more plants leased to one location, the higher the profit margin. For example, if a location has twelve plants and it takes one hour weekly to service all the plants, including travel time, the service cost per plant per month will be about $1.25. But if another lessee has thirty-six plants and service time per week is two hours, the monthly service cost per plant drops to about $0.83.

CROSS-COUNTRY TRUCKING

High Net Profit Before Taxes:	$47,000 plus
Average Net Profit Before Taxes:	$38,000
Minimum Start-up:	$16,000
Average Start-up:	$21,000

Are you a free-wheeling, independent type? Are you looking for an industry that needs new talent? Maybe it's time to hit the open road. The American Trucking Association (ATA) predicts that there will be a shortage of over 500,000 drivers by the mid-1990's. Stricter regulations, such as mandatory drug-testing policies, will take many drivers off the road—and replacements will be needed. The implementation of a national driver's license, which will eliminate the practice of carrying multiple state licenses, is also expected to remove drivers from behind the wheel.

All this translates into an increased demand for qualified, reliable truckers. If you like to travel and don't mind a nomadic existence, you can make good money and see the country from behind the wheel of a big rig.

Big Profits

Profits varied for the independent truckers we talked to. One reported a net profit of $27,000 before taxes on a gross of $93,000 and 200,000 miles. Another estimated pretax profits of $35,000 on a gross of $100,000 and about the same mileage. The average was between $25,000 and $30,000 a year on start-up investments ranging from $18,000 to $36,000.

Four Best Ways to Begin

For travel-minded entrepreneurs, there are four different ways to enter the trucking industry. The hardest way is to become an independent owner-operator and haul your own freight. This requires you to obtain an ICC authority. It will take longer to get into the business this way, especially if a protest is entered by a competitor.

A second, more practical approach is working under a contract basis for one of the large freight companies. This eliminates the need for an authority, and part of your insurance and other costs are picked up by the freight company. You still own and maintain your own rig, but the freight company generates much of your business.

A third way to enter is as a furniture mover for one of the larger moving companies. Some companies even offer training programs for aspiring truckers. Call companies in your area for details.

A fourth way to get into the trucking business is to hire on as a dockworker for a freight line, get to know the trucks and loading and unloading procedures, move up as a "second carrier" (the truck-driving equivalent of a copilot), and finally obtain your own rig. This takes the most time, but the experience is invaluable, and it allows you to "test the waters" first.

Personal Independence

Few businesses offer the independence available to the men and women who push rigs across the country night and day. It can be a rough life, but one in which you can accumulate a lot of capital in a short time. Many truckers have used the road as a stepping-stone into other businesses, or as a way to get through college or accomplish other goals.

Living expenses on the road are usually minimal: you live out of your rig and move from one truck stop to another fifty weeks out of the year. Many tax advantages also exist. As an independent contractor, numerous expenses are deductible, including depreciation of your truck and equipment, insurance, maintenance, and even food and lodging (check with your accountant for full details). With the right planning, you can end up with a fat bank account.

4

FOOD

BREAKFAST IN BED

Imagine waking up to eggs Benedict and champagne in bed, prepared by a chef in your own home and served with fine china, crystal stemware, silver, linen, and fresh flowers.

A dream come true? No, it's a nifty business idea that's sweeping the country. A professional chef and food server arrive at the client's home with their own equipment and food and prepare a breakfast fit for a king. Packages, which run the gamut from omelets and eggs Benedict to croissants and cafés au lait, make great gifts and are a terrific way to commemorate a special occasion.

We've spotted breakfast-in-bed services in several major cities, but many communities that could support such businesses don't have them. Yet this isn't a difficult business to break into. Initial start-up costs are low, and overhead is modest. Fees, on the other hand, are attractive—most services start at $65 a couple.

Consider linking up with existing restaurants, caterers, bakeries, etc., for food supplies and kitchen access. Advertise in theater programs and slick regional magazines to attract the affluent clientele you're after.

MUFFIN SHOP

High Net Profit Before Taxes:	$85,000
Average Net Profit Before Taxes:	$68,000
Minimum Start-up:	$35,000
Average Start-up:	$54,000

You're looking for something warm, hearty, and satisfying for breakfast, something you can get quickly and that doesn't cost an arm and a leg. Something sweeter than a croissant, but not as sweet as a Danish—something, in short, like a muffin. And if you're looking for a business that's warm, hearty, and profitable, then feast your eyes on the muffin shop.

Palatable Business

Most of the muffin shops we contacted, with facilities ranging from 600 to 700 square feet, gross $200,000 to $300,000 annually. That's 500 to 700 muffins a day! Profit margins can be very high because product costs are low, and muffin shops are usually high-volume operations.

What's more, since you're selling only one or a few products, you can operate with just a few employees, your production is uncomplicated, and your inventory is relatively small. Net profit before taxes is as high as 30 percent of gross sales in some successful operations. A specialty bakery that sells muffins only is a relatively new concept, so there is still plenty of room for growth in this industry.

They're Good for You

The recent muffin craze is due in part to the great American pursuit of health. While the average per capita consumption of bakery desserts is constantly increasing, so, too, is the demand for healthier baked goods. Muffins, although they do contain fat, are baked, not fried, and many are available sugar- and sodium-free. They also contain fiber, so they have a decided edge over doughnuts or sweet, sticky pastries.

Today's muffins usually weigh between ¼ and ½ pound each, measure 3½ inches across the top, and retail for $0.75

to $1.25. The flavor varieties are nearly infinite, but staples include apple spice, banana, blueberry, bran, carrot, cheddar, chocolate, coconut, corn, cranberry, prune, pumpkin, raisin walnut, and zucchini.

Muffin quality has improved with the advent of specialized muffin shops—and with those improvements have come sophisticated consumer tastes. If consumers are aware that a better-quality product exists, they're usually willing to make an extra effort to get it. For muffin shops that are well situated and offer plump, toothsome products at a reasonable price, plenty of customers and profits await.

Product Streamlining Is the Key

Muffin shops come under the category of specialty bakeries, operations that sell only one or a few types of baked goods. The most obvious success story in this industry is that of Mrs. Fields' Cookies. Debra Fields started her first cookie shop in 1977 and struggled to keep it open until people, slow to respond, eventually discovered the goodness and freshness of her products. Her subsequent success is entrepreneurial history.

Mrs. Fields and others like her helped open retail baking, formerly a highly specialized industry requiring years of experience, to businesspeople eager to start their own small bakeries with little or no previous experience. The expertise required to perfect just one recipe and production method is much more accessible than that required for a full-service bakery.

You don't have to be a pastry chef or even a good cook to run a successful muffin shop. There are food technologists and suppliers out there who will be glad to help you formulate your recipes and streamline your production so that you and your employees can manage everything. All you need is a good head on your shoulders, a realistic financial plan, sufficient start-up capital, and good old-fashioned stick-to-itiveness.

Making muffins is not the most ordinary way of making a living. On the one hand, it's a serious business, and if done right, it can earn you impressive profits. On the other hand, it's a business to have fun with. After all, what could be better than selling a product everyone loves—muffins like Grandma used to make?

HEALTH-FOOD AND VITAMIN STORE

High Net Profit Before Taxes:	$80,000
Average Net Profit Before Taxes:	$28,000
Minimum Start-up:	$29,000
Average Start-up:	$57,000

Health food isn't just for hippies anymore. The more you read about pesticides, hormones, preservatives, and chemical additives, the more you want to avoid them. The demand for organically grown produce, natural meats, healthy foods, and vitamins didn't go out with the seventies. In fact, these days the demand may be stronger than ever.

Yet the health-food market is changing. Successful shops focus less on granola and gorp and more on fresh fruits, vegetables, and meats. Yes, you can still find whole-grain bread, tofu ice cream, and brown-rice cookies in most health-food stores. But you'll probably also find a number of all-natural staples—the same foods you might find in a supermarket, only less processed and free of chemicals. Health-food shops are no longer the domain of the eccentric and the organic. They're hip, they're polished, and they're ready for the mainstream.

Profits Are in the Pink

The health-food industry accounts for 6 to 9 percent of the annual food business, between $30 billion and $40 billion strong. And there are healthy business segments within the wider market. Yogurt, for example, is a $1.3-billion industry in this country. The vitamin industry accounts for nearly $2.7 billion all by itself. Food manufacturers, processors, and growers admit that the pressure is on to respond to this growing market. That's where health-food retailers come in.

Health-food and vitamin retailers bring in healthy markups on inventory—from 54 percent to 100 percent on most items. Perishables such as organically grown produce do even better, carrying up to 300 percent markups to cover spoilage losses.

With markups at these levels, and because of limited square footage and controlled operations, health-food stores are realizing bottom-line nets in the 10-percent range. Compare this to major supermarket chains, which depend on volume to obtain net profits that barely reach 3 percent.

The smallest 1,500- to 2,500-square-foot store will typically stock between $10,000 and $20,000 in inventory, and turn it over eight to ten times a year. This translates into gross sales of $360,000 to $600,000, and bottom-line nets in the $35,000 to $45,000 area. We found sharp operators grossing $750,000 a year and more.

Everyone Wants to Be Healthy

Everyone from teenagers to office workers to upper-class homemakers and business executives is shopping at health-food stores, using them as full-service grocery stores as well as a place to pick up a snack or bottle of vitamins. We found young athletic men buying wheat-germ oil standing elbow to elbow with senior citizens stocking up on herbal remedies for everything from sniffles to insomnia.

The primary health-food shopper is female, thirty-five years and older. In fact, 75 percent of the health-food and vitamin business comes from this market segment. The secondary market is made up of women aged twenty-five to forty, who are often shopping for their families. While an increasing number of males are participating in the movement toward fitness, nutrition, and health, it is the women who do most of the shopping. Remember this when planning your advertising and merchandising strategy.

Integrity Matters

As a health-food retailer, you will enjoy several benefits that mass-market grocers do not. You won't have to run promotional contests, discount your merchandise to death, or stay open twenty-four hours.

On the other hand, you won't be able to get away with sloppy standards. True health-food aficionados know their stuff. Let them catch you with a display of Twinkies or a shipment of pesticide-sprayed apples and your credibility is shot. Take the time to educate yourself on food-related issues. Find out what health-food shoppers want—and don't want—from the food they buy. If you stock vitamins, make sure they're of the highest quality and see to it that your staff is knowledgeable.

Health consciousness is more than a fad in America. Consumers are smarter than ever about nutrition, fitness, and the perils of chemically treated food. You can offer a healthy, sensible alternative to superprocessed supermarket fare—and maintain a healthy business.

=======BRIGHT IDEA=======

FINE CUISINE AT 50,000 FEET

Hungry airline travelers know the dread of hearing "dinner" service announced and then being presented with unappetizing fare—roast beef that looks more like the sole of your shoe, mashed potatoes smothered in lumpy gravy, and sponge cake that tastes like an actual sponge. While most flyers suffer through these second-class suppers, others are dining in style thanks to Carlo and Elizabeth "Lisa" Middione.

The San Francisco couple caters sumptuous takeout meals for flyers who can't stomach the rough stuff. The meals are packaged in black picnic boxes, embossed with the Vivande Porta Via logo, and purchased in bulk from Traffic, a vendor in Vernon, California. Diners can choose from a wide variety of enticing meals, including pasta salads, fresh sausages, and baked desserts.

The Middiones began their takeout service in 1981, and business has grown steadily since then. With more and more people traveling and refining their palates, Vivande is really taking off. The company's sales volume has doubled since the business opened its doors seven years ago. Today, Vivande's mailing list includes some 12,000 names, many of them very well known. Lisa boasts, "We've sold meals to everyone from Henry Kissinger and Goldie Hawn to Catherine Deneuve."

While catering to private jets accounts for a large percentage of its business, Vivande also provides meals for commercial-airline travelers. At the request of their clients, Vivande added a few tables at its location to create a café atmosphere and also provides over-the-counter retail and full-staff service catering. The bulk of their business remains the airline-traveler takeout meals, which average about $15 to $20 a-piece. However, a complete dinner including entrée, dessert, and wine can go as high as $100 per person.

Although the company has nine chefs on staff, Carlo Middione doesn't leave all the cooking to them. "I insist on cooking," he says. "Otherwise, I would just get a job as a maître d' or kitchen manager. I'm always worrying about things like scheduling workers and making sure the soup is just right, and sometimes it gets very confusing."

If only more entrepreneurs would follow the Middiones' lead and tackle the airline-food problem head-on. The skies wouldn't only be friendlier—they'd be tastier, too.

MOBILE RESTAURANT

High Net Profit Before Taxes:	$50,000 (two units)
Average Net Profit Before Taxes:	$26,000
Minimum Start-up:	$12,000
Average Start-up:	$30,000

The catering truck sounds its horn, and for a moment normally serious, hardworking adults respond like Pavlov's dogs. Employees of every rank file out for soda, coffee, cookies, sweet rolls, sandwiches, chips, and candy. At many factories and office buildings, these trucks return twice or even three times a day. Nationwide, mobile restaurants like these serve up some $1.2 billion in ready-to-eat foods annually.

Mobile restaurants have become a kind of workplace institution. Often, factory and office managers will coordinate break times with the arrival of the sandwich truck. With a well-scheduled route, you can net $150 per day. If you prepare your own sandwiches, you can yield about $3,300 per month before taxes.

Many Areas Untapped

The mobile-food business started during World War II to service war plants that were far from restaurants and snack bars. Since then, the concept has spread across the country slowly. Some cities have never heard of the service. Others could use more. A city of 100,000 can easily support twenty catering trucks.

The business is highly competitive in some areas, but many major cities have plenty of room for newcomers. The largest factories and office buildings have their own cafeterias, but most people in America work at facilities that have fewer than twenty employees, the minimum number of people necessary to have an in-house cafeteria.

Few Independents

Industry surveys show that over 50 percent of the catering trucks are owned by companies with ten or more trucks, some employing as many as 100 units.

Most companies do not hire crews of drivers, but assign specific routes. The company supplies the truck and the route, for which the driver puts up a deposit, usually at least $500. The driver gets a fully stocked truck, which must be restocked daily from a company commissary for cash at wholesale prices (40 to 50 percent off retail). The driver also pays the company $25 to $35 a day for the use of the truck. The company pays for repair of the vehicle, insurance, health-department permits, and a business license. The driver pays for gas and oil. A driver can net $10,000 to $25,000 per year, depending on the volume of sales.

If you own your own truck, most companies will give you a route in return for a guarantee that you will buy all your food from them. However, they still require a cash-performance deposit of up to $500. The truck owner/driver will net from $15,000 to $30,000 per year.

=== BRIGHT IDEA ===

SHORE TO DOOR

Fresh fish can't swim to your door, so here's the next best thing. Puyallup, Washington, entrepreneur Kim Paeper's company, Shore to Door, delivers flash-frozen seafood to clients' homes.

The business started with a brainstorming session. "We were sitting around at my former job with a seafood company thinking of services that might be needed in the seafood business," Paeper recalls. "I was dissatisfied with the quality of fresh seafood that was available in our area and thought of a service that would deliver a high-quality product right to the home."

As simple as the concept may have been, no one else had thought of it. Paeper reports, "I did some market research in the area and found that there were no seafood delivery services," she says. "So I started Shore to Door in 1986 and operated on a part-time basis while still working at my regular job."

It didn't take very long before Paeper was able to take her unique seafood service full-time—her product was an instant hit. "Our fish is often of a higher quality than what's considered fresh fish because the fish is frozen immediately after it's caught and then it's shipped right away."

Americans certainly have an interest in buying fresh fish of late. Since the perils of eating red meat have been publicized over the past several years, more and more people are turning to fish as an alternative source of protein. Yet few things are worse than eating bad fish—and that's what's available in most supermarkets. The delivery concept makes Shore to Door contemporary: it's even more convenient than visiting the local grocer.

"I still deliver all of the seafood myself," says Paeper, "and now we've launched a catering business to complement the seafood company. It's a perfect mix, and I expect that sales will double this year."

LOW-CALORIE BAKERY

High Net Profit Before Taxes:	$ 91,000
Average Net Profit Before Taxes:	$ 70,000
Minimum Start-up:	$ 84,000
Average Start-up:	$120,000

It rots your teeth. It pads your hips. It causes rapid mood swings. Sugar has a bad rep, and it's only getting worse. Over 100 million Americans identify themselves as diet-conscious, and for most of those dieters, sugar is off limits. Millions of diabetics have to limit their intake of sugar for medical reasons. Millions of other people simply object to refined sugar as unhealthy, even sinful.

But the craving for sweets persists. After an hour of vigorous aerobics or a strenuous run, a person is apt to feel entitled to a little indulgence. It's this rationale that's prompted tremendous growth in the gourmet-food industry—and a lot of guilt as well. Sneaking a few chocolates or a slice of cheesecake here and there leaves most health nuts feeling cheap and sullied.

Our love-hate relationship with sugar has set the stage for an explosion in the sugarless-sweets business. Of course, some people have always had a taste for sugarless products. But most of us equate "sugarless" with bland, bitter, and bad. Recent consumer interest in sugarless products, though, has brought about some encouraging advances in the search for sugarless sweets.

Sugar-free Shops

Innovative retailers and food technologists have developed low-calorie, sugarless treats that are downright delicious. Don't believe it? The stores we contacted offered a wide array of candy, chocolates, ice cream, cakes, cookies, muffins, and pastries—most of which contained not a speck of sugar.

According to one successful operator, low-calorie goods available today are a far cry from the sugarfree fiascoes of years past. "We encourage people to sample," she says, "especially if they're cynical about sugar-free candy. Some of them have tried sugar-free chocolates in the supermarket, but the candy we sell here isn't the same thing. There are a lot of bad sugar-free candies out there, but we don't sell any of them." Cleverly situated next door to a health club, this sugar-free shop is enjoying the sweet taste of success. And interest in the business continues to grow.

Another shop in Las Vegas, Nevada, boasts an incredible array of 100 sugarless desserts and ninety-two flavors of sugarless ice cream offered on a rotating basis. The owner, a diabetic, makes a good portion of the sweets on his premises using carefully guarded recipes and state-of-the-art alternative sweeteners. "I don't believe anyone is going to succeed in this business on a halfway basis," he contends. "Shops that offer a few candies or a dessert here and there are not going to get the business."

The public is eager to change. Just give them a chance. Retailers are finally presenting alternatives to a nation of guilty sugar addicts. "A lot of people want to restrict their sugar," one operator notes. "The diabetics you have regardless, but if you want to capture the 100 million people who choose to stay away from sugar, you have to make yourself attractive."

Sweetening the Pot

With the right mix of products, a good location, and proper management, a sugar-free/low-calorie dessert shop can be a major hit, mirroring the success of frozen-yogurt shops in the past decade or so. The most important factor is inventory. If your sugarless sweets leave customers flat, they won't return to your shop. Bad alternatives to good desserts abound—what you need to offer is a good alternative.

Take the time to develop outstanding recipes. Experiment with various alternative sweeteners, and be careful of fat content in your food as well. If you're unfamiliar with low-calorie dessert making, consult someone who knows the territory. Diabetics are a good source of inspiration (many have tried-and-true recipes they've developed themselves). Manufacturers of artificial sweeteners are another potential source.

Also, ferret out only the best ready-made products. Fortunately for you, manufacturers are waking up to the sugar-free, low-calorie market. You should be able to find yourself a list of good suppliers. Don't fill your inventory in with second-rate products. One bad experience will confirm people's worst fears about low-calorie desserts.

Considering the proliferation of low-calorie products on the market, as well as continuing consumer interest in dieting and health, the future of the diet dessert market looks promising indeed.

==========BRIGHT IDEA==========

GOURMET POTATO CHIPS

Whether you make them or sell them, one potato chip is not just like the next. We're not talking about minute differences in size and shape here. We're not talking about the virtues of barbecue vs. cheddar cheese. We're talking about texture, flavor, oiliness, crunch—the very essence of a good chip. If you know what we mean, you aren't alone. Americans are discovering the subtle delicacy of a good chip in droves these days. And, as usual, entrepreneurs with taste are reaping the rewards.

Ken Potter, Sr., of Martin's Potato Chips Inc. in Thomasville, Pennsylvania, is regarded in the industry as the guru of kettle-fried chips. For those who don't know, kettle-cooked chips are thick cut and french-fried in small batches. Martin and his wife, Sandra (also vice-president), started selling chips in 1974. First-year sales reached $50,000. In 1987, they reported sales of $9 million. Their Kettle Cook'd brand of chips brings in about $3 million a year.

Kettle-cooked chips are by no means the norm. According to the Snack Food Association, kettle-fried chips comprised only 2 percent of the $3.8 billion potato-chip market in 1987. Moreover, the two largest chip manufacturers retain a 60-percent share of the market. But the rarity of kettle-fried chips is precisely the point. Consumers pay more for calorie-saturated DoveBars and fresh deli-case pastas—why not for a superior chip?

Do spuds catch your fancy? There are numerous ways to break into the chip industry—even on a small scale. Manufacturing high-quality chips and selling them to grocery and gourmet stores is one option. Another is to sell fresh chips retail—in a specialty shop, from a cart or kiosk in a mall, or by delivery. Potatoes may not be a glamorous food, but they are addictive: no one can eat just one.

COOKIE SHOP

High Net Profit Before Taxes:	$70,000 plus
Average Net Profit Before Taxes:	$45,000
Minimum Start-up:	$45,000
Average Start-up:	$65,000

There's a fortune in cookies, and we don't mean the Chinese kind. Homemade-cookie stands started out as a kind of fad about a decade ago. Ten years later, America's appetite for upscale cookies isn't satisfied yet.

Success Secret: the Smell

More than a few of us have been halted by the smell of freshly baked cookies while shopping in a mall. And even if your good sense resists buying a fattening snack, your sense of smell will defeat you every time. This is no accident. Whenever possible, clever cookie-store owners vent their ovens (secretly even!) into the mall enclosure, or out their front doors. Mall managers and fire departments may frown on this approach, but anyone who's fallen victim to it knows it's effective.

And there's another aromatic trick up the sleeves of successful cookie vendors: real vanilla extract. While many less-expensive packaged cookies rely on less-expensive imitation vanilla, upscale cookie makers know that real vanilla permeates the air far more powerfully. For most people, real vanilla is the smell of home-baked cookies, a smell that can stop a shopper or tourist dead in his or her tracks.

The Mobile Cookie

Cookies are an impulse item, so go where there is heavy foot traffic: shopping malls, tourist attractions, swap meets, art shows, beaches, college campuses, etc. You can even buy a van and christen it "The Mobile Cookie" and go where the action is, seasonal or otherwise. Busy cookie shops do a brisk business. We counted fifty-six customers in fifteen minutes at one bustling mall location—and that was on Tuesday, the slowest day of the week.

======= BRIGHT IDEA =======

FOOD GIFTS THAT REALLY FLY

Whenever New Yorker Gail Kleinberg-Koch went out of town, she was constantly greeted with the same question: "Did you bring bagels?"

"Let's face it," she says, "New York City's bagels are unique in the industry. Every place else claims they can make bagels, but only New York can turn out the authentic product." The constant requests from friends prompted Kleinberg-Koch to start New York to Go, an airport-based gift shop selling five varieties of bagels—"the universal edible symbol of New York"—as well as a selection of other ethnic goodies popular in the Big Apple, including bagel chips, ruggelach, and cheesecake.

Kleinberg-Koch knew that the airport was a prime location for her new business. Not only was there ample foot traffic, but she'd catch those out-of-town travelers who needed bagels for gifts of goodwill. But airport space is premium real estate, and Kleinberg-Koch knew her concept had to be good.

Before she even secured a site, she had boxes custom-designed and printed. Then she went from airline to airline with her boxes of bagels. "Some of the airlines were less adventurous than others about trying something new," she recalls. "But not one of them said no to our concept, and at least three airlines gave us the go-ahead."

Kleinberg-Koch notes that turning a regional food into a business, as she did, is something to consider no matter where you live. There are few cities or regions of the country that don't boast of at least one food that's not only a traditional favorite among locals, but a temptation to visitors. Just think about Chicago pizza, San Francisco sourdough bread, Boston chowder, Maryland crab, Philadelphia pretzels with mustard, Vermont maple syrup—the list goes on and on.

Success doesn't happen on its own, however. To make a go of such a business, you need a prime location, excellent packaging, and enough capital to fund your ideas.

Kleinberg-Koch's enthusiasm for the food business (especially her food business) is contagious. "I am giving new height and dignity to the bagel," she says, "and I plan to pepper the world with bagels." If she has her say, many more shops emphasizing the bagel will continue to open in New York. "New York to Go sort of defines a life-style," she claims. "If I could, I'd like to go to Europe and open a New York to Go."

CONVENIENCE FOOD STORE

High Net Profit Before Taxes:	$ 50,000 plus
Average Net Profit Before Taxes:	$ 35,000
Minimum Start-up:	$ 68,000
Average Start-up:	$107,000

What would you pay for convenience? If you found yourself out of snacks just before the midnight TV horror feature, or if you ran out of disposable diapers at 2 A.M., you might be willing to pay just about any price to get what you need.

That's just the thinking that makes convenience stores so popular. Annual sales at convenience stores nationwide are over $10 billion. According to a survey conducted by Maritz AmeriPoll, 57 percent of Americans visit a convenience store at least once a week. We discovered one store operating out of a paltry 400 square feet grossing $250,000 annually. Another store we investigated averages 900 customers a day with daily sales of more than $1,300. The highest-volume store we found, with 2,400 square feet, grossed almost $1 million in a single year.

Convenience stores depend on large volume. Average sales aren't large, so you'll need a fair number of customers to keep the business afloat. But keep in mind that you are selling a product that everyone needs three times a day or more—food.

Room for Everyone

Convenience food stores cater to a nation on the go. In 1957, there were approximately 500 convenience food stores with total sales of $75 million. Today, they seem to be on every street corner. Even major oil companies have jumped on the bandwagon, setting up stores in company-owned and -operated service stations.

There's still room, though, for the little guy to make a splash. With careful cost-cutting and good management you can bring in a pretax net of 10 to 14 percent—after your salary has been paid.

Happy to Pay More

Convenience food stores have the ideal customer. Your typical customer is buying, not browsing. Not only that, he is happy to pay for convenience. The average shopper visits the store four to five times per week and spends an average of four minutes shopping. This describes customers in a hurry—customers willing to pay a few cents more for a can of baked beans rather than fight the hassle of a big super-market. One shopper we interviewed said it was worth pay-ing an extra $0.30 for his favorite bottle of soda to avoid the heavy supermarket traffic.

Setting up Shop

Your most important decision will be where to set up shop. Convenience stores can operate profitably out of single-store locations, strip shopping centers, congested downtown areas, even converted gas stations. The common denominator is dense foot traffic, usually in highly populated residential areas.

Remember, 80 percent of your customers will live or work within one mile of your store. Look for a highly visible spot that can be seen from at least two directions. Parking is also essential. You should have parking for at least ten cars, pref-erably right in front of the store for easy in-and-out shop-ping. You're selling convenience as much as merchandise.

Your Shopping List

What's the secret of choosing a good product mix? It's as simple as knowing your customers and trusting your own judgment.

Most stores have an inventory of 2,800 to 3,200 basic consumer items. In order of volume, the more successful convenience stores sell the following items: tobacco, beer, wine, groceries, soft drinks, nonfoods (magazines, charcoal, etc.), dairy products, candy, baked goods, and health and beauty aids.

Once you decide on your beginning inventory, you will have to find suppliers. You will be dealing with three basic types of suppliers: wholesalers, co-ops, and route vendors.

The Price Is Right

Accurate, competitive pricing will be the basis of your success. Most stores shoot for a 29-to-30-percent overall gross spread out over their line. Bread and milk generally have only a 3-to-4-percent markup, while cigarettes and beer can carry a 40-to-45-percent markup.

High-markup items include sandwiches, coffee, and snacks. Many convenience stores are turning to the sale of fast foods to raise their total profits and increase store traffic. The customer in a hurry will gladly pay $1.50 for an egg salad sandwich that can cost you as little as $0.40.

General Operating Expenses

Because you're dealing with food, you will need to be licensed by the board of health. And if you sell alcoholic beverages, you must also be licensed by your local beverage control board. Insurance is another necessity. Since your store is open long hours (82 percent of all convenience stores are open twenty-four hours a day, seven days a week), your electricity consumption will be high.

Qualified, trustworthy help is worth paying for. Most stores are managed by the owner and one or two employees (long hours make it impossible for the owner to manage every shift).

SANDWICH SHOP OR DELI

High Net Profit Before Taxes:	$60,000 plus
Average Net Profit Before Taxes:	$40,000
Minimum Start-up:	$35,000
Average Start-up:	$69,000

For years, the sandwich has been the king of lunchtime cuisine. Millions are sold every day, ranging from basic peanut butter and jelly to gourmet variations like smoked turkey with Brie.

Palatable Profits

Nationwide, gross sales in simple takeout sandwich shops with limited seating ranged from $100,000 to $500,000. Sharp management and low product costs can yield net profits in the 26-to-31-percent range. That's a bottom line of $26,000 to $75,000 or more, and well-run places do that much business in a year.

Good Locations Everywhere

A sandwich shop can flourish at all kinds of sites in communities of almost any population. For highest volume and profit, however, look for a site surrounded by as many potential lunch clients as possible. An urban high-rise business/shopping district can be ideal, drawing heavy lunchtime traffic from office and shop employees in the area. College campuses are an added plus.

We've seen profitable sandwich shops in the basements of high-rise office buildings or apartment complexes. Isolated suburban offices and industrial parks are also locations worth considering. In any case, look for a location with limited competition. Your clientele will be further guaranteed if you're the "only game in town."

Start on a Shoestring

Some sandwich restaurants spend hundreds of thousands of dollars on elaborate theme decor and fully equipped kitchens before they open their doors for business. This is not necessary.

Under the right circumstances, you can start with as little as $35,000, particularly if you take over the lease of an existing restaurant instead of starting from scratch.

Don't be intimidated by taking over a failed venture: a high-profit operation can replace a losing one under the right conditions. Find out why the previous owner folded. The best location won't cover the mistakes of a poor businessperson.

If the location is sound, go for it. Careful shopping before the sale and good management after it will spell the difference between success and failure.

In this business, operations are simple and equipment is easily available. This means that you can set up in nearly any storefront location without high renovation costs. You won't be cooking on site, so grills, fans, and vents aren't a problem. About all you need is a small work area, a service counter, and a few tables.

SOUP BAR

High Net Profit Before Taxes:	$129,000
Average Net Profit Before Taxes:	$ 98,000
Minimum Start-up:	$ 71,000
Average Start-up:	$107,000

Soup's on—and it's also in. We found restaurants devoted almost entirely to soup grossing $600,000 a year. One outlet, selling only chili, clam chowder, and salad grosses over $300,000 a year.

Health-conscious consumers are rediscovering the virtues of soup. It's lighter than a sandwich, more satisfying than a salad, and comes in an endless variety of flavors. Soup is also an economical alternative to a big meal. For working people who buy lunch five times a week, those savings can add up.

Cafeteria-style soup bars are doing a brisk business. One we visited served 600 people during the 11-to-2 lunch rush. And even though it was raining torrents outside, many customers sat at umbrella-covered tables on the outdoor patio. Now that's popularity!

Hot Market

Who buys soup? The lunchtime crowds at the average soup bar are about 70 percent female, mostly students and office workers grabbing inexpensive meals during the lunch break. After 1 P.M. the crowd becomes older and more sophisticated—executives and affluent shoppers linger over soup, salad, and a glass of wine while conducting business or taking a break from shopping.

Lunch menus are typically limited to a selection of soups and salads, bread or rolls, desserts, and wine, beer, espresso, and other beverages. Some soup bars also serve quiche.

Cooking up the Profits

Soup bars make huge profits from items that most restaurants fail to exploit: soup and salad. Yet these items are inexpensive to make and require little overhead when served cafeteria style. Customers are willing to spend as much as $2.50 for a bowl of soup and a roll, $2.00 for a simple dinner salad, and $4.00 for a glass of wine.

There's no secret to running a successful soup bar. All it takes is a good location, proper atmosphere, keeping overhead low, and maintaining superior product quality.

The product cost for a soup bar is 23 to 25 percent; labor should be 20 percent or less; and overhead is about 25 percent. That translates into a profit margin of 30 percent or more for you. A full-menu restaurant with a similar seating capacity has about the same sales volume, but overhead and sales costs may be 20 percent higher.

Find a Busy Spot

Proper site selection is especially important for a soup bar. Most of your revenue will be generated during the lunch rush (though dinner business usually warrants staying open until 8 or 9), and this means you'll have to go where the workers are. Office workers on limited lunch schedules don't have time to drive across town.

Locating in a high-rise business district is ideal, especially if department stores, boutiques, antique shops, and other businesses that attract crowds are nearby. That way, you'll be able to serve late-afternoon shoppers as well as capacity crowds at lunch.

Once you've zeroed in on the right location, make sure the local zoning and health departments will give you their blessings. This is especially important if you plan to convert an existing structure.

You'll need a location big enough for at least 100 patrons: 2,500 to 3,000 square feet. A 1,500-square-foot location may be big enough if there is also outdoor patio space for seating. Keep future expansion capabilities in mind as well.

========= BRIGHT IDEA =========

GROW GOURMET PRODUCE

Tired of ordinary peas and green beans? Peter Forni, Lynn Brown, and Barney Welsh hope so! The three owners of Forni-Brown Gardens take advantage of the temperate climate of California's famous Napa Valley to raise exotic and baby vegetables.

If you've ever wondered where that one-inch squash or purple potato you ate at your favorite gourmet spot comes from, now you know. Specialty farmers are cultivating peculiar crops—and America's gourmet market is eating them up. Even small farms can prosper with the right selection of produce and careful growing.

We're not talking about plain old snow peas and baby corn. The trio has nurtured unheard-of vegetables: arugula, frisée, radicchio, and the beautifully striped chioggia beet. Garden greens that were staples in ancient times are making their way from the five acres of Forni-Brown Gardens to gourmet restaurants across the nation via overnight air delivery.

Tilling and weeding the ground year-round, the three cottage farmers are approaching $250,000 in annual sales of fresh produce. Now in their eighth year of business, the group has proven that specialty growing is more than a passing trend.

PIZZERIA

High Net Profit Before Taxes:	$137,000
Average Net Profit Before Taxes:	$ 87,000
Minimum Start-up:	$ 97,000
Average Start-up:	$160,000

Over the past decade, pizza has become as American as apple pie. And why not? For fast-food eaters, pizza is a nearly perfect food. Given the right combination of toppings, pizza can span all the food groups: starch, meat, dairy products, and vegetables. It can be junky—flat and tasteless and blissfully cheap. It can be trendy—topped with a tantalizing mixture of goat cheese, fresh basil, and sun-dried tomatoes. In its various forms, pizza is alternately convenient, surprising, reliable, and delicious.

And judging from recent consumption statistics (pizza is America's fastest-growing fast food), pizza is here to stay. Americans eat a staggering seventy-five acres of pizza a day. That's no fewer than twenty-three pounds per person annually.

Pizza Evolution

Remember when pizza was considered Italian food? Many older Americans can still remember their first pizza, probably sampled hesitatingly as a kind of ethnic novelty. Today, pizza is scarcely considered ethnic. Baby boomers grew up eating pizza. Over half of all teens report that pizza is their favorite food.

Moreover, pizza isn't considered junky anymore. While consumers wolfed their pizza down with guilt, now they order it with pride. Pizza is less fattening and more nutritious than we formerly believed, news that has caused many pizzaholics to unleash their culinary desires in full.

Today, pizza eaters represent varied tastes and demands. Accordingly, contemporary pizzerias are a sundry group—ranging from trendy eateries and full-service restaurants to delivery-only or take-and-bake operations. Almost every conceivable variation exists. And apparently, there is room enough for the diversity.

New Products and Services

Don't feel you have to stick to the traditional pepperoni-and-cheese routine to be successful in the pizza business. The past few years have seen a virtual renaissance of products in the pizza business. For starters, there are gourmet pizzas, topped with grilled chicken, lamb sausage, sautéed eggplant, and cilantro. Calzones—those turnoverlike pastries with pizza toppings in the middle—have burst onto the scene. Low-calorie, low-fat, and low-sodium pizzas show special promise among the health-conscious.

"It's similar to what happened with pasta," says Evelyne Slomon, owner of Pizzico in New York and author of *The Pizza Book*. "A few years ago, there was only spaghetti with red sauce. Now people will eat almost anything on their pasta. The same thing is happening with pizza."

Innovative products go hand in hand with extra services. Home delivery is becoming a standard in the pizza business. And with franchises like Domino's and Crusty's delivering the goods faster and more reliably, the standards are high in this area. If you can't stomach the idea of delivery (it is a tricky service to master), consider what a handful of pizzerias are offering: take-and-bake pies. Consumers buy unbaked pizzas at the shop, then heat them in their home ovens. The pizza doesn't get cold, the crust doesn't get soggy, and the pizzeria owner doesn't have to employ an extensive staff—or even install ovens.

Advertising Wars

Neither product nor service will matter, however, if no one knows you exist. Advertising has become more than important in this business—it's absolutely essential. Independent operators report spending more than they'd like to on advertising just to keep up with franchised competition.

Large pizza franchises have been positively merciless in their use of advertising and promotions—a boon to consumers, but a problem for many small operators. Offers like Domino's thirty-minute guarantee and various two-for-one offers make competition stiff promotionally and operationally.

Naturally, advertising and promotions are more important in some markets than in others. If you're the only pizzeria in town (or one of two), ads are less significant than if you're competing with a dozen or more shops. Consider the importance of advertising in your area. If you think it will make a difference, you may want to consider buying a franchise instead of starting your own. The support you get from franchise headquarters could make a big difference in your ability to promote.

Which Way to Turn

Perhaps the best way to summarize the pizza business is to say that it's too vast to summarize properly. Like pizza itself, the pizza market is a hodgepodge of the upscale and the down-to-earth, the basic and the innovative. There are franchises and independents. There are generalists and specialists. And while the market is certainly getting more crowded, there is room for growth.

SALAD-BAR RESTAURANT

High Net Profit Before Taxes:	$170,000
Average Net Profit Before Taxes:	$115,000
Minimum Start-up:	$ 73,000
Average Start-up:	$109,000

In many ways, the current trends toward gourmet gluttony on the one hand and diet consciousness on the other are really two sides of the same coin. You can cash in on both with a gourmet salad-bar restaurant that caters to the upscale tastes of the healthwardly mobile.

Profits Are Green

A salad restaurant in the 90-to-120-seat range should gross from $250,000 to $500,000 per year. One of the most successful we found projects $600,000 to $750,000 gross. That's about the same as a well-run coffee shop the same size, but simplicity and operating economies result in higher than 25-percent net profit pretax for its owners. That's $150,000 to $187,000 on the bottom line.

One operation we found is ideally located in a business district with a heavy lunch and dinner trade. It serves from 800 to 1,000 people per day at an average of $3.50 per meal, in a 100-seat storefront of only 3,000 square feet.

Another medium-sized operation we observed seats 100 and has served up to 500 people a day in its 7,000-square-foot store. Its owners project $400,000 in gross revenues from this newly opened restaurant at an average meal price of $4.25.

Gross-volume potential depends on location, the number of daily customers, and average price of a meal. Seating capacity is an important variable as well.

Food costs for a salad-bar restaurant are 22 to 27 percent. Labor is 23 percent, and operating costs are 27 percent. With careful management, some of these costs may be trimmed. If so, your pretax profits could exceed the average of 23 to 28 percent. A smaller restaurant or coffee shop of the same size can expect higher operating costs (35 to 54 percent)—resulting in lower net profits of 15 to 18 percent.

Huge Market

Our researchers conducted traffic studies at salad bars and found lunchtime business phenomenal. Most of the customers are healthy, weight-conscious executives, office workers, and shoppers. They have little time and/or money and want to eat light and run, between 11 A.M. and 2 P.M. At the later hours, patrons tended to be leisurely lunchers who relaxed with a salad, wine, and cheese or carrot cake.

The dinner trade tended to be lighter, but more than justified staying open until 8 or 9 P.M. Couples and families came in for soup, salad, and a quiche. Many adults had beer or wine with dinner.

Keep Front-End Investment Low

Some operators spend as much as $150,000 before opening, but it is neither necessary nor wise to invest this much up front. You can start with $75,000 under the right circumstances.

The low-end investment assumes you can take over the lease and equipment of a small restaurant that's gone broke. Here you just pay the rent and redo the premises to suit your needs. You can renovate and increase seating in a location as small as 1,500 square feet.

The simplicity of this operation and the availability of used equipment means you can set up in nearly any good storefront without high renovation costs. All you need is a small "Pullman" kitchen area with a minimum of hardware and equipment. The salad bar, tables, chairs, and decor complete the picture.

HAMBURGER/HOTDOG STAND

High Net Profit Before Taxes:	$37,000
Average Net Profit Before Taxes:	$28,000
Minimum Start-up:	$ 9,000
Average Start-up:	$19,000

All health concerns aside, Americans are addicted to hamburgers and hotdogs. Sure, we know fast-food fare is loaded with fat, salt, and calories. But true junk-food aficionados can't resist—and their ranks are large. Though there are burger and hotdog joints on every corner in some towns, this market isn't saturated yet. With ingenuity, hard work, and a little marketing savvy, it's still possible to make it big in this business.

To Franchise or Not to Franchise?

In the past few decades, franchising has extended far beyond its fast-food roots. But in this business more than any other, the question of whether or not to buy a franchise is inevitable. It's hard to ignore the successes of the major chains—and the failures of many lesser-known ventures. Is franchising for you?

The pros and cons are many. On the one hand, franchises are more expensive to start. In addition to the capital required to get the facility up and running, you'll pay a hefty franchise fee. On the other hand, you may find it easier to get financing if you are buying a franchise as opposed to starting your own. Franchises are far less likely to fail, but they also leave less room for creativity. You won't be redesigning the logo or serving up your favorite recipe if you open a McDonald's. For entrepreneurs with little business experience, franchises can be godsends—assuming, of course, that the franchise is a good one.

Your decision to franchise or not to franchise will be all your own. Certainly, it's possible to make it in this business (or any other) without the support of a franchisor. We do recommend, however, that you at least check into franchise opportunities. Contact some of the major players, and some minor ones, too. Ask specific questions about what they can offer you, how much money you'll need to get started, and how satisfied their franchisees are. Call individual franchisees yourself to get the full picture. At the very least, you'll gain some valuable insights into how the business works. Even if you don't end up buying a franchise, you'll know that much more about your competition.

Finding the Gap

You may wonder, though, how any small operator can compete with the likes of McDonald's, Burger King, Wendy's, or Carl's Jr. The trick is filling the gap in the services they provide.

For instance, one independent operator stumbled on his niche while lunching with a friend. While running errands, the two decided to stop at a major chain to pick up a burger. His friend asked for well-done fries and was informed that fries were cooked one way and one way only.

At that point, the operator realized that his local chain was not meeting everyone's needs. While millions of people are perfectly willing to accept the dictates of the franchise (i.e., golden-fried potatoes), there is a significant portion of the market that prefers and will demand service tailored to their specific tastes. This particular operator resolved to open his own outlet where customers could get whatever they wanted however they wanted it. Over twenty years later, this operation still thrives—even with a new McDonald's operating just down the street.

Stress Individuality

One way to make your business stand out is to emphasize your unique quality. Serve only the best hotdogs. Use only the freshest buns. Grill the burgers to order over an open flame. Sell homemade pie. The more outstanding your business is, the more likely it is to make an impression.

In the fast-food business, just about everyone is a potential customer. People are eating out more often these days, and they demand variety and quality in the foods they eat. Your business can be a nice departure from standardized franchise fare. From teenagers to working couples, busy parents to retirees, everyone is looking for an inexpensive, convenient way to eat out.

Service can also make your business stand out. While big-chain operations are hiring the young and illiterate to man their drive-thru windows, why not seek out polite, articulate people to work at your operation? Customers will be grateful just to be able to converse with your employees.

Innovate, Innovate, Innovate

Quality food and good service are the basics of success in the independent burger business. Now let's consider some of the more interesting ideas to crop up in the past few years.

If you believe a burger is just a burger and a hotdog just a hotdog, think about modifying your operations to give yourself an edge. We've reported on drive-thru-only operations, burger delivery outfits, upscale gourmet burger joints—the variations on this theme go on and on. Americans eat billions of burgers and hotdogs each year. Innovations in this business are not only welcomed, they're devoured.

===== BRIGHT IDEA =====

THEY ONLY HAVE FRIES FOR YOU

Years ago, hamburger stands discovered the value of paring down a whole restaurant menu to a simple hamburger and fries. Now one Maryland business wants to cut the hamburgers out of the formula. At Ellicott City–based Boardwalk Fries, there are nothing but fries on the menu.

While selling only spuds may sound a little minimalistic to you, consider that doing so reduces your equipment requirements, simplifies your ordering, streamlines your operations, and—well, you can save a lot of money on those plastic menu letters.

And according to cofounder David DiFerdinando, fries don't require a hard sell. "People buy our fries and make a meal of them," he says, "or they carry them around as a snack and continue to do their shopping." To complement the fries, Boardwalk tempts customers with toppings like cheese, gravy, and chili. It may sound like a fattening proposition, but DiFerdinando maintains that it's not. A sixteen-ounce serving of his fries weighs in at a petite 112 calories, not much more than a banana.

In any case, customers seem to be gobbling the idea up. Boardwalk Fries is franchising its concept, and they're even thinking of adding onion rings or fish to the menu—sometimes the urge to expand is irresistible.

FROZEN YOGURT SHOP

High Net Profit Before Taxes:	$40,000
Average Net Profit Before Taxes:	$25,000
Minimum Start-up:	$54,000
Average Start-up:	$60,000

Just call it ice cream without guilt. Frozen yogurt is the darling of the dessert industry—and with good reason. A far cry from the sour, icy "health food" entrepreneur Walter Simonsen invented almost twenty years ago, today's frozen yogurt is smooth, creamy, and rich tasting—everything that ice cream is except fattening. It's a dieter's dream come true.

In 1988, frozen yogurt sales hit the $1-billion mark, up from a mere $40 million in 1982. From all indications, the nation's appetite has only been whetted. According to surveys, only 57 percent of the American population has ever tried frozen yogurt, and 43 percent say that they will eat more frozen yogurt this year than last.

Top This Concept

Frozen yogurt is healthy stuff. A four-ounce serving of custom-made vanilla contains only ninety calories and 2½ grams of fat. You don't have to produce the yogurt yourself. Mix is available from a number of suppliers: you simply pour the mix into a soft-ice-cream machine and let the equipment do the work.

Yogurt isn't everything at most frozen yogurt shops. Toppings are what make the difference. Adding chocolate-chip-cookie crumbs and chopped-up Snickers bars to an otherwise healthy yogurt might not do much for good health, but it can enhance your profits. Most yogurt shops also offer a variety of fresh fruit and syrup toppings. Each topping adds about $0.50 to the total price.

Small yogurt shops usually have two dispensers with two flavors each. You can make shakes by adding a little skimmed milk to the yogurt and putting the mixture through a regular shake blender. Offering soft drinks, fruit juices, cookies, chips, or lunch items is also a possibility.

Not Without Competition

The frozen yogurt industry is booming, but don't think this fact has escaped potential competitors. In fact, the competition in this industry is hotter than ever. Innovative products, sharp marketing strategies, and solid management are critical for future growth and even survival.

If you're serious about starting a frozen yogurt shop in your area, you may want to investigate franchise opportunities. As the competition becomes ever more fierce, linking up with a large organization could work to your benefit. Even if you opt to open an independent shop, learning about the various franchises available could give you fresh insights into the business. This may not be the wide-open market of ten years ago, but there's still room for smart operators who have a flair for marketing and management.

DOUGHNUT SHOP

High Net Profit Before Taxes:	$75,000
Average Net Profit Before Taxes:	$30,000
Minimum Start-up:	$40,000
Average Start-up:	$75,000

You couldn't call them health food, but doughnuts continue to be a perennial favorite among American snackers. We're hooked—and that's good news to the doughnut shops of America, who bring in profits that smell of sweet success.

Doughnut shops offer the entrepreneur rich profits and relatively simple operations. Automation and dirt-cheap product costs can translate into gross-profit margins of 75 to 80 percent. Even the fanciest doughnuts cost only pennies apiece to produce in quantity. Yet they sell for $0.20 to $0.45 apiece, or even more—one at a time or by the boxful.

Operating expenses for a good high-volume location are minimal. Keeping expenses in the 50-to-56-percent range means net profits on the bottom line of 20 to 25 percent before taxes.

About $685 million worth of doughnuts are sold every year in franchised outlets alone. All told, doughnuts comprise about 15 percent of the $30-billion retail-baking industry. Though recent concerns about excess dietary fat don't seem to bode well for the doughnut industry, doughnuts boast a loyal contingency in this country. Moreover, many doughnut shops are meeting consumers halfway by offering low-fat alternatives like muffins in addition to the usual pastries.

Volume Is the Key to Profit

One of the most successful operations we found opened only two years ago in a tiny store behind a gas station. Phenomenal growth based on high quality has led the owner to open his ninth store recently. Average gross volume in each store is estimated at $100,000 plus.

We also found a single-location shop owned by a former pharmacist. His 900-square-foot shop now grosses $200,000 a year. As an absentee owner, he spends about eight hours a week in his store supervising baking. He told us that he nets almost 25 percent, and could do even better if he chose to work in the store every day himself. He's been so successful that he's renting out his services as a doughnut-shop consultant.

The secret to success in this business is volume. To gross $150,000 a year, you need to make and sell 125-to-150-dozen doughnuts, or more, per day. This takes into account 20 percent of sales from beverages.

Owners enjoying the highest returns were doing everything possible to improve their retail-sales volume. They had carefully selected a site for their shops, and were not afraid to stay open around the clock by staffing lean.

A good location will make its bread and butter at night— well worth the extra effort of staying open. Booming shops had a surprising number of patrons through the night, from midnight snackers to night workers.

Business in some stores was especially brisk after the bars closed, when night people were looking for a place to go and unwind over coffee. Many of these patrons would buy takeouts for breakfast the following morning.

Product costs get smaller and smaller as volume increases. The successful stores we investigated for this report had overall product costs of about 25 percent of gross sales. This depends on the price paid for and the quality of mixes, frying shortenings, and toppings.

CINNAMON ROLL SHOP

High Net Profit Before Taxes:	$105,000
Average Net Profit Before Taxes:	$ 87,500
Minimum Start-up:	$ 44,000
Average Start-up:	$ 65,000

Move over, cookies! Step aside, croissants! Here comes the cinnamon roll . . . and it's hot!

Sometime around 1984, consumers started noticing the sweet smell of cinnamon wafting through their local malls. This irresistible aroma lured them to tiny shops serving giant-sized cinnamon rolls, which have since become the hottest item in the baking industry.

The Temperature's Rising

Popping up in shops from coast to coast, these cinnamon rolls are anything but ordinary. Weighing in at a whopping half pound each, these all-natural treats have specialty bakers rolling in the dough. One cinnamon roll entrepreneur reports that after only three months her shop was grossing $25,000 per month. Another operator we contacted claims that each of her two shops grosses between $400,000 and $500,000 a year.

Cinnamon-roll-shop operators note a number of factors contributing to their success. For one thing, Americans are more conscious than ever about what they eat. Leery of preservatives and food substitutes, people prefer to buy items they know are made fresh from natural ingredients (like cinnamon rolls). This, and the fact that busy people have little time to devote to baking, explain why there is such a demand for fresh-baked goods like cookies, muffins, and cinnamon rolls.

"Think big" seems to be the motto of successful specialty bakers, and cinnamon-roll-shop owners are no exception. Their colossal rolls enfold layers of butter (or margarine), sugar, and cinnamon, as well as a syrup that is poured over the top to give the rolls a sticky appearance. Upon request, warm rolls are laced with thick, white icing for people with a serious sweet tooth. One cinnamon roll aficionado claimed he would rather jog an extra mile so he wouldn't feel guilty about indulging in a delicious roll. All in all, they're pretty irresistible.

Easy to Operate

A cinnamon roll shop is fairly easy to run since it only offers one main menu item. The operators we spoke to had no professional baking experience before opening their shops. And in fact, many suppliers offer ready-made mixes with complete instructions on how to bake the oversized buns.

Success doesn't come without some work, though. Successful owners recall working long hours, seven days a week, during the early phases of their businesses. You can get around some of the hustle and bustle by hiring a manager to run your shop. But of course, hiring a manager costs money. Your decision whether to hire a manager right away or act as a manager yourself during the start-up phase will depend mostly on the amount of operating capital available.

The Scent of Cinnamon

All the successful operators we spoke to agreed that location, sometimes even more than a tasty product, is a key to success. A cinnamon roll shop can be successful in a small town or in a big city, as long as it is located in a mall or strip center with heavy foot traffic. "People don't really go to a mall to buy a cinnamon roll," notes one operator. "They're shopping and they want something to eat, and if we keep the rolls coming out fresh, then they'll stop."

How do you lure people into your shop? Two tactics are especially effective. One is smell. The more potential customers smell your fresh-baked rolls, the more often they will end up buying them. In selecting a location, look for one that has good scent potential—for instance, one that borders on a walkway. Hiding your shop in a corner away from passersby could cut down on your business considerably, so follow your nose. The second simple tactic is handing out bite-sized samples. Once customers get a taste of your sweets, they won't be able to resist.

Trend or Fad?

If you're worried that cinnamon rolls may be just a fleeting success or that the market may soon be glutted with cinnamon roll shops on every corner, listen to entrepreneurs who are already in the business. When asked if the recent explosion of cinnamon roll shops is a trend or just a fad, most said they think the rolls are here to stay, and shops are reportedly doing "better every day." Even as more and more cinnamon roll shops open nationwide, owners express little worry about the competition, secure that the market for cinnamon rolls is large enough to keep them and their new competition in the dough.

COFFEE SHOP

High Net Profit Before Taxes:	$ 92,000 plus
Average Net Profit Before Taxes:	$ 73,000
Minimum Start-up:	$ 85,000
Average Start-up:	$118,000

There are three basic factors that make coffee shops popular. The first is that restaurant menu prices are not rising as quickly as the price of groceries, which makes dining out an appealing choice. Second, as more and more mothers enter the work force, time to cook homemade meals is waning. And third, more people live alone today than ever before. Singles often prefer dining out to eating alone at home.

The average 100-to-125-seat coffee shop will gross about
$12,000 per week. Many twenty-four-hour operations collect
more than $1.5 million per year. Profit margins increase
dramatically with volume. A high-volume operation nets in
excess of 25 percent before taxes and depreciation. An average shop will net about 15 percent for an absentee owner.

Investment Variables

For an absentee owner the optimum-size coffee shop has
125 seats. An owner-operator, however, can make a 50-to-60-
seat shop profitable. Location plays a major role in the success of a coffee shop. If, for instance, you're the only roadside
restaurant for fifty miles along the interstate, you will enjoy a
fair amount of built-in business. On the other hand, if you
start a place fifty miles from nowhere, miles outside the
nearest city limits, you can't count on much drive-by traffic.

Initial investments on coffee shops range from about
$85,000 to well over $500,000. Why the disparity? Start-up
costs vary with land or leasing costs, the amount of work
needed to get the place in order, equipment and furnishings,
and so on. If you have only a limited amount of cash to
invest, consider looking for a location that's housed a restaurant before. Not only will you be able to negotiate favorable
terms, but you may also inherit valuable equipment and
fixtures.

Shop around for good used equipment; that, too, can save
you money. As a rule of thumb, try to build as large a restaurant as you can comfortably afford. A 100-seat coffee shop
requires only a few thousand more dollars to set up than a
50-seater, because they require the same basic outlays for
major equipment.

The Keys to Success

We asked the executive of a coffee-shop chain what he felt
were the most important elements of a profitable shop. His
answer was threefold: location, location, location. Of course,
a restaurant must be well managed, but from our surveys, we
tend to agree with the chain executive. Other important
factors for independent operators include moderate prices
and quick, twenty-four-hour service.

Establishing an Image

In and around every city there are a few restaurants that are well known for one specialty item: the biggest, juiciest hamburger; rare roast-beef sandwiches sliced and piled high at your table; world-famous Texas Tom's chili; Anderson's homemade pea soup; Jacques's famous crepes, Granny's clam chowder—the list is endless.

Try to establish a dish on which to base your fame, whether it be falafel or charbroiled chicken or homemade apple pie. Advertise your specialty prominently on your signs and menu. The Marie Callender chain started out primarily as a coffee shop, but became famous for its pies. People buy what they are sold: if you offer them a world-famous dish, they will try it just to see what makes it famous.

And don't overlook larger dietary trends in putting your menu together. While most coffee-shop fare tends to be pretty basic, don't be afraid to add a few exotic items to the menu. Low-calorie, low-sodium, and low-fat dishes are also especially popular. Offering items that other coffee shops don't is one way to get an edge on the competition.

======================= BRIGHT IDEA =======================

LUNCH DELIVERY

Some people just can't tear themselves away from their work—even for lunch. But then in some neighborhoods there isn't much incentive to do so. Lunch delivery services make eating in appetizing, with homemade sandwiches, microwavable hot dishes, salads, pastries, and snacks.

Starting a lunch delivery service can be as simple as finding a supplier (try local caterers who need weekday work or local restaurants/delis that want to boost their business), buying an ice chest and a set of wheels, getting a license, and finding a route. Or you can opt to start bigger with your own kitchen facilities and a team of well-outfitted delivery people. Either way, you're likely to encounter an eager market for your services.

If your food is palatable and your management sound, you could end up making a mint. Los Angeles entrepreneur Billy

Kostoff started L.A. Daily with a partner in 1970 on an initial investment of a few hundred dollars. Now Kostoff oversees a network of fifty independent delivery people and sells about 3,000 sandwiches, salads, and entrées a day.

HOMEMADE CAKE SHOP

High Net Profit Before Taxes:	$85,000
Average Net Profit Before Taxes:	$30,000
Minimum Start-up:	$ 4,000
Average Start-up:	$30,000

Not until consumers started relishing superpremium ice cream, Mrs. Fields' Cookies, and gourmet brownies did they find real fault with the same old bakery cakes. Forget the rainbow sprinkles and frosting flowers—where was the gooey denseness of a real, honest-to-goodness homemade cake?

Certainly it wasn't at home. As more and more women join the work force, the concept of baking a cake from scratch becomes increasingly antiquated. Yet most bakery cakes fall woefully short of the cakes Mom used to make (even for those of us whose mothers couldn't bake a can of beans).

There's a void to be filled here, and innovative new bakeries are doing just that. Instead of the usual bakery fare, they're offering everything from poppyseed-and-raspberry concoctions to cheesecakes, pies, and super-rich candy-laden chocolate layers.

All ingredients are fresh, and everything used is "natural," which is to say no artificial vanilla, synthesized fruit flavorings, or preservatives. Be a stickler for quality. Your product should taste like it comes from a home kitchen—even if that means making your production a little more labor-intensive. In return, you'll be able to charge higher prices for your goods.

The Cake Market

You may sell your goods through a retail operation or limit your baking to wholesale sales—usually to restaurants or other retail outlets. Additionally, products may be custom-baked to order for weddings, birthday parties, and the like.

Your primary market will be affluent. These people will be able to pay more for your goods and will have the palates to appreciate your fine baking. Truly determined foodies will travel great distances to out-of-the-way locales to obtain gourmet fare, so it pays to cultivate this market. That doesn't mean, however, that you should ignore less affluent consumers. People of all economic levels will pay for quality goods. For some, a well-made cake is an affordable luxury. In other cases, a gourmet cake lends an air of elegance to a birthday, wedding, or other special event.

The possibilities for aspiring cake bakers are nearly limitless. In addition to basic cakes, consider the following specialty baked goods:

—Health-food cakes: Using whole wheat flour, fresh fruit, and no sugar (honey is the preferred alternative), you can attract health-conscious consumers who wouldn't be caught dead in a regular bakery.

—Cheesecakes: In many cities, a good cheesecake is hard to come by. Perfect your recipe for the basic item, then branch out into chocolate, amaretto, pumpkin, lemon, bourbon-pecan, and whatever else strikes your fancy.

—Ethnic baked goods: Anyone for Chinese pork bao? How about Mexican pan dulce? Japanese manju? Italian panforte? Indian barfi? You get the picture. Ethnic stores often have a built-in market (provided there are people of that ethnicity in your neighborhood), and they also attract adventuresome gourmets in search of something different.

—Chocolate: If you haven't heard as much about chocolate in the media lately, it's not because people aren't devouring the stuff. Rather, they're so busy eating that they don't have time to report on it. Homemade chocolate cakes, candy, tortes, cupcakes, mousses, and confections are still strong sellers, especially if you have a flair for decadence.

What's your specialty? Is your apple pie to die for? Are you a wizard with fresh-fruit tarts? Can you whip up an outrageous chocolate mousse extravaganza? Run with it. Specialize in something that suits you. The personal investment you make in your products will show in your sales.

It Starts in the Kitchen

Though many successful bakers started out at home, don't plan on following suit. In most cities, commercial cooking from home is prohibited. Check with your local health department to make sure, but this usually isn't a legal option for new bakers.

Instead, consider buying out an existing bakery. One cake baker we visited bought a bakery-gone-broke for $3,000. It had a pizza oven, stove, refrigerator, and worktable. Additionally, she invested $15,000 in equipment and decor, but even then the facility was a bargain.

If your new business will stress the wholesale, look for a commercial kitchen without retail access. Eventually, your new concern will probably need a space of its own, but to start you may be able to share quarters with another business. Restaurants may be willing to rent their kitchens to you after hours, or check with local catering firms. Church kitchens are often inspected by the health department and are usually available during the week.

Your equipment costs will vary, depending on your volume, the types of goods you'll be making, and whether or not you buy used equipment. All told, you'll probably spend anywhere from $8,000 to $20,000 on equipment, but we've seen net profits as high as $50,000 a year in this business, proving that America's appetite for baked goods is anything but waning.

FRIED-CHICKEN TAKEOUT

High Net Profit Before Taxes:	$92,000
Average Net Profit Before Taxes:	$61,000
Minimum Start-up:	$47,000
Average Start-up:	$84,000

Fried-chicken takeout restaurants have some of the lowest failure rates in fast food. A well-run chicken-takeout restaurant in the right location can net upward of $150,000 annually before taxes—and it doesn't have to be a famous chain, either.

Find a Location and Start Cooking

Much as it seems as if the big chains are everywhere, the fact is they aren't. Research shows that most chicken-take-out restaurants draw business from only a one-to-three-mile radius. That leaves plenty of gaps for independents. With steady advertising, conscientious service, and a good product, you can compete with the big chains for neighborhood business.

The key to making this business work is location. A good location has 20,000 to 30,000 people within the immediate area, with the majority of the adults being young—aged twenty to thirty-one. The location should be freestanding on a street heavily traveled by local traffic, and it should be near a local shopping area.

Nevertheless, the net for an independent, absentee owner-operator rarely drops below 30 percent before taxes—and obviously, that percentage is higher with greater volume.

Your Own Secret Recipe

Don't be intimidated by the competition's secret recipes. In truth, they aren't so mysterious—just the result of some experimenting in the kitchen. You or any good cook you know can probably concoct something equally delicious. Break out the cookbooks and start creating—your secret recipe could take the chicken industry by storm.

================= BRIGHT IDEA =================

FOOD IN A BIN

It's a sad scenario, but a familiar one. Your stash of butter cookies has turned to dust and your stock jar of tarragon smells like cheap furniture polish. You just didn't use them in time. We all yearn for variety—a few raisins here and there, a handful of pistachios. We long for the spice of life, but recoil at the high prices of herbs, usually sold in bottles most of us will never live to see the bottom of.

That's why bulk-food shops are popping up in all corners of the country. At bulk-food stores, consumers shop for a pinch of this and a handful of that—and they only pay for what they buy. They don't pay for any expensive packaging, either. Instead, they bag their own goodies from a selection of 1,000 to 1,500 items lined up in uniform bins.

Sound like a good time? According to bulk-food addicts, it is. Not only do they have more control over what they buy, they have more access to it. In bulk displays, shoppers can see the food, smell it, and (though retailers don't condone the practice) taste it.

What fits in a bin? Anything from dried soup to nuts. Pasta, dried mushrooms, cookies, candy, dried fruit, spices, nuts—even staples like sugar and flour. Seasonal items like Valentine hearts and Christmas candy add variety. And specialty items like low-calorie snacks and salt-free tidbits are also popular.

Bulk-food shops fit America's changing eating habits. Smaller households, more frequent visits to restaurants, and a growing interest in diversity all add up to new demands on food retailers. For now, bulk-food shops seem to have a winning formula in the bag.

GOURMET WINE AND CHEESE SHOP

High Net Profit Before Taxes:	$ 85,000 plus
Average Net Profit Before Taxes:	$ 62,000
Minimum Start-up:	$ 73,000
Average Start-up:	$135,000

Just a decade or two ago, buying wine and cheese meant picking up a package of sliced American and a jug of cheap Chablis at the local market. Today, such pedestrian selections just won't do. Contemporary consumers know their Brie from their Camembert and their chardonnay from Chenin Blanc. They want quality—and they're willing to pay for it.

For many, gourmet foods are an affordable luxury—a well-deserved reward for hard work. And though we've witnessed a near renaissance in the supermarkets (international-food sections, fresh pasta and seafood bars, shelves full of gourmet items, well-stocked wine departments), most don't stock the full array of gourmet products available to the public.

The Gourmet Approach

Unlike supermarkets, where the markup is small and a net of 2 percent on gross sales is a good profit, novelty-food stores use markups of 100 percent and more. As a gourmet retailer, you don't have to stress low prices. Play up the superior quality of your merchandise. Take the time to teach your employees all about wine, food, and the finer points of being a gourmet so that they can exercise good salesmanship. People are willing to pay more for truly outstanding wine and food, but only if you can demonstrate what makes your goods so outstanding.

In addition to wine, cheese, and pâté, consider stocking accessories: hand-blown wineglasses, deluxe picnic baskets, cheese boards. You may also wish to branch out into prepared foods. Keeping a variety of pasta salads, quiches, sandwiches, or takeout entrées can broaden your appeal and bring customers in on a more regular basis.

5

RETAIL

HAND-ME-DOWNS FOR SALE

After the birth of her daughter, Karen Lynch had a problem to solve. "It seemed like every time I changed my daughter's clothes, she outgrew something," Lynch recalls. "She outgrew her clothes; she outgrew her crib, her stroller, her high chair. She never had a chance to wear anything out." Lynch surveyed her daughter's closet with a frustrated eye: "Most things were still perfectly good."

Lynch's solution was—and is—a booming children's resale boutique in Newburyport, Massachusetts, where mothers like Lynch gather to buy and sell "perfectly good" clothing, furniture, and accessories. It's one of the few places where mothers can land designer dresses for as little as $5.00, or Aprica strollers for $60 or $70. Parents can expect to save a tidy 75 percent at Children's Orchard, but Lynch warns that hers is not a thrift shop.

"We take only the best items that people bring in," she reports. "We don't take anything with stains or rips, and we look for quality." Instead of messy bins of unsorted clothes, all items at Children's Orchard are neatly pressed and hung on racks according to size. "We look like a regular children's

146

boutique," Lynch maintains. "It takes some people a while to realize we're a resale shop."

Since it opened in 1980, Children's Orchard has been just as popular as Lynch projected. Impressive sales confirm Lynch's suspicion that she was not alone in her frustration. "I thought that other mothers were probably going through the same thing I was," she says. "Our market is middle- to upper-middle-class people who want quality clothing and brand names but are frugal."

Customers are as anxious to sell as they are to buy. Lynch purchases inventory by appointment only, often booked months in advance. Mothers are clearly delighted to put their children's outgrown goods to use, particularly since Lynch pays cash for everything she accepts.

Children's Orchard attracts more than one kind of potential seller, however. From the very beginning, customers have inquired about starting children's resale boutiques in their own towns. Since 1985, Lynch has been franchising the concept. "We've had tremendous interest from around the country," she says, "but we're trying to keep the growth controlled to make sure we can provide all the services we want to offer."

PET SHOP

High Net Profit Before Taxes:	$120,000
Average Net Profit Before Taxes:	$ 25,000
Minimum Start-up:	$ 25,000
Average Start-up:	$ 55,000

What do Lassie, Tweety, Toto, Scooby Doo, Morris, Garfield, Mr. Ed, Tom and Jerry, Gentle Ben, and Sylvester all have in common? Yes, they're all animals, but more than that, they're all beloved pets. You can count on it: Americans love pets, and for pet-shop owners, this fact means a solid business opportunity.

Pets and pet supplies represent a $10-billion industry in the United States. Nearly 600 million pets run, crawl, swim, and fly around American homes. A *Better Homes and Gardens* survey revealed that 52 percent of the respondents owned at least one dog, and 34 percent owned at least one cat.

With many Americans currently experiencing an increase in discretionary income, pet sales are on the rise. In a survey conducted by *Pet Age* magazine, 39 percent of the respondents said their shops' gross sales revenues were $200,000 or more. Less than 1 percent said they grossed under $50,000. A well-run nonaquatic pet store can net around 25 percent before taxes. Profits increase if fish and aquarium supplies are added.

The Perfect Pet?

Pet shops come in a variety of shapes and sizes. Yours should reflect your customers' tastes and interests as well as your own personality. For example, right now Akitas from Japan are the hot "yuppie puppy." On the other hand, in an area populated by a lot of apartment dwellers, a 100-pound Akita probably won't sell well. In apartment-dominated neighborhoods, fish sell best. In suburbia, people buy animals to inhabit their backyards: dogs, cats, rabbits, etc.

For an entrepreneur with limited capital, stocking aquarium supplies makes good sense. While a dog, bird, or cat owner may spend $25 to $50 on accessories for his pet, a single aquarium setup can cost from $25 to $1,000.

Because sales patterns vary greatly from area to area and from store to store, each owner must decide what percentage of his stock will be animals vs. dry goods. Generally, because of the volume involved, pet supplies bring in more revenue than the pets themselves. On the other hand, pets can bring in foot traffic. Passersby who stop in to look at the puppies and kittens are more likely to buy something while they're in the shop.

Experience Pays

One thing most experts agree on is that the more related experience a new owner has, the better his or her chances are of being successful. One owner, for instance, took a correspondence course in becoming a veterinarian's assistant. The course supplied basic knowledge about animal care, and the owner recommends it to his employees.

If you don't know how to keep animals happy and healthy, team up with someone who does. Develop a good relationship with a local veterinarian—the association could benefit both your businesses.

T-SHIRT SHOP

High Net Profit Before Taxes:	$200,000
Average Net Profit Before Taxes:	$ 35,000
Minimum Start-up:	$ 5,000
Average Start-up:	$ 9,000

Even in the "Dress for Success" eighties, novelty T-shirts are here to stay. The sale of T-shirts has become as dependable as sales of the backbone of the casual-apparel business: blue jeans. T-shirts have also become a mainstay of the promotional business: from movies to national parks, from instant rice to college humor. T-shirts offer comfort and style at a low cost. And they go great with a pair of jeans.

Fit the Market to a "T"

That isn't to say, however, that nothing's changed in the T-shirt business. In addition to the slogan T-shirts that ushered in the craze over ten years ago, there are hand-painted T-shirts, exotic-print T-shirts, spin-art T-shirts, T-shirts bearing the logos of famous restaurants (for instance, the Hard Rock Café)—the list goes on and on.

The T-shirt market can be divided into two basic categories: commercial and retail. The commercial market is often overlooked, but can be lucrative. One retail store specializing in custom T-shirts writes $5,000 a week in business orders for shirts geared toward advertising and promotion. As advertising costs continue to skyrocket, customized T-shirts look more and more attractive to retailers, restaurateurs, and other companies.

The retail market makes up about 70 percent of a T-shirt shop's sales. This would include individual consumers (most are under thirty-five), gift givers, and people with special affiliations (sports teams, companies, etc.). Catering to both the retail and commercial markets isn't difficult; in fact, it's probably the best way to maximize revenues and profits.

Model T's

With proper planning, the start-up investment for a retail shop can be less than $10,000, though $15,000 to $20,000 are probably more realistic figures. Your personnel, space, and equipment requirements will also be low. And once you're up and running, the operation is simple to manage.

The essential piece of equipment for any T-shirt shop is a heat-seal press. It features a large plate upon which you place the T-shirt, a press plate, and time and temperature controls. The technology of these presses is improving constantly, and as they improve, the prices drop. As of this writing, small presses can be had for about $400 new. A more substantial press (the better bet for a retail operation) costs more, but can usually be purchased on payments.

Your inventory will consist of a few dozen assorted styles and colors of shirts and 30 to 100 transferable patterns. Look for a location with 300 to 400 square feet of floor space. In addition, you'll need shelves for your shirt inventory, racks for displaying the shirts, and a dressing area with mirrors. Compared to the average retail operation, your needs will be minimal.

For stores catering to the individual retail market, making $100,000 gross is not uncommon. Stores that deal with both business and retail customers can do as much as $300,000 a year in the right location.

================ BRIGHT IDEA ================

SOCK OPTIONS

For years, Americans have frequented shoe stores for footwear. But what about socks? Until recently, most people settled for garden-variety, department-store socks. That is, until the advent of the specialty sock shop.

If you're still of the belief that a sock is a sock is a sock, take a second look at the socks out there. Women's hosiery, once limited to basic beige panty hose, now come in a rainbow of colors, textures, prints, and styles. Athletic socks in a variety of weights and fibers are also popular. And men's socks are undergoing a positive renaissance. Men who grew up on tube socks and basic black are sporting slick silks, wild prints, and ultrasoft cashmere.

"When people come into the store, their reaction is, 'We've got to have it!' They're kind of awed by what they see," says Norman Carter, owner of the Soc Shop in Orem, Utah. "We've made a commitment to quality socks. As a retailer, you can either go for the low end, or you can make a commitment to quality and try to sell it."

Selling socks, we admit, is not necessarily as easy as selling shoes. Because the public is just becoming aware of the sock options available, people aren't yet accustomed to visiting special shops to buy socks. The market is there, however, for the dedicated. If you're serious about the sock market, be prepared to seek out high-quality merchandise that can't be found in most department stores. Also be ready to sell. With a superior inventory and a strong knowledge of foot fashions, it's possible to keep a sock business on its feet—and in the pink.

PLANT SHOP

High Net Profit Before Taxes:	$85,000
Average Net Profit Before Taxes:	$20,000
Minimum Start-up:	$12,000
Average Start-up:	$18,000

Over the past years, decorating magazines have implanted, nurtured, and confirmed the notion that having plants in your home is a sign of good taste. In fact, having no plants can imply that you're cold, insensitive, unfriendly, and not especially intelligent. How conditioned are we to plants? Try going to a home or office that's plantless. Chances are, you'll find the decor a bit spare.

From Art Gallery to Plant Shop

A young artist with a small storefront gallery in the artsy section of town decided to add some plants to his shop to pick up a few extra dollars. The plants were soon selling better than the artwork. In the end, the fellow gave up his artistic ideas and opened a new, larger store in a more up-scale area. We doubt he's painted a stroke since.

Now he's grossing over $700,000 a year with a projected net of $200,000 before taxes. Not bad for a young man with no starting capital to speak of and no business experience.

His artistic talents aren't totally wasted on his new venture. He specializes in the unusual. He has plants potted in everything from spittoons to rusty coffeepots. He pays kids $0.50 an item to hunt down and bring back potential pots from junkyards, city dumps, or wherever. Using this system, his profit margin is impressive. His cost for the plants averages $1.25; the pots set him back $0.50. Planting itself takes less than five minutes. The retail price is $8.95.

The store's atmosphere is also a work of art. Decorated with waterfalls, antiques, and a veritable forest of plants, the shop gives the customer the feeling of strolling in a rain forest. Just browsing is a good time.

Case History Number Two

Another shop owner doing a similar volume uses the same kind of interior setup, but also capitalizes on people's ignorance about plants. Most plant buyers have problems keeping their greenery healthy, so this operator promotes free classes in plant care. He holds these seminars daily and nightly.

To provide the best possible assistance, he convinces salesmen from nurseries, pottery companies, seed companies, and so on to give lectures. Sometimes, he borrows films from the Department of Agriculture. He's also careful about hiring the right staff. His salespeople know and love plants, and are able to offer more than standard service.

These employees hold casual instruction sessions free to anyone who comes in during the day. In the evening, the owner has a regular course for twenty students, three nights a week for four weeks. These classes are also free. When he hires instructors—usually foremen from local nurseries, college instructors, landscapers, etc.—he pays them $20 a night for a two-hour session.

The shop owner advertises consistently in local newspapers, emphasizing his two major selling points: an unusual selection and free daily lessons.

Doubling as a Teahouse

To add to the colorful setting, he gives away free wine, cheese, tea, coffee, and cookies to his patrons. And throughout the store he has paintings, sculptures, and other crafts that he takes on consignment from local craftspeople. These provide free decoration and a tidy profit on the side. The store that we've just described does $500,000 in gross sales per year, and has an average inventory of $18,000.

═══════════════ BRIGHT IDEA ═══════════════

GOWNS FOR HIRE

Where can you find evening gowns from top designers like Yves Saint-Laurent for as little as $75? Believe it or not, New York's Madison Avenue is the spot. The only hitch is that these dresses are not for sale—they're for rent! An innovative service called One Night Stand has tapped into a market that was once reserved for men only: formalwear rentals.

At the rent-a-dress shop, a gown can be had for a three-day period for $75 to $300, plus a deposit of a few hundred dollars to ensure its safe return. This revolutionary shop attracts budget shoppers who can't afford designer dresses, as well as socialites who want a different gown for every social event. After ten rentals, the gowns are taken off the racks and sold to customers at wholesale prices.

This new twist in the women's apparel industry is starting to catch on. Gowns-for-hire shops have opened in Dallas, Chicago, and Boston. Joanna Doniger, who founded One Night Stand, plans to add three more shops to her operation. The party isn't over yet.

MEN'S CLOTHING STORE

High Net Profit Before Taxes:	$72,000 plus
Average Net Profit Before Taxes:	$53,000
Minimum Start-up:	$60,000
Average Start-up:	$95,000

If you think women are the only people who are born to shop, guess again. Today, record numbers of men can be seen browsing at and, more important, buying clothing in, men's specialty shops across America. Traditionally, men have let their wives or girlfriends select their clothing for them. However, men today are becoming increasingly fashion-conscious, and they're exploring malls and independent clothing shops on their own.

Why So Casual?

One trend that's making a splash in menswear is casual clothing. Casual duds are not limited to weekend wear anymore. Office dress codes around the nation are becoming less rigid, allowing men to discard the traditional suit and tie for more relaxed clothing. Even major corporations like Xerox and General Motors are loosening up in favor of a more humanistic approach. Shops that cater to this trend—toward dressy casual clothing—are making tidy profits.

Aren't dressy and casual two conflicting styles? Not anymore, according to the successful shops we talked to. Sport coats, designer pants, and casual shirts in natural fibers are the core of this look. You might call it a little to the left of the cookie-cutter wool suit and a little to the right of jeans and a T-shirt. The hottest looks are formal enough for the office without being so formal that the client looks ready for a funeral.

Dress for Success

Men's-specialty-shop owners are reaping the benefits of the growing interest in men's fashions. Since many traditional men's stores don't offer this kind of merchandise, small entrepreneurs are able to capitalize on the new trends. Our research found the average gross revenue of a new men's casual-apparel store to be between $250,000 and $400,000.

According to the successful menswear-shop owners we contacted, location is a prime factor in a store's success. The best and most expensive locations are in malls and strip centers with heavy foot traffic. Locating in busy downtown areas or around college campuses is another good option.

A good location goes hand in hand with excellent service. Your location can entice first-time shoppers, but if you don't offer a good selection, outstanding service, and a pleasant shopping atmosphere, customers won't keep coming back.

Also bear in mind that men, unlike many women, weren't born to shop. So a little extra salesmanship and attention goes a long way. Helping customers coordinate colors (many men are color-blind), select flattering styles, and find the right accessories will make a big difference—not only in their perception of your shop, but also in increased sales through merchandising.

Increased Competition

As in any industry, the proliferation of men's shops means more competition for existing operations. In the men's apparel industry, however, the increasing numbers of shoppers who are buying and spending more than ever before means that the market is far from saturated and competition has not yet become fierce.

CHARACTER MERCHANDISE STORE

High Net Profit Before Taxes:	$59,000
Average Net Profit Before Taxes:	$40,000
Minimum Start-up:	$40,000
Average Start-up:	$75,000

Mickey Mouse appeared in his first cartoon, "Steamboat Willie", over sixty years ago. It was the start of two fortunes— Walt Disney's and the licensing industry's. Walt's came quickly; the licensing industry's has just arrived.

Recent interest has sparked billion-dollar sales and has put character merchandise at center stage. Retailers are bringing out the Mickey Mouse dolls, Bullwinkle T-shirts, and Snoopy posters like never before. Many stores sell nothing but character merchandise, and for the owners, business has been both fun and profitable.

Grown-up Market

The character merchandise store specializes in licensed products bearing images of popular cartoon and entertainment characters. Such stores sell everything from Gumby key chains to Elvis scarves, to Raggedy Ann watches and Mickey Mouse coins, and as many kinds of stuffed dolls as there are cartoon characters. These fun, flashy shops cater to the kid in all of us.

Character merchandise has always been popular, especially with kids. But now adults have joined the fun, pushing sales figures to extraordinary heights. According to one Los Angeles franchisor, adults now comprise a large percentage of the $55-billion character merchandise industry's annual sales. And these adults aren't buying for children: they're buying for other adults.

With adults making the majority of purchases, the merchandise mix at these stores is surprisingly grown-up. While some children's toys remain, most of today's character merchandise is upscale and expensive, geared toward adult tastes and pocketbooks. In addition to the T-shirts and sweats, retailers also carry watches, clocks, and jewelry. And there is a growing market for limited-edition and collectible items, such as cartoon cells and character coins.

Be Seen and Heard

Because most sales are made by impulse shoppers, character merchandise stores rely on high visibility and heavy foot traffic for adequate profits. The experts agree that regional malls offer the best possibility for both. Most operators locate their stores in malls, and within the mall they seek the highest-traffic areas.

Capitalize on your visibility with snappy storefront displays. "We have a television in the front window playing cartoons and movie videos," says one smart operator, "and we have a rainbow that stretches across the front of the store, which grabs a lot of shoppers' attention."

Sales service and inventory are also critical factors. One store owner reports that about half of her shoppers are looking for gifts, but have no idea what they want. The other half, she says, want to buy something for themselves, but hesitate to spend the money. Friendly service and good salesmanship make the difference between mediocre sales and healthy profits.

Keeping the right mix of characters also requires skill. Today's hot character could be tomorrow's has-been, so keeping on top of trends is essential. The most successful stores maintain a balance between the current favorites and the classic characters. While the favorites bring high volume and quick sales, the classics provide steady, reliable sales, continuing to sell long after the favorites have become passé.

Start Small or Big

Opportunities abound in character merchandise stores. You can open a store inexpensively, buying a small inventory and renting a kiosk (a small, temporary mall structure). Or you can buy franchise rights with one of the national chains and start out with a large inventory and ample room to grow.

Many store owners who initially operated from kiosks until they saved enough money to open a store say that the kiosk experience helped prepare them for the greater responsibility of running a retail shop.

But starting small isn't necessary. Many shop owners open up successfully with limited experience, either with the help of a franchise organization or on their own. One operator started out with no retail experience and was so successful that she opened a second location only eight months later.

Though the future looks bright for character merchandise stores, even this business has its worries. "There are nights," confides one successful operator, "when I lie awake wondering if I should be having this much fun at work."

======== BRIGHT IDEA ========

BOXING BUSINESS SCORES A KNOCKOUT

Today, hundreds of thousands of people change residences every year, and at least one smart entrepreneur is capitalizing on the growing demand for packing boxes. Jeff Sheyka's customers buy used cartons from him at bargain prices and avoid the mover's nightmare of scrounging for boxes in trash dumpsters.

Sheyka's business, Carry All Cartons, began when Sheyka approached the owners of several moving companies and offered to pick up their used packing cartons from customers. Some companies do their own collection (a service that is often part of a moving contract). If state law permits, some moving companies sell these used boxes. After seven tries, Sheyka contracted with two moving companies whose managers welcomed the idea of disposing of a client's used boxes easily and at no cost to their business.

They agreed to give Carry All Cartons' phone number to their customers, who phone Sheyka and arrange to have him pick up empty boxes after a move. "I always get back to the customers on the day they call, and set up an appointment to pick up and flatten the boxes," says Sheyka. "Customers are also told I won't take trash, water-soaked boxes, or the like." Sheyka and his employees also consolidate the clean packing paper and haul it and the cartons to a twenty-four-hour, commercially zoned storage unit.

About twice a week, Sheyka spends a couple of early-evening hours making two or three pickups, which average thirty boxes each. On nights when he's not collecting boxes, he's selling them. Carton consumers meet him at a scheduled appointment time at the storage unit, where they can buy the boxes in good condition for half the cost of new ones. Sheyka donates the packing paper to civic groups for their recycling programs.

One advantage to a used-carton business is that it can be profitable when operated on the side while maintaining a full-time job, as Sheyka does. Sheyka nets about $25 an hour, working an average of ten hours a week.

Do-It-Yourself Framing Shop

High Net Profit Before Taxes:	$46,000
Average Net Profit Before Taxes:	$35,000
Minimum Start-up:	$33,000
Average Start-up:	$43,000

You don't have to be Picasso or live in Paris to become an important member of the art world. With a little training and a lot of hands-on practice, you can open a do-it-yourself framing shop in your own community. And you don't need the financial resources of J. Paul Getty to do it, either.

Frame-shop owners are hardly starving artists. We found do-it-yourself framing operations grossing $250,000 a year or more, and netting as much as $87,000, or 35 percent, before taxes. According to *Decor* magazine, the average per-store annual gross is $136,298.

Nationwide, Americans are exhibiting an unprecedented love of art. Prints of famous paintings and original graphics make art collecting a newly affordable hobby (you can now hang the *Mona Lisa* in your living room). And prints are only the tip of the iceberg. Interest in original oils and water-colors, limited-edition prints, and other framables is keener than ever. Over $100 million is spent annually in framing shops getting artwork ready for the wall.

Take Advantage of the Do-It-Yourself Bug

Framing shops have been around for centuries. In fact, fine framing is an art form in its own right. But high-quality framing isn't cheap. For the average person, who may already have blown his or her budget on the artwork itself, a custom-made professional frame may be simply too expensive.

Do-it-yourself framing presents an alternative. A do-it-yourself frame shop is set up so that customers can make their own frames with the help and advice of a trained profes-sional. Customers select from hundreds of different molding patterns and mat colors, putting together their own frames for the fun of it—and saving up to 40 percent off what they might pay a custom framer.

Some shop owners offer only do-it-yourself and devote their entire operation to the concept, but most offer custom framing as well. Custom work generates higher gross and net profit returns per customer. Also, many customers need time to get used to the idea: they will try making their own frames only after seeing the process in action. Conversely, others will feel that the savings are not worth the time and effort, and will come back for custom work next time.

Handsome Profitability

The gross revenue in most established do-it-yourself shops is split on a sixty-forty basis between do-it-yourself and custom work. With material costs between 26 and 32 percent, gross profit falls in the 68-to-74-percent range.

Though the popularity of do-it-yourself frame shops in recent years has made this business more competitive, the demand outstrips the supply in many communities. Industry reports indicate that this is especially true in the Midwest, but opportunities certainly aren't limited to that region.

WOMEN'S ACCESSORIES STORE

High Net Profit Before Taxes:	$59,000
Average Net Profit Before Taxes:	$39,000
Minimum Start-up:	$52,000
Average Start-up:	$75,000

High fashion has always been too expensive for the working woman, so the majority of women have depended on lower-priced popular fashions to fill out their wardrobes. Today, however, even popular fashions have become expensive. To combat the high cost of fashion, women are turning to accessories to add variety to their wardrobes. This trend has created a new opportunity for entrepreneurs: the accessories-only store.

Minor Items, Major Sales

Sales in the accessories industry have increased dramatically over the past decade or so. Between 1977 and 1987, wholesale accessory sales more than doubled, jumping from $5.1 billion to $12.1 billion. And on the retail level, the National Retail Merchants' Association reports that accessories specialty chain stores outperformed department stores' accessories divisions, with a gross margin of 49.8 percent compared to the department stores' 46.5 percent.

Women's accessories stores sell a broad category of goods including scarves, handbags, jewelry, and leather goods.

Stores may carry designer, popular, or private labels—or a combination of all three.

American women are discovering what European women have known for years: you can stretch a wardrobe almost endlessly with the right accessories. Old dresses look updated, new dresses take on a different flavor, and everything looks more polished when finished with the right accessories. And as clothing prices continue to soar, accessories are far more accessible than just about any other wardrobe enhancers.

Who Sells Accessories?

Department stores probably represent the most formidable competition. Their size and purchasing power give them greater access to accessory markets and enable them to buy in large quantities. This combination gives department stores a distinct advantage.

But personal service and a superior selection make all the difference at accessory boutiques. To remain competitive, many department stores have scaled down their sales staff, hampering their ability to provide good service. Because accessories stores are much smaller, they are able to provide better service with less personnel.

Accessories stores also offer merchandise not available in most department stores. Recent mergers have reduced the once diversified retail industry to a few conglomerates. Consequently, a small group of buyers select the accessories for a number of department stores. The result? Most department stores carry essentially the same selection of accessories. Independent accessories stores help break the monotony.

Accessory Success

Accessory items are generally impulse purchases, so stores rely on heavy foot traffic. While many stores do well in strip malls, most locate in regional malls where foot traffic tends to be heaviest. One operator opened three locations in strip centers before discovering that regional malls were more profitable. "The mall store was successful from the beginning because of heavy foot traffic," she says. "The store draws more than 200,000 customers a week."

Inventive displays are a critical factor in accessory success. Window displays lure customers in. Additionally, many stores make merchandise accessible to the shopper instead of keeping it in a display case or behind the counter. "Shoppers are more likely to buy a product if they are comfortable with it," reasons one store owner, "and they are more likely to be comfortable with a product if they have access to it."

Accessories stores that highlight jewelry cannot allow as much accessibility because of the threat of shoplifting. Instead, they put the expensive jewelry in a display case and the less expensive jewelry on display stems.

Opening the Store

While the cost of opening an accessories store varies from one area to the next, it is possible to start up with relatively little expense. A minimum of $25,000 will get you started, though the average figure is probably closer to $45,000. Accessories stores are generally small—between 800 and 1,200 square feet—so the overhead is usually low.

Because the stores are small, few fixtures are required, and they need not be costly. While a variety of fixtures can be used, a glass case for jewelry and shelving for other items are all that is really needed.

Even the cost of inventory can be kept within reason. Some accessories are more expensive than others, so during start-up, the owner can keep inventory costs down by concentrating on the less expensive items until the business can support the more costly ones.

As clothing prices rise, accessories-store owners will continue to enjoy success. "I've been in the business for seven years," one owner told us, "and it gets better every year."

===================== BRIGHT IDEA =====================

TAKING RETAIL BY STORM

Speaking of the weather, would you believe it's the subject of a successful New York retail outlet? Proprietor Fran Ziskin opened the shop in May of 1986 to help people cope with the changeable weather in the Big Apple.

Although weather might not appear to be the catchiest of themes for a specialty store, Ziskin has made her idea shine with an imaginative, high-quality inventory and attractive seasonal displays. The store itself has been decorated to look like a summer beach house. Colorful displays of raincoats, umbrellas, and rain boots line the walls. Light streams in through an artificial skylight. According to Ziskin, a synthesized thunderstorm goes off every ten minutes.

Pointing out that most department stores stock merchandise for the coming season instead of the current one, Ziskin says that customers appreciate the chance to buy accessories suited to the day's weather.

"Our merchandise is in stock in season," she stresses, "and it's all in one place." Those unprepared for a sudden downpour or a surprise snow flurry are especially grateful to stumble upon Ziskin's extensive collection of fashionable waterproof gear. She is quick to add, however, that the Weather Store's sales do not dry up when the sun comes out. In the summer, they stock beach gear, sun hats, and Hawaiian baseball caps.

LIQUOR STORE

High Net Profit Before Taxes:	$120,000
Average Net Profit Before Taxes:	$ 85,000
Minimum Start-up:	$ 84,000
Average Start-up:	$137,000

Any way you look at it, Americans like to drink. Every occasion—festive or bleak, momentous or forgettable—has the potential alternately for a toast or a ceremonious drowning of sorrows. In good times or bad, come negative publicity or prohibition: nothing will prompt Americans to abstain from drinking.

Liquor sales represent a vast industry in America. Each year Americans buy some $10 billion worth of wine, $25 billion worth of distilled spirits, and $38 billion worth of beer for total retail sales of $73 billion.

Changing Patterns

Americans clearly buy enough liquor to keep a multitude of stores open and thriving. But the liquor market is changing, and so is the face of successful liquor retailing. For instance, moderation is now in vogue—which doesn't mean people have stopped drinking, just that they're doing so less recklessly than before. Concerns about health, fitness, and alcohol abuse have consumers rethinking their drinking habits.

In response to these concerns, the liquor industry has begun promoting low-calorie and low-alcohol beverages. "Light" beers and wines that boast either fewer calories or less alcohol—or both—have been appearing on retailers' shelves more frequently of late. As an odd side effect, light-colored spirits (rum, tequila, and gin) also have an advantage over so-called "brown" goods like scotch, bourbon, and brandy, even though white spirits aren't "light" in any other respect.

Another trend that's helped compensate for decreased alcohol consumption is a growing interest in upscale liquor. Consumers figure that if they're going to drink less, they might as well drink something good. Sales of boutique wine, imported beer, and premium liquor are consequently on the rise. Selling premium products, however, requires superior salesmanship. Simply putting a bottle of twelve-year-old Irish whiskey or pear liqueur on your shelves isn't enough: you must also know enough about the spirit to sell it.

Individual Pursuits

The first step in establishing a liquor store is learning who the consumers in your immediate market are. This is likely to be a highly individual process, since the liquor market is divided up into small, distinct segments. Moreover, liquor stores are subject to a score of legal and commercial variables that make every store a unique entity, differing from state to state and from street corner to street corner.

State regulations affect the liquor business profoundly. The first thing to do if you're considering a liquor business is to check with your state government for rules and regula-

tions. State laws can affect what you sell, when you sell it,
and how you promote your business.

Local tastes also matter. Wine sales are up across the
country, and many liquor retailers are keeping profits up by
emphasizing their wine departments. But some retailers report that their clientele could "care less about wine." In some
neighborhoods, wine coolers, beer, and basic spirits are
much bigger sellers.

Establish an Identity

Because the market is segmented by nature, almost any
kind of liquor store is feasible, provided it's properly located
and well maintained. Choosing your location should be your
primary consideration. In addition to the obvious pitfalls—
poor locations and unpopulated areas—you should also consider the personality of your proposed store. Opening an
exclusive wine boutique, for example, wouldn't make sense
on skid row.

Once you've selected an accessible, appropriate location,
think about how you're going to promote your business.
Though liquor stores in the past have not been in business
purely for sport, as a group they haven't shown a genius for
merchandising, either. Creating the kind of atmosphere that
will make your store stand out doesn't require a great deal of
invention or interior design—just a basic knowledge of retailing fundamentals.

Service, of course, can't be underestimated—though it
can be overdone. Especially now, when public sentiment
seems to be vehemently anti-intoxication—if not antidrink-
ing—liquor retailers must know the difference between
salesmanship and the hard sell. Thinking of yourself as a
source of information and not persuasion is probably the
safest policy in the current climate.

If you pay close attention to local demographics, set up an
attractive, well-organized store, develop an eye for in-store
displays, and stay on top of your customers' needs, your
liquor store should be a success. In an industry that has
largely neglected the fine art of retailing, a little knowledge
and enthusiasm go a long way.

ANTIQUE STORE

High Net Profit Before Taxes:	$100,000
Average Net Profit Before Taxes:	$ 20,000
Minimum Start-up:	$ 5,000
Average Start-up:	$ 33,000

A young woman attending an estate sale spotted a cane-backed walking-stick rack. Apparently it had been stored in the attic. It was grimy and had a loose joint that needed regluing. She guessed its date of origin at around 1900. She paid $2.00 for it, and another $1.00 for a three-tiered salad colander.

As she returned to her car with the loot, an antique dealer—who was just arriving at the sale—approached her and offered to purchase the walking-stick rack. His first offer was $25, which she declined. His final offer, which she accepted, was $55. Though he offered an additional $25 for the colander, the woman left—with a $52 profit and a new prize for her collection.

This kind of story is commonplace in the antique business—a field that practically anybody can enter with some basic knowledge of antiques and a minimum of cash.

Profitable Hobby

One successful part-time antique collector started out with an initial investment of less than $50. Each afternoon, she drives to auctions and estate sales, and investigates classified ads in the local newspaper. Occasionally, she rummages through junk shops in the poorer sections of town.

Every other weekend, she places classified ads for the items she's found, using her garage as a showroom. The first weekend, her sales were $308 on items for which she had paid $42. Profits have ranged from a low of $50 to a high of $820 on her biweekly sales.

She began with very little knowledge, so she researched the history of each item she purchased carefully. Today, she has an extensive collection of books on American antiques and is as knowledgeable as most full-time dealers. Learning about antiques is essential to success in this business.

Acres of Antiques

In most cities, antique dealers congregate in the same area or along the same street. In some cities, there are even antique shopping centers, where collectors and retailers gather to hawk their wares. Along the roads leading to the Catskills resort area in an eighty-four-square-mile area in the Hudson River valley, there are over a hundred dealers' shops. Merchandisers with huge outlets are getting into the act. There are several in the New York City area whose showrooms are as large as football fields.

Where antiques are concerned, bigger is often better. One outlet in the Los Angeles area boasts three acres of floor space. It's drawing customers from as far as 300 miles away, and selling items priced as high as $10,000.

Investigate the Market

America's interest in antiques has just begun. If you're serious about getting into antique sales, take some time to see what's selling in your area. Are mahogany armoires the hot ticket? Or does wicker from the forties move faster? While truly old merchandise is hot, so is merchandise that's relatively recent. In many cities, trendy furniture from the fifties and sixties is making a comeback. Investigate regional preferences in your area, and do your best to cater to those tastes.

You can even try this business part-time, like the collector we talked about earlier in this section. Invest in some salable pieces and try your hand at informal sales.

===================== BRIGHT IDEA =====================

TOYS FOR GROWN-UPS

Once upon a time, only children were allowed to run amok in stores. They would zip up and down the aisles, open boxes, and try out the newest toys—much to the dismay of the toy-store owner.

Now things are different. There are actually stores where play is encouraged. And they aren't for kids: they're for adults. Selling toys for grown-ups has several advantages—adults are less likely to cause permanent damage, adults are often more difficult to buy for than kids, and adults have more money to spend.

Grown-up toys run the gamut from state-of-the-art fitness equipment to video phones, high-tech dog leashes, and massage chairs. For people who think they have everything, these shops open whole new vistas in consumerism. For entrepreneurs, a knack for spotting clever items and a way with merchandising can pay off big in this field. One operator with twelve shops estimates sales at $10 million to $20 million.

To start a store of this sort, you'll need a fair amount of capital. You should make it a policy to carry only the most unusual, most ingenious items. To achieve this kind of inventory, you'll have to invest plenty of selection time and money. Your store must also be attractive—as interesting and well designed as your merchandise. With the right spirit of innovation and fun, you can help people rediscover the children within.

FLOWER SHOP

High Net Profit Before Taxes:	$50,000
Average Net Profit Before Taxes:	$40,000
Minimum Start-up:	$41,000
Average Start-up:	$62,000

Fueled by renewed consumer interest, America's flower industry is coming up profits. Between 1977 and 1987, retail sales of floriculture products nearly tripled, from $2.9 billion to an estimated $8 billion, according to the U.S. Department of Commerce Bureau of Economic Analysis.

Reasons for the boom are many. One contributing factor is the installation of floral departments at many supermarkets—not exactly a boon to individual flower shops, but a clear indicator of current demand. Consumers are more interested in buying flowers for everyday occasions and for decorating than they were in past years. Even the institution of new holidays has had an impact: Secretary's Day, for example, is now a major sales event for florists.

Whatever the reasons, increased sales spell hope for florists and would-be florists all across America. Yet the changes taking place in the industry have as much to do with style and savvy as sales volume. Successful flower shops are becoming more attractive, more service-oriented, and more efficient. These advances open up opportunities for dedicated, quality-driven operators in a market that should continue to blossom.

Business Is Blooming

The flower business is a fairly venerable retail industry. Since the days when vendors wandered the streets hawking baskets of blossoms, florists have existed—and prospered. Florists learned early on the advantages of selling a specialized product. Long before yuppies existed, florists responded to the demand for convenience—hence, the floral wire service. While other industries are just starting to adopt delivery services, florists have been delivering their products for years.

But during the same time period, the floral industry also remained relatively quaint. Even today, most of the nation's 30,000 florists are independent shops. Flower shops have been a traditional favorite among entrepreneurs looking for inroads into retailing. Flower shops require a relatively small initial investment (an average investment is about $62,000), don't have massive staffing requirements, and enjoy a certain amount of built-in business on holidays and special occasions like weddings.

Moreover, the floral industry hasn't yet been dominated by franchising. For the moment, at least, the individual operator is the standard in the florist business. This makes the flower shop an attractive entrepreneurial venture today, though the ground rules for running a flower shop do appear to be changing.

A Rose Is a Rose

On one hand, Gertrude Stein's memorable assessment is wrong: all roses are not created equal. Nor is a freesia just a freesia, nor a mum a mum, and so on. The one advantage that flower shops are able to maintain over their mass-merchandiser competitors is quality—and the bigger the advantage the better.

Freshness is one important criterion. Many florists offer guarantees on their blooms—five days, for example, or your money back. Another discriminating factor is selection and style. Stocking unusual flowers like peonies, delphiniums, and lilacs can put you ahead of the competition. Likewise, offering superior design can bring in customers. Some of the most successful florists make it a point to study continually—everything from Japanese ikebana to lush English arrangements.

Trimming the Costs

On the other side of the coin, sound management will also play a big role in the future success of America's flower shops. Maintaining a fresh inventory may be good marketing, but it also requires a meticulous system of care and rotation. Not only do florists juggle a fragile and perishable inventory, but they also balance a wide variety of tasks—from design to wire services. In between, they must map out marketing strategies and keep pace with the books. Many flower shops have branched out into items like greeting cards, gift baskets, and balloons. These, too, require work.

The future looks decidedly upbeat for the floral business, but only for those ready to make a commitment to the trade. This is no place for the grouchy, the dull, or the slovenly. The ideal flower-shop owner will have both business sense and a love of flowers. For the entrepreneur with a passion for peonies and a yen for yucca, owning a flower shop could be the most enjoyable way to bloom as a businessperson.

WEDDING SHOP

High Net Profit Before Taxes:	$70,000 plus
Average Net Profit Before Taxes:	$50,000
Minimum Start-up:	$55,000
Average Start-up:	$90,000

Weddings are back—and bigger than ever! Say hello to fancy dresses, engraved invitations, traditional showers, and celebrations with all the trimmings. Couples are returning to big, formal weddings—and that spells good news for the booming bridal industry.

Saying "I Do" to Spending

These days, couples are waiting longer to get married, often until careers are established. That means they're better prepared to contribute financially to their own weddings— usually supplementing the money their parents will spend. It also means they're more strapped for time. Working brides can't run from one shop to another to handle the details of their weddings. They want one-stop shopping at an establishment that offers service and quality.

For a relatively low investment of only $55,000, you can help brides-to-be accomplish all their shopping under one roof—yours. Net profits range from $50,000 to $200,000 before taxes.

Basic services include wedding-dress sales and tuxedo rental, but that's just the tip of the iceberg. The entire bridal party needs dressing. You can even make money as a wedding consultant, matching couples with the services they need for their weddings—photographers, florists, musicians, and so on. One consultant we know charges a flat fee of $1,000 for each wedding, and handled more than 800 weddings last year for a gross of $800,000.

If on-site consulting sounds like more work than you're ready to tackle, at least consider adding a referral service to your shop. Work out a co-op arrangement with local florists, photographers, and so on, where they provide the services and you take a percentage for the referral.

One operator broke down his $1.2-million gross as follows: $400,000 in wedding-dress sales, $350,000 in tuxedo rentals, $65,000 in photography and videotaping, $35,000 in floral contracting, $102,000 in catering, $109,000 in equipment rental, $72,000 in music, and $82,000 in printing and invitations.

Outstanding Service Is the Key

The wedding industry is highly competitive and there are many major companies going after the bridal dollar. Successful shop owners are finding that size is not the determining factor: service is. That's good news to small operators and would-be small operators, since service is one area in which small shops can compete effectively with large outlets.

CHILDREN'S CLOTHING STORE

High Net Profit Before Taxes:	$65,000
Average Net Profit Before Taxes:	$24,000
Minimum Start-up:	$19,500
Average Start-up:	$30,000

Though children's clothing is not a new item, it's playing to a whole new market these days. Parents today—most of whom hail from dual-income households—have money to spend, and they're spending it on their kids.

What's more, children are not the unfashionable slouches most of us were when we were small. On the contrary, today's kids are hip—and that includes children too young to know what the word means.

This on top of an already attractive opportunity. Because even before children became fashion plates, they exhibited a constant need for clothes. By definition, children grow. So even if they get new wardrobes one month, chances are good they'll be back three months later buying all new outfits. With a market like this, it's no wonder that children's apparel stores are doing a booming business.

Find Yourself a Specialty

Like any other kind of apparel retailing, children's clothing offers a variety of niches. Discount clothes make up a large portion of the market, but this end of the business is dominated by large stores like K-Mart and Sears.

Catering to a more upscale clientele is a better bet. By handling exclusive, fashionable clothing, you can develop a following with money to spend. And you won't have to worry about the discount stores carrying the same outfits for a few dollars less. Your customers will be shopping for quality and fashion, not price.

The Right Location

In this business, location is vital. Open your shop in a neighborhood with plenty of young upper- or upper-middle class families with children. Most successful children's-apparel-shop owners told us that 90 percent of their business comes from a five-mile-sqare area around their shops. This is something to keep in mind when advertising as well. Local newspaper and fliers, your least expensive form of advertising, should be all you need.

Look for a location that's near stores that promote browsing—bookstores, men's clothing stores, and specialty shops such as jewelry and antique stores. Make sure the area has heavy foot traffic.

Keep in mind that it pays to take advantage of evening shopping. With more and more mothers holding down jobs, the morning hours may not be as important as the evenings.

It Pays to Be Different

The best way for a person to succeed in this business is to be different. If you create an unusual atmosphere, your customers will enjoy shopping.

Theme decorating is one popular concept. Adding superheroes, circus characters, or cartoon characters to your decor will make you an instant hit with young clients. By working with skilled free-lance designers and woodcrafters, you should be able to design and prepare an innovative interior affordably.

Other extras to consider: a television and VCR to show children's videos (it keeps children occupied while their parents shop), and a play area with toys and/or books. The more attractive your store is—to parents and children alike—the better your sales will be.

Mark It Up

The largest portion of business in children's apparel is in the two-to-four-year-old age group. Within this group, the largest amount of business—about 60 percent—comes from color-coordinated outfits. Though your major stock will probably consist of the traditional pastel colors, don't be afraid to be daring. Hot colors, as well as basic black (it's true!), are becoming more and more common in children's closets. For an increasing number of fashion-conscious parents, no price is too dear for exclusive, designer children's wear.

When you have an exclusive item, take a healthy markup. Pricing it as high as three times the wholesale cost is not out of line. Of course, you won't be able to do this on every item. But if you have goods that parents can't buy anywhere else, they'll pay the price for fashion—whatever that price might be.

Mark It Down

At the same time, don't hesitate to mark down any items that aren't moving as quickly as you'd like. Most retailers take far too long to mark down slow-moving merchandise. If you have clothes that aren't selling quickly, mark them down immediately. Generally, about 7 to 9 percent of your stock will end up being marked down.

=========== BRIGHT IDEA ===========

BOOKSHOPS WITH A TWIST

If you've been losing sleep because you can't find a book that will help you sharpen your knife- and tomahawk-throwing skills, you can rest easy—it's at the How-To-Do-It Book Shop in Philadelphia.

If tomahawk throwing isn't your style, how about comic books? Los Angeles entrepreneur Bill Liebowitz has an inventory that attracts collectors and connoisseurs alike to his shop, Golden Apple Comics.

Plain old bookstores are out. For true aficionados, only a specialty bookstore will suffice. As chains become increasingly dominant in general book sales, many book-minded entrepreneurs are adopting specialties—how-to books, comic books, mysteries, biographies, children's books, science-fiction warehouses, and so on.

Ginger Curwen of the American Booksellers Association

in New York City has witnessed this trend. "We've seen a tremendous increase in specialty [book] retailers over the last decade," she says. "For instance, the number of children's bookstores has jumped from about 30 shops ten years ago to about 300 or 400 today."

All told, there are about 2,300 specialty bookstores in the United States, compared to about 6,600 general bookstores, according to the 1988–1989 American Book Trade Directory. Clearly, specialty bookstores are getting a healthy percentage of the $17 billion to $18 billion spent on books annually.

For the entrepreneur, selecting a specialty has additional advantages, including smaller space requirements, instant identity, and perhaps the only way to go head-to-head with the major players.

LINGERIE SHOP

High Net Profit Before Taxes:	$41,000 plus
Average Net Profit Before Taxes:	$27,000
Minimum Start-up:	$37,000
Average Start-up:	$58,000

In the past several years, American women have rediscovered lingerie. Not that they went without it before—but today the selection of bras, camisoles, slips, and garters is more than just basic. Silk, satin, and lace abound, as do special bras for jogging and aerobics. Sleepwear, too, has gone beyond simple flannels and pajamas. Some nightgowns sell for as much as $150 or more; silk peignoir sets sell for about twice that.

Lingerie is a hot item today, and shops that specialize in fine-quality items are capitalizing on the demand. Our research shows that the average purchase is $20 in a specialty lingerie shop, and $200 sales are common. This is well above the average sale in a regular department store.

Big Profits Are Possible

Small specialty lingerie shops can realize a net pretax profit of 25 percent during the second year in business, based on $150,000 in annual sales. One owner-operator, who stocks an incredible array of intimate apparel, has a 1,500-square-foot shop that's constantly bustling with customers. The shop yields a gross in excess of $200,000 annually, and she's been in business only four years. Her net profits are close to 29 percent before taxes.

Another owner-operator, who opened his 700-square-foot lingerie boutique a year and a half ago in a supersized shopping mall, grossed $120,000 the first fiscal year with 16-percent net profits before taxes. He expects to reach $200,000 in sales this year, with a 35-percent net-profit margin.

Low Investment Gets You Started

We found one 500-square-foot shop that opened several years ago in a busy suburban shopping center. The owner-operator started with a $14,500 investment and is now grossing $50,000 a year.

It's possible to start a lingerie shop on very little money. However, if you can invest at least $45,000, you have a better chance of beating the competition and making a sizable profit. With a more substantial investment, you'll be able to stock a larger inventory and develop your store's image. An inviting atmosphere can be critical to your success.

Huge Market

Though your potential market includes virtually all women, the market to focus on for nontraditional, exclusive intimate apparel is young women between eighteen and thirty years old. Increasingly, women over thirty represent a strong market as well.

The customers who frequent specialized lingerie stores are very much aware of themselves and current fashion trends. Often they're looking specifically for something sexy and out of the ordinary—regardless of price. Don't overlook opportunities to merchandise: a customer buying a single bra is usually game for a few pairs of matching panties. Lingerie lends itself to coordinated buying, so be prepared to sell.

Women aren't the only customers, either. Men are predict-ably enthusiastic about buying lingerie for their wives or girlfriends. One store we observed had a clientele that was about one third male. Men are especially open to buying matching camisoles and tap pants or expensive negligees: again, good salesmanship can make a big difference.

TROPICAL FISH STORE

High Net Profit Before Taxes:	$51,000 plus
Average Net Profit Before Taxes:	$25,000
Minimum Start-up:	$35,000
Average Start-up:	$50,000

Forget the cynics who claim that fish are boring pets—they don't realize that dullness is the point. For millions of stressed-out Americans, aquariums provide an element of calmness and serenity that other pets can't. They're even popular in offices these days. What better place for a stress-reducing aquarium than a dentist's waiting room?

The fish business isn't an easy one. You'll need to put in a lot of hard work and determination. It's not enough just to love fish. This is a competitive business that requires skill in buying, displaying, and maintaining livestock. Your clients will also need plenty of advice on equipment and fish. You must know your inventory backward and forward in order to be a good manager and salesperson.

Profits, however, are often reward enough for your hard work. You can net between $20,000 and $35,000 a year before taxes. We found owner-operators who were grossing as much as $150,000 pretax with profit margins of 27 to 34 percent, including income from servicing home and office aquariums. Most owners start with small inventories of high-quality livestock and build a reputation for quality and service that draws customers from miles away.

Fast-Growing Hobby

Enthusiasts visit stores regularly seeking new breeds of fish, the latest equipment, and supplies. Tropical-fish-store customers spend an average of $8.00 per visit for accessories and food. Aquarium setups cost between $35 and $1,000, depending on the size of the tank, fish, and decorating accessories.

Better equipment, lower costs, and improved shipping methods have all contributed to the recent popularity of tropical fish. Not only are they tranquilizing, but fish take up very little room, don't eat a lot, never need to be taken for walks, never bring home dead rodents, and are a beautiful addition to any home.

What It Takes to Start

We interviewed store owners who started out with only $12,000 to $15,000. They stocked only a basic working inventory of equipment, supplies, and fish at the beginning and built the business into successful operations by expanding as profits grew.

One owner-operator we spoke to opened a 1,000-square-foot store several years ago with $6,000 for equipment and inventory and only $1,000 for building improvements. He has more than doubled his inventory since that time and is now expanding into a vacant store next door.

Start-up costs vary with the size of the shop and the types of fish sold. Saltwater fish are extremely popular (not to mention pricey) among contemporary enthusiasts, but setting up marine display tanks will cost you extra money up front. Plan to spend at least $50,000 opening a well-stocked store in a 1,000-square-foot space. It is better to install top-quality aquarium equipment to minimize replacement costs later. Plus, you have the advantage of opening as a "going business" rather than a low-end operation.

Hot Trend: Servicing Tanks

Here's a way to break into the aquarium business—or supplement an existing shop—with a small initial investment and virtually no inventory or lease costs. Aquarium services are becoming increasingly popular with both home and office enthusiasts. With as little as $1,000 and a working car, you can start making your rounds.

If you start out with a service only, you can save the money you make to open a shop. Or, if you plan to open a shop anyway, consider offering a service as an additional profit center. Several store owners have incorporated this concept into their established operations with great results. A service can be exceptionally profitable if run correctly. Some operators net up to 35 percent pretax due to service contracts with affluent homeowners, businesspeople, and professionals. These contracts go for $10 to $50 a month or more plus the cost of equipment, usually paid by the customer.

Find a Good Location

Tropical fish stores can thrive in unlikely locations if they have outstanding reputations and knowledgeable personnel. You can guarantee a high volume, however, by locating in a middle-class area in a city with a population of at least 300,000 people. Even though you may attract hobbyists from thirty or forty miles away (depending on competition), you need a strong base of customers in the immediate vicinity.

Look for a location with good visibility, a heavy flow of auto traffic, adequate parking, and a sizable volume of foot traffic. Though aquariums aren't a classic impulse item, good displays and healthy stock can go a long way toward convincing even casual browsers to take the plunge.

LARGE-SIZE WOMEN'S APPAREL STORE

High Net Profit Before Taxes:	$250,000
Average Net Profit Before Taxes:	$ 50,000
Minimum Start-up:	$ 25,000
Average Start-up:	$ 40,000

Among the most promising specialty retail businesses this year is a seemingly unlikely candidate: the large-size women's clothing store. The market itself isn't exactly new—large women have always existed. But perhaps for the first time, they're being considered a legitimate, vital fashion market.

The garment industry has only recently discovered that large women, just like their smaller counterparts, will gladly bedeck themselves in sequins, miniskirts, suits, and shorts. In fact, they represent about $10 billion worth of clothing sales. Today, certain innovative, intelligent retailers are helping this long-neglected market realize its potential. And that potential is nothing less than formidable.

The Forgotten Market

Somewhere along the line in America, we developed the mass opinion that a woman should weigh 110 pounds, and that any woman who deviated from that ideal was somehow bizarre. We believed, in short, that every large woman deserved scorn. But the fact is that an estimated 35 million American women wear a size 14 or larger. Large women are not an abnormality in this country. Rather, a full third of all American women do not conform to the "thin is in" ideal.

Yet until just a few years ago, large women were forgotten by the fashion industry. Carole Shaw, editor of *BBW: Big, Beautiful Woman,* a Tarzana, California–based fashion magazine (circulation 300,000!), recalls with outrage her attempts to buy fashionable large-size clothing. "All we had in 1979," she recalls, "were dumb polyester pull-on pants and maternity blouses. There was nothing that by any stretch of the imagination could be called fashion."

"It's as if retailers believed that once a woman wore a size 14 or over, she had no taste, no buying power, and no problem with shopping in an obscure corner of the department store," laments one large-size retailer, who became so fed up she opened her own chain of shops and in one year grossed just under $7 million.

Plenty of Room for Growth

In years past, the large-size market was one giant muumuu of monotony. But today, large-size fashions reflect the diversity of the market. After all, large women are one out of every three women in America—and that represents a wide range of ages, interests, and life-styles.

The most successful retailers are focusing on variety, not only within their stores, but between themselves and their competition. Aspiring large-size-store owners should take careful note of what their immediate market needs. In some areas, department stores and discount chains may be the only competition around. In others, established specialists may already exist. Either way, there is room enough for new ideas in most communities.

One thing most successful large-size retailers agree on is that fashion sense is no longer optional, but a fact of life. And while the advent of fashion in the industry has opened up new opportunities for entrepreneurs, it's also made the business tougher. Large-size retailers can no longer rely on entire stocks of polyester basics to carry their shops.

Good Sense, Good Business

Of course, it takes more than a few attractive dresses to succeed in this business. Like any retail operation, a large-size women's boutique requires careful planning, smart buying, good management, an excellent location, and savvy marketing. Retain experience isn't a must, but it certainly helps.

Assuming that you do have the good business sense and panache to do it right, however, large-size retailing represents a solid opportunity. After years of neglect, there's a lot of pent-up demand for interesting clothes. And not only is the market just coming into its own, but it will continue to be substantial even as it levels off. "Nobody really needs to buy a lot of clothes," says one successful retailer. "But you do buy clothes because you want something new, or you want a new color. It's something you do to enhance your image." Now that the large-size market has awakened to the idea of fashion, there's no turning back.

The ranks of large women have existed virtually forever: The ranks of fashionable large-size retailers is just beginning to catch up. Few other retail markets can boast such potential. In this growing field, there is ample room for new ideas and new, higher standards.

COOKWARE SHOP

High Net Profit Before Taxes:	$48,000
Average Net Profit Before Taxes:	$37,000
Minimum Start-up:	$52,000
Average Start-up:	$75,000

American consumers are on a cookware binge. You can help yourself to a healthy portion of those sales by opening your own gourmet cookware store. With the right inventory and a good location, you can cook up profits of up to 52 percent before taxes.

Many small gourmet cookware shops bring in annual sales in the six-figure category. One 600-square-foot shop currently grosses $120,000 a year and nourishes the owner with net profits of 21 percent before taxes. Another owner with three shops boasts combined annual sales of more than $1 million.

An owner-operator who is familiar with gourmet cooking can make annual net profits between 22 and 33 percent before taxes, based on a minimum inventory of $25,000. Adding cooking classes at $15 to $30 each class per person can boost gross profits by as much as 12 percent.

The profit margin on merchandise is attractive in this industry. Basic cooking and serving products are generally marked up 105 percent. Unique accessories are slightly higher, and items like specially blended tea can go as high as 300 percent. Customers can't wait to buy. Industry studies indicate that $15 is the average national purchase in a gourmet cookware shop. Participants at in-store cooking classes generally spend up to $100 for the purchase of items used in each session.

Strong Appetite for Gourmet

The affluent eighties brought about a culinary awakening in America. Even average consumers discovered the best of things: imported cheeses, boutique wines, gourmet chocolates, and food of every type and ethnicity. Kitchen gadgets became plentiful, not only the ubiquitous food processor and microwave, but also such labor-saving wonders as the pasta maker, ice cream freezer, salad spinner, and electric wok.

In the nineties, the trend continues. Now that the nation's appetite for gourmet cooking has been whetted, the market is open for all kinds of new cookbooks, tools, equipment, and gadgets. Cooking classes are also a hot ticket, since most people still don't know the first thing about cooking Thai food or cooking without fat, to name just a few potential topics.

Opening Investment Is Modest

A minimum investment of $52,000 will put you into a small 500-square-foot shop with excellent profit potential. This includes equipment, building preparation, and a well-rounded opening inventory. One owner-operator we spoke to opened an 800-square-foot shop with $19,000 a few years ago. Second-year sales reached $168,000 and continue to increase dramatically.

Invest in a prime location. Although the merchandise required is basically the same in any size shop, more available capital will improve your working inventory. Keep in mind that an annual inventory of $27,000, turned between four and five times, will result in net profits of $25,000 to $30,000 before taxes. That's in addition to the salary you would draw as an owner-manager by running the shop yourself.

Ingredients of Success

The most successful owners have an in-depth knowledge of their markets. While the gourmet craze is touching every socioeconomic level, the primary market is the well-educated, upper-income consumer. People who have the discretionary income to spend on cookware and an interest in exotic cuisine are your best potential customers.

The typical customer is thirty-five to forty-five years old, has a family, and earns a middle-to-high income. He or she enjoys creating new dishes and likes entertaining at home. Singles make up an important secondary market. Young professionals with incomes of $15,000 and above are interested in products that simplify meal preparation and save time in the kitchen—food processors, blenders, and similar gadgets are especially popular.

========= BRIGHT IDEA =========

CARBURETOR COFFEE TABLES?

Ever since Americans gazed in amazement at the first Model A, cars have held a certain fascination for us. More than just a mode of transportation, the automobile has always been held in reverence by American teenagers and their parents. The baby boomers still reminisce about those big-finned beauties of the fifties, and today's teens dream of owning exotic, foreign sports cars like Porsches, Lamborghinis, and Ferraris.

While these car-struck lovers may not be able to afford their dream cars, they can stock up on auto replicas, art, and memorabilia at Car's the Star in Kansas City, Missouri. Owner Philip Schroeder explains how he came up with the idea to open this one-of-a-kind operation. "I spent five years selling furniture like love seats, bars, and tables that I made from auto parts. And I found a tremendous demand for 'automobilia.' The store really is a celebration of the car."

And celebrate it does. With products ranging from $1.50 postcards to a $25,000 love seat that looks like a 1952 Imperial, Car's the Star is catering to an upscale crowd that doesn't mind dipping deep into their wallets to buy mementos of their favorite vehicles.

But don't mistake this shop for an auto-parts store. You won't find any spark plugs, wiper blades, or distributor caps here. Instead you'll find trendy art, model cars, clothes, and stylized jewelry.

Since its opening in October 1988, Car's the Star has been an instant hit. And although Schroeder won't reveal sales figures, he boasts, "Our Christmas sales were 15 percent higher than we had projected." The store's popularity doesn't stop with its customers, either. Schroeder has plans to franchise the operation, and he's already fielded hundreds of calls from potential franchisees. Apparently, Car's the Star is in the fast lane to success.

SPECIALTY GIFT SHOP

High Net Profit Before Taxes:	$50,000 plus
Average Net Profit Before Taxes:	$26,000
Minimum Start-up:	$70,000
Average Start-up:	$90,000

These days, just about everyone is the person who has everything. In this age of affluence, it's hard to find a gift that's unique, thoughtful, and something the recipient hasn't already purchased for himself.

To find that special something, more and more shoppers are turning to specialty gift shops. While most department stores stick to basics, specialty shops can be more adventuresome. Consider the case of one New York retailer that carries only men's underwear. From bikinis to boxers, this shop has every conceivable form of underwear, plenty of which wouldn't be found in the average department store.

If underwear isn't outlandish enough, how about a lamp shaped like a cat? Or a giant lighted replica of the Empire State Building? Or an inflatable palm tree? Many Los Angeles gift shops specialize in trendy (if not out-and-out useless) items. Though you couldn't call them practical, they are fun, witty, and different. And best of all, they sell.

Specialty gift stores come in all shapes and sizes. Whether you're selling crystal, designer throw pillows, chocolate novelties, or teddy bears, the secrets to successful gift retailing are an imaginative, well-planned inventory and good salesmanship.

Aim for Broad Appeal

One California entrepreneur decided to break into the specialty gift market by selling only crystal chess sets. The sets were beautiful and certainly different, but the store didn't survive. Why? Only a small percentage of the local population wanted crystal chess sets. The store generated a lot of curiosity and walk-through traffic, but very little revenue.

Nearby, another retailer specializes in crystal dolls and music boxes, but also features Royal Doulton, Hummels, and collectible dolls of various types from around the world. The appeal is broader, and the store grosses $275,000 annually.

Whatever your specialty, try to stock merchandise that will appeal to a broad market. Cater to as many styles, tastes, and price ranges as possible. You can sell crystal chess sets if you like, but sell other items as well.

Make Location a Priority

Location can make or break a specialty gift business in two ways. First, make sure your business suits the surrounding community. Don't open a shop full of yuppie gadgets in a low-income neighborhood or a beach shop in Nebraska. Since affluent customers are probably your best target market, look for a shop in an upscale area.

Also try to find a shop with a high volume of buying traffic (not just shopping traffic). Malls are a good bet or, if you're wary of high rents, stand-alone buildings in residential shopping districts can also work. Before you sign a lease, take some time to scout the location thoroughly. One retailer recommends counting the people carrying bags in the vicinity of your prospective shop: that will tell you whether or not the location is a hot spot for serious shoppers.

Your Shopping Skills Count

Along with location, selecting the right inventory is critical to your new venture. Use your own good shopping skills. One way to get ideas is to attend gift shows. There, you can look for intriguing merchandise, make contacts with national and overseas distributors, and get the broadest possible picture of what's available. Check with your trade association for details on shows in your area.

You should also start contacting merchandise suppliers. Don't overlook unusual sources of supply. Local artists and craftspeople are ideal sources of original merchandise. Think of suppliers that other stores might overlook. For instance, if you start a luggage, purse, and leather-goods store, consider contacting manufacturers of designer dog leashes and collars. Remember, going one step beyond what the department stores do is going to be your trademark.

For your initial inventory, be careful not to go overboard with any one particular item. Overbuying at the outset is particularly unwise in the specialty trade. Ordering in smaller quantities will not only decrease start-up costs, but will help you analyze customer preferences. Then you can replenish your inventory based on what sells. This monitoring of your sales will be a constant process, and the key to maximizing revenues.

CHRISTMAS TREE LOT

High Net Profit Before Taxes:	$10,000
Average Net Profit Before Taxes:	$ 5,000
Minimum Start-up:	$10,000
Average Start-up:	$17,000

Each year, millions of Christmas trees are sold in this country. Cheerful operators of Christmas tree lots filled their stockings with net profits as high as $10,000 before taxes—and that's just for a month's work.

Several small retailers we spoke to sell an inventory of 700 trees and walk away with gross profits of $5,000 to $7,000. They net close to 17 to 18 percent before taxes. Tree lots with inventories of up to 1,500 trees average sales of close to $30,000 and can net from 25 to 32 percent for the season—even more under the right circumstances.

The secret is in the markup, which runs between 200 and 300 percent. A six-foot Scotch pine, for example, may wholesale for $7.80, including delivery, and retail for close to $20. If the tree is flocked, there's a 65-percent increase in gross profit. And the consumers will buy, regardless of cost.

The Fresh Smell of Success

Studies by the National Christmas Tree Association say that people buy real trees to capture the old-fashioned feeling of Christmas. The artificial trees that were once popular are now being left in the closet. They simply don't look—or smell—like a true Christmas tree.

For as little as $10,000, you can open your own small tree lot, staff it with your family, and still be home in time for Christmas. Start with at least 700 trees in a good residential location.

Many operators work on a permanent seasonal basis. Every year they set up in the same location, building a faithful cleintele that returns year after year for their trees. You, too, can make Christmas tree sales a thriving annual business. The demand is as reliable as the appearance of old Santa himself.

FURNITURE STORE

High Net Profit Before Taxes:	$135,000 plus
Average Net Profit Before Taxes:	$ 88,000
Minimum Start-up:	$ 43,000
Average Start-up:	$ 80,000

Here is yet another necessity of life: furniture. Furniture stores can be big money-makers, whether they sell fine, expensive furniture, middle-line merchandise, modest furnishings, or budget goods. Each type of store has its own style, and its own set of pros and cons.

Starting a high-end furniture shop usually entails a large investment. Moreover, courting an elite clientele takes time and money. Though exclusive furniture is fun to buy and affluent clients are a desirable target market, this isn't the business for everyone. You need cash and a good deal of decorating know-how.

You don't need a large investment or a decorating degree to start a budget furniture store. But these operations usually thrive on credit and hard salesmanship. They are most effective when they carry their own contracts. Financing your own credit instruments requires a tremendous amount of capital, even though the profit margin is high.

Aiming your shop somewhere in between these extremes is probably the simplest alternative. The initial investment is relatively low and the operations are probably the least complicated. Experience in sales is about all you'll need.

Upholstered Furniture Is Custom-Made

You don't sell upholstered furniture from the floor. Every piece of furniture in your store is merely a sample on which you take orders. The upholstered furniture is custom-made by the factory and delivered direct. As a result, you don't have to stock an extensive inventory—just enough samples to fill your showroom.

Some large operations do just the opposite. They stock unbelievable quantities of upholstered goods and claim to sell them at the lowest prices. But their system requires a high gross-profit margin to maintain a reasonable net. Don't be discouraged by big chain stores in your area. With careful management, you can compete favorably with the big chains in terms of both price and service.

TO Sales System Doubles Closing Rate

Most low-to-middle-line stores use a TO sales system (TO stands for "takeover" or "turnover"). It works this way: if the salesperson cannot close the sale, he or she finds out what the customer's objection is and then calls in another salesperson to take over, presenting the salesperson as the sales manager, decorating expert, buyer, or other in-house expert.

Even though the takeover person tries to answer the customer's objection and often does—thereby closing the sale—he or she impresses the customer with the power to make a deal in order to make a sale. A special deal is offered, dropping the price as an enticement to buy now. The percentage of sales at this point is high, and the procedure saves a lot of sales.

The theory is that it is better to take a small profit than none at all. In the furniture business, the number of people who promise to come back and do so is very low, so it's important to clinch a sale on the spot.

There is plenty of latitude for price-cutting, since furniture of this type is generally marked up 100 percent plus 10 percent. (Most store owners add the 10 percent to pay advertising costs.) That is, a sofa that cost the dealer $100 sells for $200, plus $20, or $220. The lowest drop allowed the TO person is a "half number," or 25 percent of the total price—in this case $55. The customer's special price is now $165. In the trade, this is called a full-number markup and a half-number drop.

Specialize in the Biggest Market

The highest volume of furniture sales is in upholstered goods—living-room sets and accessories. Bedroom furniture runs a slow second, with bedding sets and miscellaneous pieces coming in third. Dining-room sets are fourth.

Once a salesperson has closed a sale for a living-room set, usually the value of a sale can be doubled with add-ons: tables, lamps, etc. Most customers finance their own purchases, and an additional $5.00 to $15 a month doesn't seem like much to them when they visualize a completely new living room. Also, bedroom, den, and dining-room furniture are easily promoted once the initial sale is made.

WOMEN'S APPAREL STORE

High Net Profit Before Taxes:	$123,000
Average Net Profit Before Taxes:	$ 70,000
Minimum Start-up:	$ 41,000
Average Start-up:	$ 75,000

Miniskirts, sequined capes, and thigh-high boots may go out of style, but shopping never does. For many female shoppers, women's apparel stores and boutiques are the places to have fun, increase a wardrobe, and spend money.

Sizing Up the Market

The market for women's clothing stores is great, and it keeps increasing for several reasons. The contemporary woman, especially one of the 55 percent who work full-time, does not want to spend valuable time finding her way through a department-store maze or rummaging through acres of overstuffed racks. She expects courteous service, attention to her clothing needs, and an organized, relaxed shopping atmosphere. Smaller shops that cater exclusively to women can provide all these extras and still maintain competitive prices and a healthy profit.

In general, women tend to make more clothing purchases than men, and those purchases generally have higher price tags. Women spend about $25 billion a year on clothing—accounting for 38 percent of total retail sales. The outlook for independent women's apparel stores is favorable—each year there is a marked increase in the number of new stores opening. These stores range from small, specialized boutiques to medium-sized, high-variety shops like The Limited.

The market for women's apparel is nearly limitless. Clothing is highly disposable merchandise, not only physically (i.e., colors fade, fabrics wear out), but aesthetically as well. Once something's gone out of style (and this happens fast!), it's time to get something new. Women, especially, are susceptible to the changing whims of fashion—their wardrobe turnover is nearly twice that of men's. One always needs new clothes, and it's up to the retailer to encourage frequent wardrobe updates by stocking those items that appeal most to customers.

Making a Difference

The keys to competing with major chains and department stores are simple: service and specialization. Women will return to a store that takes the time to consider their needs, whether through personal attention or extra services like alterations.

Moreover, the trend for smaller retailers seems to be specialization. Look around at the proliferation of shops devoted exclusively to maternity wear, lingerie, large sizes, petite sizes, accessories-only, leather goods, formalwear, sportswear, dancewear, careerwear, and teen apparel.

This kind of sharply focused merchandising makes it that much easier for beginning retailers to stock inventory. Instead of having to decide what percentage of the store to devote to outerwear, pants, dresses, shirts, accessories, and so on, they can proceed directly to the lines and styles they want to carry and the image they want to convey.

Your Wares

After deciding what kind of store would be best in your market and location, the next big step is buying your inventory. This is the element that can make or break a new store. And it's not easy. There are thousands of manufacturers out there, with hundreds of thousands of styles, sizes, colors, and prices to choose from. How do you go about purchasing apparel that is right for your store?

Each retailer seems to have his or her own formula for selecting an inventory. If you need help, remember that the retail industry has an immense support system—numerous trade associations, publications, institutes, and research centers. Competitive as the business may be, there are experts out there who can help you get started, in the form of both paid consultation and free advice.

Manufacturers are very aware of the bright future for

small women's apparel stores. They also know that since the department stores and chains have been stocking more of their own private-label items, smaller stores are prime customers for their lines. Manufacturers' reps are usually willing to help out the new retailer with advice on what and where to buy. You should have a minimum start-up inventory capital of about $20,000 to $25,000.

Try It On for Size

Today's women are sophisticated shoppers. They have grown up with department stores, designer labels, and discount outlets. The retailer's challenge is to keep up with her. The smaller specialty store is growing in significance, in small towns and big cities, because women are demanding special attention to their fashion needs and are willing to pay for it.

HOBBY SHOP

High Net Profit Before Taxes:	$110,000
Average Net Profit Before Taxes:	$ 17,000
Minimum Start-up:	$ 13,000
Average Start-up:	$ 52,000

Start a model business—that is, a business that sells model cars, airplanes, boats, and more. Scale modeling is a popular hobby among children and adults alike. Hobbyists building or collecting model planes, railroads, racing cars, and sailing ships keep hobby shops busy supplying kits, equipment, and tools.

Better still, hobby shops can be models of profitability. We found several owners grossing $500,000 and more, netting as much as 22 percent pretax. The average shop grosses about $100,000 and has a 38-percent gross-profit margin before taxes. Many established small stores net in the 10-to-12-percent range, providing a modest salary and takeout for owner-operators who are happy to be making a living from their former hobbies.

Are you a hobby enthusiast? You can spend most of your

time building models for display and making a decent living if you're willing to put in some hard work for low pay to get to that point.

Hobby shops are not "get rich quick" operations. In the first year or two, most owners put profits (except for a modest salary) back into their stores to satisfy inventory requirements. A supplemental income, or substantial operating capital going in, may be necessary at first.

We found some owners who opened stores on a shoestring and built them into very successful businesses. One opened a few years ago with only $5,000, which does not include the $4,000 put into inventory and $1,000 for fixtures for a 2,100-square-foot store. Now he grosses $320,000 per year and has between $50,000 and $60,000 in inventory.

Another started in a tiny storefront with borrowed capital, and over several years built up a five-store chain now valued at $1 million. The opportunity is there for impressive long-term financial success—or a comfortable living, depending on your goals.

Know Who the Buyers Are

Your primary market will be males in their twenties to early forties with an interest in model building. The majority are middle-income homeowners and family men, although a growing number of single men have also taken an interest in hobbies.

Buyers are most often skilled workers, professionals, or businessmen who have the leisure time and the income necessary to make larger-than-average purchases for themselves or their sons.

Preteens and teenage boys are the second key market. But average purchases by kids and teens are smaller when they buy for themselves. By the midteens many youths set aside their interest in model planes and trains—about the time they take up an interest in dating.

A Final Word

For true model enthusiasts, opening a hobby shop can be a dream come true. Though this business does take some skill and determination to run profitably, for many, the financial rewards are secondary. Very few people are able to make a hobby their life's work. This is one business that affords that chance.

DISCOUNT FABRIC SHOP

High Net Profit Before Taxes:	$71,000
Average Net Profit Before Taxes:	$50,000
Minimum Start-up:	$34,000
Average Start-up:	$54,000

Reap rewards from what others sew. Today, 25 percent of all women's clothing in the United States is made in the home. Over 50 million women—half the female population—are sewing everything from simple shorts to the latest designer dresses.

Retail sales of home-sewing goods exceed $5 billion each year. Over 600 million articles of clothing and other items are made by home sewers annually and nearly 50 percent of all fabric sold to the consumer is purchased in fabric shops.

As a result, the small-yardage shops we investigated are grossing between $150,000 and $250,000 a year. One national retail chain specializing in home-sewing supplies grossed $177 million in 1977. That's an average of over $600,000 in sales for each of the company's 280 shops.

Surprisingly, the highest gross and net profits in this business are made by small discount fabric shops. Small fabric discounters, we found, buy substantially below the wholesale price—often for as little as $0.10 on the dollar. Gross-profit margins of 80 percent, which means a markup over cost of 400 percent, are commonplace.

Discount shops specialize in seconds, irregulars, end cuts, and closeouts from mills, distributors, clothing manufacturers, upholstery and drapery companies. Skillful buying allows substantial savings to consumers, while these fabric discounters can compete successfully even with the largest retail fabric chain stores.

A discounter obtains these leftovers or high-grade seconds for a fraction of the regular price that a retailer must pay. So a fancy fabric that sells for $9.00 a yard down the street can be sold for, say, $5.00 per yard to cost-conscious patrons, all at a high gross-profit margin.

The Little Shop Can Win Big

Huge retail chain operations move slowly and miss out on the majority of great buys in fabric seconds and closeouts, while the smaller independent discounters aggressively canvass the nation's garment districts and textile-company buying offices in search of high-quality merchandise at dirt-cheap prices.

The rising (some might say ridiculous) prices of women's clothing make home sewing a good bet for the coming decade. Many people are also turning to sewing as a means of self-expression.

There's Room for You

The market is definitely there for a small discounter. In 1967, only about 2,300 retail home-sewing centers were scattered across the country. Today, there are over 20,000. With record growth forecast for the coming decades, there's plenty of room for a smart operator.

Department stores and retail chains specializing in inexpensive fabrics constitute the greatest competition. But their service and product quality are characteristically poor. We found small discount fabric shops providing top-quality fabrics (seconds and closeouts) and expert personal service existing quite profitably alongside major retail chain operations.

Smart shoppers rarely buy without checking around first. Locating near a large impersonal chain can work to your advantage if your goods and services are superior.

You Must Know the Business

You have to know what you're doing to compete effectively in this business. Merchandising fabric goods requires sharp buying techniques, pricing, and inventory-control methods. Technical knowledge of fabrics is not a requirement, but a working knowledge of fabric types and how to buy them is critical. If you like to sew and have an eye for fashion and fabrics, you're halfway there already. With careful attention to detail and the application of sound business sense, there's no reason you can't become a rags-to-riches success.

PARTY GOODS/GIFT STORE

High Net Profit Before Taxes:	$100,000
Average Net Profit Before Taxes:	$ 40,000
Minimum Start-up:	$ 45,000
Average Start-up:	$100,000

For party throwers and goers, retail stores specializing in good-time merchandise—party goods, gifts, novelties, and decorative ware—are the answer to hours of going from one store to the next in fruitless pursuit of the right decorations and other items. Gift shops may carry greeting cards and a limited selection of party goods, but they usually don't have everything needed to create the right festive atmosphere. And neither do department and discount stores. Enter the one-stop, everything-under-one-roof party-goods and gift shop. For consumers and entrepreneurs alike, the party starts here.

Surprisingly, party-goods and gift sales bring in a whopping $5.6 billion annually. Industry insiders estimate annual growth in this business at 25 percent. The bulk of that growth comes from small-time operators. "This industry is governed by these mom-and-pop shops all over the country," says David Gooding, editor of *Party and Paper Retailer* magazine. "They're attracted to this industry because they've always dreamed of working with party items, pretty papers, and greeting cards. They enjoy being a part of a fashion business."

Pulling Out the Stops

Starting a successful party store is much like throwing a good party: skimping isn't allowed. Setting up shop can cost you anywhere from $45,000 to $150,000 and more, depending on the size of your shop and the extent of your inventory.

One of the biggest priorities is location. For retailers, location often spells the difference between success and failure, and a party-goods store is no exception. You can start up in a strip center, mall, or freestanding location and make your business a success, as long as there's adequate traffic and manageable rent.

Seasonal fluctuations are a natural part of the party business. Typically, strong sales of wedding invitations and decorations in the spring taper off until the Halloween-through-Christmas rush.

With these fluctuations, many party-goods retailers walk a very fine line in terms of cash flow during the lean months in deciding when and how much inventory to order for the spring and holiday seasons. It's not uncommon for party retailers to have to borrow from bank accounts to meet overhead and inventory costs when sales begin to slump.

Of course, busy seasons more than compensate for the slumps in terms of annual profits. Planning-wise, however, it's good to anticipate slow months. Retailers combat seasonal slow times by hosting sidewalk sales, beefing up their marketing efforts, and stocking a selection of regular merchandise like greeting cards and gifts.

Average pretax net in this business is $40,000, but profits of $100,000 are not uncommon. And in addition to the financial rewards, there's the fun and creativity of planning parties every day. "The nicest thing about being in this business is that the store is a happy place," one party-goods retailer told us. "The people who come in here are looking for things to celebrate a happy event."

PAINT AND WALLCOVERING STORE

High Net Profit Before Taxes:	$56,000
Average Net Profit Before Taxes:	$45,000
Minimum Start-up:	$47,000
Average Start-up:	$67,000

Paint and wallcoverings represent a $3-billion industry in the United States. You can cash in on this vast market with a paint and wallcovering store of your own.

A good paint and wallcovering store can become a mecca for local do-it-yourselfers. Sales personnel provide assistance with paint selection, as well as helpful information about preparation of surfaces, color coordination, and application techniques. In return, store owners are realizing high annual sales with solid markups 1.7 times inventory costs, based on $8,000 to $15,000 in stock.

We have seen tiny operations, run by owner-operators in good locations, grossing $125,000, and netting 25 percent before taxes. Established companies with more than one location are pulling in $150,000 to $200,000 in gross annual sales at each store.

Home Improvement Is Big Business

Given the high price of housing in most major cities, it's no wonder that more and more homeowners (and even apartment dwellers) would rather redecorate their current homes than buy new ones. In fact, many have no choice but to improve their present surroundings. Paint and wallcoverings are among the simplest, cheapest, and most effective home improvements around. A fresh coat of paint can make even the dingiest room seem new again.

You can set up a bare-bones operation for about $45,000. This approach is profitable if you maintain a basic, workable inventory and emphasize customer service. We found one store cleaning up in a small suburban shopping center. The owner-operator had opened less than four years before with a $9,500 investment and soon was grossing $80,000.

Most stores operate on a 40-to-46-percent profit margin for paint and wallcoverings. Brushes, rollers, and other sundry supplies operate on even higher margins. Sundries are impulse items and can account for one third of your store's sales. In addition, they provide the customer with one-stop shopping, a very important aspect of this service-oriented business.

Find the Buyers

Profitability depends largely on reaching the right markets. For instance, many apartment dwellers are showing a new interest in personalizing their surroundings. People who settle into apartments for 1½ to 4 years don't want institutional white walls—they want color. Apartment dwellers currently make up approximately 40 percent of the population and are important customers to consider.

Contractors and decorators also make up a large portion of a store's trade. A survey of independent store owners shows that an average of 40 percent of total sales was to smaller painting and decorating contractors in 1977. There are over 250,000 independent painting contractors in the United States today. They generally purchase volume amounts of paint and/or wallcovering, and can play an essential role in reaching your inventory-turnover goals.

Annual retail per capita spending in specialty paint and wallcovering stores is about $14. So you can figure that in a community of 20,000, your total store sales will easily reach $125,000 a year, counting on only half of the available decorating dollars for the area. Keep in mind that the cost of paint and sundries per room can vary from $15 to $50, depending on the type and amount of paint used.

BABY SHOP

High Net Profit Before Taxes:	$ 55,000
Average Net Profit Before Taxes:	$ 30,000
Minimum Start-up:	$ 85,000
Average Start-up:	$100,000

The recent baby boomlet has created a full-fledged boom in the baby market. According to the Juvenile Products Manufacturers' Association (JPMA), sales figures for the industry have reached their highest mark ever. In less than a decade, sales have more than doubled—from a meager $700 million in 1979 to $1.67 billion in 1986. And if you include clothing and toys, sales of baby products have skyrocketed to over $16 billion.

According to a recent report from the National Center for Health Statistics, the number of births in the United States jumped 3 percent last year to 3,829,000—the highest level since 1964. But a surge in the birthrate is only one factor in the baby-products boom. Parents' changing attitudes and the makeup of the modern family are also fueling the rash of sales.

Baby boomers have come of age, and their spending habits have matured along with them. Statistics show that women of childbearing age are waiting longer to have children. Figures compiled by *American Demographics* magazine show that one in four babies is born to a mother over thirty. And this trend doesn't seem to be waning. *American Demographics* concludes that an increasing percentage of women are spending more time in college and entering the work force later—evidence that the trend will continue.

Older parents have more money to spend on their growing brood. And what's more, they're having fewer children, which means that they're more likely to splurge on the children they have. The trend toward smaller families also means that more children today are firstborns and therefore need more clothing, furniture, and miscellaneous paraphernalia.

The Designer Baby

Babies are more than just offspring these days: they're status symbols in an image-conscious America. Today, parents want their kids to keep pace with the "Dress for Success" life-style—and why not? Children are in the public eye much earlier than they once were. Many attend day care from the time they're infants.

Hence the flowering of infant couture. Drab terry-cloth sleepers and ho-hum rubber pants simply won't do for hip youngsters. New fashion lines like Wee Boxers from Los Angeles-based Baby Boxers, Inc., are taking the infant market by storm. And while $14-to-$60 price tags may seem a bit high, they don't seem to faze modern parents.

The fashion trend isn't limited to clothing, however. Baby-store owners also offer some very pricey furniture, toys, and accessories. At one shop, satin baby quilts sell for $100 each.

A Shop Is Born

Shifting spending patterns and higher-priced items add up to big profits for retailers who cater to discriminating shoppers. One baby-shop owner we found grossed $150,000 in his first year of business and expects to gross more than $250,000 in his second. To parallel this kind of success, would-be retailers need three things: a good location, superior merchandise, and sufficient operating capital.

Bear in mind that new niches are open to baby retailers. Our successful operator established his business in an area where another discount baby shop was already thriving. This fact didn't daunt him, however, because he planned to target an upscale market. A small community probably won't support several similar baby shops. But if you can differentiate yourself from the current offerings, you have a good chance of surviving.

In a facility of about 2,000 square feet, space will be limited, so inventory will have to turn over frequently to reach projected sales figures. Since volume is the key to maximum profits in this industry, many baby stores end up expanding—either by additional square footage or additional locations or both.

To stock a 2,000-square-foot store, plan to invest about $50,000 annually in inventory. Choosing the right products can be tricky, especially with the proliferation of products available on today's market. Consult trade magazines and visit trade shows to keep up with the latest offerings. Ultimately, making wise choices will depend on your knowledge of the industry and a little luck.

Is the Growth Spurt Temporary?

Entrepreneurs considering this business might be concerned about how long the booming baby market will continue to grow. But today's successful retailers say there's no need to worry about the future of baby stores. Climbing sales figures—and climbing birthrates—indicate that the designer baby is here to stay. Those little bundles of joy can represent big bundles of profits for entrepreneurs who cater to the kiddie craze.

USED-BOOK STORE

High Net Profit Before Taxes:	$47,000 plus
Average Net Profit Before Taxes:	$30,000
Minimum Start-up:	$18,000
Average Start-up:	$27,000

Can't bear to throw an old book away? Open your own used-book store and turn old books into new bucks. Bibliophiles who can't pass up a good book can use their talents toward a profitable end. A personal collection accumulated over the years could be the basis for your starting inventory.

New and Used

In addition to finally clearing your bookshelves, opening a used-book store offers several business advantages. Risks are high and profits thin in selling new books. Without a fair amount of capital and some solid experience in the trade, making a new-book store work can be tricky.

But used books can be had for a fraction of their original costs. By watching the best-seller lists, you can determine the sales potential of a book before you buy it—unlike most conventional bookstores judging a new release.

If you're an avid book lover, chances are you're already familiar with a variety of titles. Before you open your own store, gain additional experience at an established used-book store. Find out what people will buy, how much they will pay, and how to create a well-rounded selection.

What Are They Reading?

Our researchers found that only one in every thirteen Americans buys books. Thus, a sizable community of 50,000 or more is needed to support a used-book store. Moreover, not every book buyer is alike. What do people read in your community? Evaluate your market in terms of population, life-style, income, education, and age levels. Also, determine what you can offer that the competition does not.

Bear in mind that college students do the most reading—for pleasure and for classes, followed by college-educated adults with higher-than-average income. Locating near a college campus will give your business an automatic leg up. An ideal community will also include a high percentage of literate, middle-income, mobile apartment dwellers (moving is a common reason for selling books to a bookstore).

Don't Just Buy: Exchange

Many used-book stores trade paperbacks on a two-for-one or three-for-one basis. There are some problems with this: paperback prices vary, so the dollar value of the trade is not consistent. Also, a two-for-one trade isn't attractive to you financially, while three-for-one doesn't attract traders. Many stores have given up this policy in favor of a new concept: exchange.

An exchange works on the basis of credits. Sellers get credit slips good for 25 percent of the list price, provided that the book is quite new and in mint condition. These credits can be used to buy other paperbacks for 50 percent of the list price. This is a good markup, but the volume must be quite large to make it financially viable, because on a $2.00 paperback, the owner will make only $0.50 per book. In a conventional used-book store a $2.00 paperback will make the owner $0.75 to $0.85.

The exchange or credit approach is very popular, and it's an excellent way to build volume—especially among the dollar-conscious college crowd. It's also cost-effective to the bookstore operator, because he or she can acquire new stock without cash.

What You Can Expect to Make

Here's what we found out from a typically successful used-book store. Our sample store was open six days a week, Tuesday through Sunday, from 10 A.M. to 9 P.M. (until 5 P.M. on Sundays). The owner closes for two weeks a year, and on some holidays like Christmas and New Year's Day.

The average gross is $175 a day, or about $50,000 a year. Rent for the store is $450 per month. Utilities, phone, and so forth add another $100 a month to this. Salary expense varies; the owner has added as many as eight part-timers—most are teens who work for minimum wage with their parents' permission. Average weekly salary expense rarely exceeds $200 per week or $10,000 per year.

The owner is just now taking out a salary. For the first year he was just taking out his expenses while trying to get the business going. Gradually his take rose to $500 a month, then $800, and it's still on the rise.

The balance of the store's income goes toward replacing and increasing the stock—he depends heavily on exchanges and plans to add a mail-order section soon. He hopes this will add 50 to 100 percent to his gross. Added income will be spent on the stock and more employees so that he can have more free time.

MATTRESS SHOP

High Net Profit Before Taxes:	$50,000
Average Net Profit Before Taxes:	$30,000
Minimum Start-up:	$20,000
Average Start-up:	$35,000

U.S. consumers spend over $2 billion each year for mattresses and foundations. Though most of us overlook the mattress industry, the market is only obvious: everybody needs a place to sleep.

Specialization and steady advertising account for their growing share of the market. A specialized business is simple to run. It requires a relatively small inventory in only one basic product. Few employees are necessary: most shops employ only two people. And this business is ideal for absentee ownership.

The primary reason that chain stores gross more is larger advertising budgets—typically $23,400 annually per unit as compared to $18,200 for the single-store owner. Predictably, individual-store owners who spent more on advertising registered higher sales.

Markup High

Some operators only mark up their merchandise 60 to 85 percent. The smart ones, we found, sell at 100 percent over cost. A mattress set with a wholesale cost of $100 will be marked $185 by most operators. But the most profitable businesses add on an extra 10 to 15 percent to absorb part of the advertising costs.

CRAFTS CO-OP GALLERY

High Net Profit Before Taxes:	$48,000
Average Net Profit Before Taxes:	$32,000
Minimum Start-up:	$27,000
Average Start-up:	$37,000

Capitalize on the current craze for crafts. After years of celebrating the prefabricated and functional, American consumers are rediscovering the charm of handmade items. Everything from Shaker furniture to southwestern pottery and handmade earrings is in demand. The news couldn't be better for America's artists and craftspeople.

Yet many artisans are looking for effective ways to hawk their wares. The age-old stereotype of the starving artist isn't entirely defunct. Individually, most don't have the resources to open their own galleries or boutiques. Most sell their goods on consignment or in person at flea markets, art shows, gift shows, and other weekend events—hardly a way to make a killing, even though the market is promising.

The Retail Alternative

Arts-and-crafts co-ops offer an attractive alternative to artisans who can't afford to open their own retail outlets. And for the co-op owner, this is an easy and profitable way to break into the burgeoning arts-and-crafts market.

The arts-and-crafts co-op benefits everyone involved. Buyers gain access to unique and difficult-to-find items conveniently and at reasonable prices. Co-op owners can bring in monthly sales of as much as $30,000 to $50,000 with no initial inventory costs and minimal overhead. And the accessibility and traffic of a mall location lure artisans as well. Successful crafts co-ops have long waiting lists of craftspeople eager to pay for the excellent exposure. Often the cost to them is less than that of a good booth space at a desirable weekend flea market. Best of all, they don't need to spend their time selling and can devote their energies to what they like best—creating.

How does a co-op work? Most successful co-ops are in high-traffic malls. They charge craftspeople a flat fee for displaying the goods, plus a commission on each item sold (30 percent is typical). Working with a variety of craftspeople, a co-op owner can offer his or her clientele a wide selection of wares for virtually no money up front.

Setting Up Shop

First you must lease a location, either in a mall, cluster shopping complex, group of browsing shops, or other high-traffic area. An area of 3,000 to 4,000 square feet should be ample.

Then start shopping for craftspeople. Remember that your business depends on the quality and marketability of the crafts: select artists and merchandise carefully. Rental fees to craftspeople range from $25 to $75 a month, depending on the store location, amount of space, and owner's overhead. The rent you collect from craftspeople should just about cover your monthly rent payment.

If you decide to provide display space and lighting, be sure to add that cost to the cost of rent. Alternatively, you may want to make artisans responsible for providing their own displays and lighting. If so, make sure they follow your guidelines to keep displays consistent throughout the store. Usually, lessees stock their own displays, set their own prices, and provide their own insurance coverage.

6

SPORTS AND ENTERTAINMENT

BALLOON SOJOURNS

You don't have to keep your feet on the ground to succeed in business. Just ask entrepreneurs around the country who are cashing in on America's newfound love of hot-air ballooning.

No, average citizens are not running out and buying giant balloons for their backyards. Rather, they're flocking to scenic country spots to take whirlwind champagne tours for $100 or more. And touring isn't all. According to David Wilsey, founder of Balloon Adventures Inc. in Quakertown, Pennsylvania, the ballooning field is more diverse than meets the eye.

"The most obvious commercial market, of course, is in passenger flights," Wilsey says. "However, ballooning has enormous market potential as a functional advertising medium. Local retailers could hardly do better than a balloon with their logo on it for high-impact, identifiable advertising."

Tethered rides, which are increasingly popular at fairs and festivals, also generate considerable income. For a tethered flight, the balloon's basket (in which the passengers ride) is anchored to the ground, and its ascent is restricted to about 80 or 100 feet. Balloonists usually receive about $800 from patrons for a two-to-three-hour tethered ride.

To start your own balloon tour company, you'll need a pilot's license. Wilsey's is just one of the companies around the country that offers training. "Candidates train under a commercial pilot," he says. "For about $2,500, we offer all the training needed to qualify for a private pilot's license. That includes both ground school and flight school." By logging an additional thirty-five hours of flying time, you may qualify for a Federal Aviation Administration commercial license.

The balloon itself isn't as expensive as you might think. A complete rig (balloon and basket) starts at about $12,000. Of course, deluxe models cost considerably more. The average price for a four-passenger balloon is approximately $18,000.

The trendiness of hot-air ballooning makes this an attractive business to get into from a marketing standpoint. But don't overlook the fringe benefits. "The main element is a love of flying," says Gene Grace, president of Spectrum Balloons in St. Louis, Missouri. "Ballooning is a captivating experience. You see the world below from an entirely different perspective. On a single flight, the altitude can range from above 2,000 feet right down to stream level. There's nothing like skimming a lake or river, and racing your own reflection."

ATHLETIC-SHOE STORE

High Net Profit Before Taxes:	$85,000
Average Net Profit Before Taxes:	$35,000
Minimum Start-up:	$40,000
Average Start-up:	$78,000

Don't wear your tennis shoes unless you're on the way to the court. These days, you need a different shoe for every activity. Walking shoes just won't do for running, and God forbid you should wear basketball shoes to aerobics class (they're too hot). With demand for athletic shoes multiplying with each new endeavor, it's no wonder that athletic shoe stores are making a mint.

Foot Fetish

Once upon a time, people bought sneakers at the supermarket and called them adequate. Today, buyers sift through dozens of upscale styles, brands, colors, and sizes. Just witness the burgeoning of athletic-shoe manufacturers. Nike and Adidas used to be the only games in town. Now, there's competition from Reebok, LA Gear, Avia, Saucony, Puma, and more.

Sporting goods are a multibillion-dollar industry in America. And increasingly, those goods are sold in specialty stores. There are jogging shops and walking shops—and athletic-shoe shops, where customers can browse through the hundreds of options available to them under a single roof.

In addition to shoes, most athletic-shoe stores offer a limited selection of accessories—socks, gym bags, T-shirts, and sweats. The emphasis remains on shoes, however. One Southern California chain specializes in just tennis shoes—rows of tennis shoes and socks, but no equipment. And the store is a hit.

We investigated a new store that's part of a nationwide chain. In its first six months in business, its average gross was $24,845 per month with a net profit of about $4,200 monthly. Naturally, as the gross sales increase, the profits rise. A $400,000 annual gross with a 20-percent net is considered par for a healthy, well-run store in this field.

Shopping-Center Location

A specialty business can survive successfully in any easily accessible location. You don't have to set up in an enclosed mall. One store we investigated was situated in a shopping center near a sporting-goods dealer who carries a complete line of footwear and clothing as well as the usual sports gear—yet business didn't seem to suffer.

This store is in an area populated by lower-middle-class wage earners. Within six miles there is a higher-income area that contributes to the store's volume.

Cheap shoes are still available for about $20, but the sophisticated weekend athlete is looking for professional quality and is willing to pay for it. A $75 price tag is not out of line for running shoes. And if they're used regularly, they'll need replacing in about six months.

Serious athletes aren't the only customers, however. Fancy $50 sneakers are a stylish choice for just about anyone—grandmothers included—who wants basic footwear for running around. While ten years ago, men made up the majority of the athletic-shoe market, women are becoming a more important segment. And brand-name leather hi-tops are a must for the toddlers of every self-respecting yuppie.

=== BRIGHT IDEA ===

PROFESSIONAL PRANKS

New York entrepreneur Tracey Moore has always been a practical joker. When she was growing up in San Francisco, friends referred to her as the class clown. Even now, her husband calls her Lucy Ricardo because of her mischievous nature. But what sets Moore apart from any ordinary prankster is that she makes a living playing practical jokes.

Moore is founder and owner of the Joke's On You! Inc., a company that performs elaborate practical jokes on "victims" based on requests from friends, family, or coworkers. Professional actors and actresses are used to pull the stunts off. At $175 for a typical job, Moore's services don't come cheap, but her jokes are guaranteed to raise some eyebrows.

Moore started the Joke's On You! on April Fools' Day, 1985, with nothing but $2,000 and a sharp imagination. She now has a repertoire of practical jokes that are used as models when developing scripts for clients.

The Joke's On You! has been received with plenty of enthusiasm. After ads in *New York* magazine and a stint on "The Joe Franklin Show," a local New York television talk show, where two of Tracey's actors posed as skin-care specialists in order to toss two pies in the host's face, the word of mouth began to spread.

Now in her fourth year of business, Moore is thinking of expanding the Joke's On You! through franchising. Though nothing is set in concrete, Moore remains hopeful about the future of her venture, noting that financial success isn't everything. "I'm in the business of having fun," she says. "I enjoy making people happy and having a good time."

PHYSICAL-FITNESS CENTER

High Net Profit Before Taxes:	$130,000
Average Net Profit Before Taxes:	$ 85,000
Minimum Start-up:	$ 76,000
Average Start-up:	$117,000

Back in the Stone Age, hunting and gathering kept people in shape. But in the 1990's, they need help maintaining their aerobic fitness, building their muscles, developing their strength, reducing stress, and warding off the fat cells. Ten years ago, avowed exercise haters predicted that fitness was just a fad. Now their worst fears have been realized: fitness fanaticism is here to stay.

Americans spend billions of dollars a year joining exercise clubs. From Nautilus to swimming, aerobics to power walking, fitness is a big business. And as long as there's overeating in America (let's face it, it's a national pastime) there will be a need for health clubs.

A small club in Georgia run by a husband-and-wife team is grossing $1,500 per week. An executive health club in Louisiana brings in $500,000 per year and is getting bigger all the time. Every successful health club we investigated— whether a simple gym or an elegant spa—shared one thing in common: healthy pretax nets. Some even hit the 40-to-50-percent range.

Health-Club Junkies

A study done by an audience-testing house confirmed that 90 percent of the public isn't happy with the way it looks. Some 40 million Americans are estimated to be overweight and out of shape, and they spend over $60 billion annually on diet and weight-reduction drugs, books, equipment, and classes. More important, they also join physical-fitness clubs in hopes of losing those extra pounds—and keeping them off.

Almost every community in America is a prime market for your health club, even if other clubs are operating. Our research indicates that health-club junkies are a notoriously fickle bunch. They will investigate any new operation in town that offers more for their money.

We asked the president of one of America's most successful health-club chains to describe his company's potential market. "How many Americans are there?" he asked. "Anyone who's living and breathing between the ages of fourteen and eighty is a potential customer."

The Coed Appeal

Though the fitness craze provides more than enough momentum for your exercise club, health clubs have an additional appeal: they're great places to meet people. All-male and all-female clubs do well in many communities, but the majority of today's health clubs are coed. That way, you can market your club as a social center as well as a place to stay fit.

No matter who your market is, you don't have to start out with fancy facilities. Many operators start small, offering little more than workout facilities and showers. As profits increase, add other profit-making amenities like saunas, steam rooms, Jacuzzis, health-food bars, massages, and retail outlets. Until you get a good membership, however, keep your operations simple and thus more immediately profitable.

Location: A Weighty Decision

When choosing a site for your health club, consider population density. Experts in the industry look for a population base of 50,000 to 75,000, both residential and transitory (office workers students, etc.).

We found health clubs in a variety of locations, but most of the profitable ones were in strip shopping centers. Don't be afraid to pay for a good location: exposure and convenience are important.

Advance Sales

Advance sales is the name of the game. Start selling memberships the minute you sign the lease. Your biggest job, along with the details of starting up, buying equipment, and getting off the ground, is to sell the benefits of your club aggressively—before you open your doors.

Advance-membership fees can pay for most of your equipment. One club in San Francisco sold 500 advance memberships at $300 each and paid for its equipment in full before opening.

Sales Tips

Hard, realistic selling is the key to your success. Skilled professionals use every sales technique from advertising, fliers, direct mail, and phone calls to hot-air balloons to guarantee large memberships up front.

All your sales pitches must feature the implied benefits of your club: good looks, a great time, and improved health. In other words, sell the sizzle with the steak.

Tomorrow's Looking Good

The market for profitable health clubs is just being tapped: a healthy market share is still open. There doesn't seem to be any letup in America's preoccupation with looking and feeling good.

========================= BRIGHT IDEA =========================

SELLING TEAM SPIRIT

How do amateur players build team identity? The same way the pros do: with uniforms. And the market for amateur-sports uniforms is probably more lucrative than you think.

Jay Deal, owner and operator of the Sport Deal Co. in Grafton, Virginia, supplies uniforms to sports teams ranging from high-school football squads to peewee baseball players, as well as company softball teams, and any other organizations that need sportswear.

Unlike a full-time retail sporting-goods store, Deal's venture required little start-up capital (about $1,500) and offered enough flexibility for him to keep his regular job. Moreover, Deal works from home, thus saving himself the expense of renting a separate location. He doesn't see working from home as a handicap, either. In fact, he believes it's added a personal touch to his business: he makes all his presentations at the customer's place of business and delivers the goods there as well.

"I think organizations like dealing with me because I'm out in the field showing samples and delivering orders, unlike some of the stores in the area where you have to go to them," says Deal. "I try to make [purchasing my products] really convenient for clients." And since his overhead is low, Deal can offer discounts as well. "I do a lot of research on markup and generally undercut my competition by 10 percent," he says.

However, if Deal's operation is small now, it doesn't mean he isn't thinking big. He believes the team-uniform market warrants its own shop, and he thinks he's just the person to staff it. "I hope to open a store in the future that will specifically deal with team sales," he says.

BAR OR TAVERN

High Net Profit Before Taxes:	$126,000
Average Net Profit Before Taxes:	$ 60,000
Minimum Start-up:	$ 47,000
Average Start-up:	$ 75,000

Through war, drought, and depression—interrupted only once by Prohibition—America's taverns, bars, and pubs have survived. For centuries, the neighborhood bar has provided the twin assets of good drink and fellowship to customers. Better still, bars also provide high profits to their owners.

Managing a bar requires a host of skills. You must be free with your hospitality, but strict with your portions. You have to know when to offer one more for the road and when to refuse service to an intoxicated guest. Starting a successful bar takes plenty of hard work. Once the business takes off, though, the profits are more than worthwhile.

The bar business is not without risks—and idiosyncrasies. One bar in a town of 26,000 averages $900 a night in gross receipts. Another bar in a town of 75,000 banks weekly receipts of only $9,000. Why?

With the potential for high profits come risks. Bars are highly regulated by the government. Federal, state, county, and sometimes city officials will be monitoring your business regularly. Also, bar customers are fickle. They're quick to investigate any new spots, taking their patronage (and your profits) out the door with them.

Four Ways to Go

Your first step is to decide what kind of bar you want to set up. There are four broad categories: neighborhood tavern, pub, nightclub, and dance club. Each has different start-up costs, setup and locations requirements, and marketing plans. Avoid locating a tavern where a dance club would be a better bet.

Size up your local market. To open a profitable drinking establishment, you have to know the habits and spending tastes of your community inside and out. Find out the average age, family size, and the types of occupations and incomes most people in your community have.

After you've done your nuts-and-bolts research, narrow in on a site. Be advised: a nightclub or dance club requires more than a different address from a bar or tavern—it must also have particular physical attributes.

Plan the Layout of Your Bar

Just as you have to know where your market is, you're going to have to decide on the right decor. The environment sets the mood, and you want to get people in the mood to sit in your place and have a few friendly drinks together.

Don't be afraid to get top-notch equipment. In any bar today, space-age bartending is the smart way to go. State-of-the-art computerized bartending equipment can make any neighborhood pub owner an efficiency expert.

You're going to be coping with problems like bouncing out drunks, repairing the ice machine, and tracking down a customer's favorite label. Plan ahead for special drinks of the month to help your customers try out new tastes. That's also an intelligent approach to racking up a higher markup.

Inside Secrets of Alcohol Sales

Markup in the alcohol business runs in the hundreds of percents. And that doesn't account for extras like cover charges. The more exclusive you make your bar, the more people will want to get in. There's even a profit in such things as plain old coffee and nonalcoholic cocktails for nondrinking friends of drinkers, as well as the happy-hour crowd. If you offer entertainment, you can charge anywhere from $3.00 to $10.00 for a cover charge.

Tomorrow's Bar Scene

Statistics indicate that adults will continue to meet in establishments to drink and socialize for years to come. This is a business that's not only timeless, but recession-proof. Some bar owners report increased business during recessions. The trick to long-term success is keeping up with the trends. As tastes become more sophisticated, bars will have to stay in step with the times.

SPORTS MEMORABILIA STORE

High Net Profit Before Taxes:	$204,000
Average Net Profit Before Taxes:	$133,000
Minimum Start-up:	$ 50,000
Average Start-up:	$ 95,000

Entering a sports memorabilia store conjures instant childhood memories of shooting for "leaners" and "flipping" baseball cards on the school playground . . . lugging your collection of cards around the neighborhood in a shoe box . . . finally attending your first professional sports game. Stepping through the door, a grown adult is transformed into a bug-eyed child.

Today, more and more customers are stepping through those doors. Sports memorabilia is now a broad-based, multimillion-dollar industry, which includes retail businesses ranging from huge professional sports apparel and merchandise stores to little corner hobby shops that sell baseball cards as a sideline.

Nuts about Sports

From the late fifties to the midsixties, elementary- and junior-high-school kids bought nickel wax packs of baseball cards just for fun and the love of the game. Born in the "Leave It to Beaver" era, this childhood hobby has grown up. Thanks to adult collectors with plenty of money to spend, baseball card (or "sportscard") mania has soared higher than a Reggie Jackson pop-out—industry sales topped $1 billion last year.

Sales of sports apparel are booming as well. Whether your customers are Little Leaguers, diehard Orioles fans, or Cubs backers, nothing gives them more pride than pulling on a snug-fitting official major-league baseball cap. And what kid, young or old, can resist slipping on a satin warm-up jacket with the emblem of the Dodgers, Yankees, Mets, or Reds? As the owner of a sports memorabilia store, you can make money helping fans live out their favorite sports dreams.

Two Major Themes

Sports memorabilia shops can be divided into two major categories: those that specialize in collectible cards and other memorabilia, and those that sell licensed sports apparel and accessories.

If these inventories sound narrow to you, be assured that they aren't. Although shops do specialize in a rather focused field, the diversity of products available is staggering. For instance, there's a mind-boggling array of licensed sports merchandise on the market. Caps, jerseys, jackets, sweatshirts, sunglasses, socks, shirts, pens, key chains, mugs, beer steins, belt buckles, money clips, magnets, trash cans, wall hangings, and posters—just to name a few items—can all be imprinted with the names of college, National Basketball Association, National Football League, National Hockey League, or major-league baseball teams. There are even lamps and telephones made out of football or baseball helmets.

And just for the record, memorabilia is enough to keep most shop owners busy. Actual sporting goods—mitts, balls, and bats that aren't collector's items, for instance—are rarely sold in a sports memorabilia shop.

Just a Game?

The financial impact of the sports souvenir industry is huge. The NFL, for example, makes so much money on the sale of officially licensed merchandise that they won't even divulge the amount. The NBA estimates 1988 gross retail sales of licensed merchandise at $250 million. NHL sources suggest their sales are about $80 million. And the front office of major league baseball says that 1987 sales were approximately $500 million.

Officially licensed merchandise is expensive. A red satin baseball jacket may cost the retailer $15 and sell for $30. The same jacket with a major-league-baseball-team emblem might wholesale for $30 and retail for $60. In general, retailers charge twice the wholesale price for sports merchandise.

With such a healthy markup for sports apparel and accessories alike, profits for sports souvenir stores are impressive. According to one leading franchisor in the field, gross sales for the company's franchises range from $200,000 in smaller markets to over $600,000 at mall locations.

In the Cards

Baseball cards are a booming subcategory in sports memorabilia retailing. But aren't baseball cards simply child's play? Not according to industry figures, which peg sales of baseball cards and related products at $1.5 billion. Aside from baseball cards, a minor-league market exists for football, basketball, and hockey cards—hence the term "sportscards."

Serious collectors will drive a long way for the right card. And what's more, they'll gladly pay the going price. In the case of certain cards, value can actually appreciate over time. "Baseball cards are one commodity where if you do not sell, the inventory actually appreciates in value," says the owner of one successful sportscard shop. "Amazingly, if an item does not sell today, it will probably be worth more tomorrow."

Naturally, learning the ins and outs of collectible sportscards is a major task. People who already have an interest in collecting cards have a considerable leg up in this complex business—a fairly startling revelation in itself. Apparently, Mom was wrong when she told you playing with baseball cards would get you nowhere in life.

===== BRIGHT IDEA =====

CHILDREN'S FITNESS

"Unfortunately, kids are in lousy shape," says Dr. Jean Rosenbaum, director of the American Aerobics Association in Durango, Colorado. "Children's fitness programs are the next wave of the physical-fitness boom."

It's surprising but true: America's kids are in poor condition. The 1986 President's Council on Physical Fitness reported that 30 percent of children under sixteen had hypercholestremia (extraordinarily high cholesterol). Forty percent of boys ages six to twelve cannot do more than one pull-up, and one out of four cannot do any. Fifty percent of all girls cannot hold their chins over a raised bar for more than ten seconds. About 50 percent of surveyed girls and 30 percent of boys cannot run one mile in fewer than ten minutes.

Kids who spend hours in front of televisions or video-game screens don't develop much muscle strength, endurance, flexibility, or cardiovascular fitness. Parents are realizing—perhaps through their own experiences—that bad childhood habits often carry over into adulthood.

Fortunately for today's kids, new options present themselves every day. For instance, SuperClub in Virginia Beach, Virginia, offers children the chance to participate in dance, gymnastics, tae-kwon-do self-defense classes, creative movement, sports skills, aerobics, strength conditioning, and individual training. For about $39 per month, children have access to a wide range of instruction, as well as a computerized learning center and afterschool bus transportation.

The real emphasis is on fun. "Let's face it," says Ken Johnson, who owns SuperClub with his wife, Jan, "Eighty percent of kids do not participate in organized school sports activities. We emphasize that we are a fun place with all kinds of activities. You don't market a facility by saying, 'Mom, your kid is out of shape!' You can't just have fitness machines—that wouldn't keep their interest."

Children's fitness presents unique challenges. Kids like to try new activities, but can't master new skills as quickly as adults. Creating programs that are fast-paced and accessible can tax one's creativity. On the other hand, there are numerous ways to market good programs—through clubs like SuperClub, through individual classes, and even through public schools, which are often looking for affordable ways to enhance their existing programs.

=== BRIGHT IDEA ===

THE PUCK STOPS HERE

Would you like to see a piece of black rubber coming at you at 100 miles per hour? Neither would most hockey players. Considering the hazards involved, it's no wonder that Canada's recreational and minor-league teams frequently have trouble finding a goalie willing to play in Sunday-afternoon scrimmages or weeknight games. Never fear, Puckstoppers Goaltending Services have come to the rescue.

Mike Wademan, who as president of the company still works full-time as a forklift operator for Chrysler, charges teams $18 an hour for a scrimmage and $20 for an actual game to rent the athletic services of an experienced goalie. With 25 goalies ready to go, Wademan does his best to match the skill level of the player to the caliber, league, and standings of the team in need.

Puckstoppers, in Brampton, Ontario, has grown in two years to include a half-dozen franchises in other Canadian cities. Wademan offers his goalies guaranteed wages even if they don't play, and gives them discount prices on equipment. The company also has an eight-week instructional program for junior goalies during the summer.

Of course, a goaltending service can't break the ice in every town. But in some hockey-crazed cities, it's a fun and novel way to make money. For Wademan, at least, the reception has been anything but icy.

PINBALL AND VIDEO-GAME ARCADE

High Net Profit Before Taxes:	$128,000
Average Net Profit Before Taxes:	$ 59,000
Minimum Start-up:	$ 8,000
Average Start-up:	$ 82,000

Video games and pinball are more than just child's play—they're the basis of a lucrative business that's ideally suited to absentee ownership. Though some might argue that they're making a flock of vidiots out of our nation's youths, video games are undeniably addictive. And if run properly, pinball and electronic-game arcades can provide youngsters with a healthy social gathering place.

Neighborhood Arcades

Today's amusement centers are shedding their seedy images and cleaning up their acts. Many are located in shopping malls, where developers welcome them with open arms. A well-run video arcade can keep teenagers busy and controlled—and pull in additional profits for mall management.

The new atmosphere demands new standards of security and operation. Smoking, food, and beverages are usually prohibited. Personnel are well trained, and strict operating procedures are maintained.

An operator in one large shopping center grosses $10,054 a month. He has one full-time serviceperson for sixty-five machines, and two change-making managers covering a twelve-hour day, six days a week. His net before taxes averages $78,900 per year—not bad for an absentee owner with simple operations.

We've seen another equally successful shopping-mall operation. The operator could lease only 1,200 square feet for his arcade, which limits the number of machines and people he can handle. But his volume averages $8,000 a month, and the arcade is packed most of the time.

Neither of these operators was allowed a food concession in his lease because of nearby stores that serve food. But if possible, consider carrying soft drinks, ice cream, candy, gum, and in some cases popcorn—all of which add a nice profit to an already healthy profit margin. Arcades require little or no promotion to get rolling. Every one that we've looked at was jammed with local kids from the moment it opened.

Midwest and Eastern Cities Most Promising

Arcades do best in cities with seasonal climates, as in the east or the Midwest. In states with a warm climate year-round, kids have a larger selection of activities to divert their attentions. One arcade we discovered in the east consistently grosses over $15,000 a month.

These video emporiums or family amusement centers immediately become hangouts for the ten-to-eighteen-year-olds in the area. Don't be put off by the word "hangout"—these kids have money to spend and only a few places to spend it.

===================== BRIGHT IDEA =====================

SAILING SCHOOL

Shocking as the concept might be to full-time students, some people actually go to school on their vacations—Offshore Sailing School, that is. And why not? The emphasis at this Fort Meyers, Florida, school is on recreation and fun, not heavy learning.

Stephen Colgate, an avid sailor, decided to open the school in 1964, when he realized how difficult it was for the average person to learn sailing. "The only way you could get into sailing was through yacht clubs, which was how I did it," Colgate explains, "but I could see that there was a big market out there of people who didn't belong to yacht clubs."

In addition to the original school on City Island in New York and the one in Fort Meyers, Colgate and his wife, Doris, who is company co-owner, now have schools in such hot spots as Captiva Island in Florida, and Tortola in the British Virgin Islands.

The Colgates have found that aligning their sailing school with a luxury vacation at a top-flight resort gives them more visibility and lowers their overhead. "The resorts let us use the facilities we need, such as dock space, and they also do a lot of their own advertising," says Stephen.

The Colgates now put some 3,000 students through their schools each year. In the past twenty-five years, Offshore Sailing School's fleet has gone from two boats to more than forty, and the sales receipts have kept pace: 1988 gross receipts hit $2.5 million.

Even if sailing isn't your forte, you can consider a similar enterprise. Combining the basics of horseback riding, tennis, baseball, or wilderness exploring with some basic R&R can result in a profitable, fun venture for customers and owners alike.

BALLOON VENDING

High Net Profit Before Taxes:	$50,000 plus
Average Net Profit Before Taxes:	$19,000
Minimum Start-up:	$11,000
Average Start-up:	$18,000

This business is deceptively simple. You might think that filling a bunch of plain old balloons with helium, tying the ends with string, and selling them at the nearest tourist area would be too easy to bring in any money. But that simply isn't so.

Consider the case of a businessman who owns a balloon concession at a major amusement park. He sells, on average, 1,000 balloons a day. During the summer months, his sales have exceeded 3,000 balloons in a day. If he sells 360,000 balloons a year at $1.00 each, his gross is a cheerful $360,000.

Now add up the costs. The colorful eleven-inch balloons he sold cost $0.04 each in volume. He pays $30 for a cylinder of helium that inflates over 400 balloons, averaging out to

$0.07 per balloon for gas. Insurance, labor, and related costs add up to about $30,000 a year, which includes a manager's salary of $10,000.

The man behind the operation lives 400 miles away from the actual location. He visited the business once a month. Before taxes, he netted around $100,000 each year. Of course, his location was outstanding—one that would be difficult to duplicate anywhere else—so his volume was extraordinary. The principle, however, can be copied with a little skill and planning.

7,200 Balloons per Month

Another young fellow we met had been introduced to the balloon business by an uncle who had worked carnivals in his youth. This man landed a balloon concession in a new year-round indoor tourist attraction. His helium supplier told us that he's buying eighteen tanks per month, except during the summer when he orders twenty-eight tanks a month. That works out to 7,200 balloons—or a gross of $3,600—for most months, and a $5,600 gross during peak seasons.

Rent takes 15 percent of his gross. His average monthly wages come to $1,600—which includes a $600 salary to a young man who runs the operation. The owner spends most of his time looking for additional locations and going to the bank every day.

Part-Time Profit at Flea Markets

We also found a retired gentleman who hawks balloons at swap meets every weekend. Swap meets are flea markets held in drive-in theater lots, and they draw amazing crowds—5,000 to 20,000 people every day. This old fellow empties almost two tanks of helium every weekend for a gross of over $400.

===============BRIGHT IDEA===============

BICYCLE TOURS

Ten years ago, the thought of going on a bike tour for a vacation would have horrified most of middle America. But today, nearly 100,000 cyclists spend up to $2,500 to peddle away their vacation days.

Pioneering the concept of bicycle tours, Vermont Bicycle Touring in Bristol, Vermont, first put vacationers on two wheels eighteen years ago. And since that time, approximately 70,000 people have ridden in the company's guided biking vacations, according to owner Bill Perry. This year, Perry expects about 6,000 vacationers to experience the pleasures of touring on two wheels.

Bike touring shifted into high gear with more than 200 bike-tour companies now offering thousands of different vacations. And each year, more and more Americans don helmet, shorts, and jersey for anywhere from two to twenty-one days to get away from it all. Don't be mistaken, though. "[Customers] are not all diehard cyclists," says Perry. "They're reasonably active people looking for a different kind of vacation."

And they're willing to pay for it. At Vermont Bicycle Touring, the prices range from $199 for a weekend tour to $2,299 for a nineteen-day tour through New Zealand. For consumers, this means an adventurous vacation. For tour companies, it translates into high-speed revenues. Perry says that Vermont Bicycle Touring is "shooting for $5 million in gross revenues this year."

NO-ALCOHOL BAR

High Net Profit Before Taxes:	$100,000 plus
Average Net Profit Before Taxes:	$ 40,000
Minimum Start-up:	$ 68,000
Average Start-up:	$100,000

For many Americans, drinking doesn't hold the same cachet it once did. According to a recent Gallup survey, 37 percent of all adult Americans over twenty-one do not drink alcoholic beverages. Some abstain from alcohol for health reasons, or because of former drinking problems. Some have religious objections to drinking. But many others simply don't like to drink: they don't like the effects or the taste.

Yet bars and clubs are a major source of socializing. And just because some people dislike social drinking doesn't mean they dislike social interaction. Nondrinkers represent a viable market, and you can reach that market with a bar that caters specifically to their preferences. We spotted one such bar that draws customers from as far as 100 miles away—in fickle Southern California.

Tipsy on Profits

From a business standpoint, a no-alcohol bar has special advantages. A nondrinkers' bar can produce greater profit margins than a traditional bar, and there's no need for an expensive liquor license. Also, as drunk-driving laws get tougher across the country, bar owners face a raft of potential legal problems. Moreover, if you serve alcohol, you must weed out minors trying to buy booze illegally. You can avoid these worries by serving only nonintoxicating drinks.

Better still, nonalcoholic cocktails can be sold for virtually the same price as their alcoholic counterparts, but with lower ingredient costs. And you won't need to stock a $3,000 inventory of liquor.

A nondrinkers' bar can legally remain open twenty-four hours a day. To optimize profits and maintain a manageable overhead, opening at 11 A.M. and closing at 2 A.M. may be a smarter idea. This schedule allows you to pick up the afternoon crowd for light lunches, drinks, and the use of game machines, pool table, or jukebox before the evening's bar and entertainment business gets under way.

Profits will fluctuate daily, with weekends and certain weeknights hotter than others. If the bar is open seven days a week, with good entertainment and lots of activities for customers to get involved in, weekly profits can be consistently high.

In the evening, charging a $2.00 minimum per person at the tables (but not at the bar) isn't so stiff as to turn customers away, yet protects against people who nurse one drink all night long. A straight cover charge or entry fee may not work as well, unless it is common in your area and you have good entertainment. Another option is instituting a two-drink minimum.

Taking over an existing bar with equipment is the best way to start a no-alcohol bar. The second best option is to renovate a small coffee shop or restaurant. This will probably be more costly than redoing an existing bar, considering the costs of bar equipment, fixtures, and furniture, as well as improvements to plumbing, electricity, and carpentry.

A rule of thumb among bar-equipment distributors and designers is to allow a $300-to-$500 per-seat investment for new bar equipment. This is a heavy investment, but most distributors will provide financing with as little as 20 percent down.

Know Your Market

The market for a nondrinkers' bar has much in common with that of a conventional bar, but there are additional needs. Like a regular saloon, your nonalcohol version should be near the entertainment and shopping areas of the community, where there is a naturally heavy flow of people after work and on weekends.

Because the no-alcohol bar represents an alternative form of entertainment, you must locate in a community with a population large enough to include a substantial nondrinking element. While a regular bar can be profitable in a tiny community, the no-alcohol kind should be considered only in a metropolitan area with a population of at least 500,000.

Hipsters to Evangelists

A nondrinkers' bar can do well in diverse locales—from trendy metropolitan areas where hip residents seek the latest innovation in evening entertainment to dry counties where liquor is illegal. Even in the Bible Belt of the south and Midwest, where Christian temperance still has clout, there are strict liquor laws to match. In these areas, you may be able to get away with a smaller population base.

Your main clientele will be middle-class people who have the discretionary income to frequent your bar, and are probably also into the current health trends. Less affluent people may prefer drinking in a regular bar, while the truly wealthy will probably opt for more upscale entertainment—like the latest hot spot in town.

Your Vital Regulars Will Be Ex-Drinkers

The people who will make you a success in this business are recovering alcoholics and their families. Along with the friends they bring with them, these people will be your regulars, because only you can offer them the environment they miss—and a place to go without worrying about falling off the wagon.

It is essential to do everything you can to cultivate this market. With all your efforts to attract a wide spectrum of clients, never lose sight of the fact that these regulars are your bread and butter.

Visit local Alcoholics Anonymous clubs to spread the word about your new bar before you open for business. Hire members as your bartenders, waiters, and waitresses. This will not only help solidify your relationship with the vital AA community, but will also provide you with reliable employees.

Word should spread quickly within the tight-knit AA group, and ex-drinkers will come from miles around to your bar, especially on weekends (weekends are a particularly depressing time for recovering alcoholics because they have time to kill and few places to go that are congenial and "safe").

Make sure that members of local AA clubs are free to hold meetings at your place—or to come over after meetings for a bite to eat and some conversation with friends.

===============BRIGHT IDEA===============

TEEN CLUB

Here's a variation on the no-alcohol bar: a nightclub just for teens. Faced with a society that urges them to "just say no," teens need some form of entertainment and socializing to which they can say yes. A club that offers teenagers a safe, drug-and-alcohol-free environment where they can dance, talk, and hang out benefits everyone—teens, parents, and entrepreneurs.

Club ReFlex, located in El Toro, California, opened in March 1989 to cater to the enthusiastic under-twenty-one market. The owner, Chris Corrales, knows the need for teen clubs firsthand—he's only eighteen himself.

"The club is run by teenagers," explains Corrales. "We have a security crew of eight that checks identification to make sure that no one over twenty-one is admitted."

Corrales says he opened the club so teens would have a place to go to dance that was safe, clean, and fun. However, starting the club wasn't easy—it took him two years to find the perfect location and to gain the support of investors.

COMPACT-DISC STORE

High Net Profit Before Taxes:	$105,000
Average Net Profit Before Taxes:	$ 60,000
Minimum Start-up:	$ 57,000
Average Start-up:	$ 75,000

Since they were first introduced in 1983, compact discs have taken the music industry by storm. They're so popular, in fact, that familiar vinyl records are going the way of the 78— replaced by the high-fidelity, virtually indestructible CD.

That's why smart entrepreneurs across the country are opening stores that sell nothing but compact discs. According to people in the business, CD-only stores can provide better selection and a more personal environment than big music chains. Many people are put off by large, loud, commercial stores. They're confused by the layout of the store— where are the CDs? Where is the sale rack? Where are the salespeople?

A limited product line is easier to handle and highly profitable, especially as a small business. One store in Los Angeles grossed $1 million in its first eighteen months of operation. It is now a franchise. Several other independent stores around the country are grossing upward of $200,000 annually. And you can plan on making anywhere from $20,000 to $100,000 in pretax profits if you plan carefully.

Taking Inventory

What kind of person can make a success of a CD-only store? Usually it's someone with a love for and knowledge of music. Since your inventory won't be as extensive as a regular record store's, you can afford to invest in many titles that your customers can't find elsewhere. One store owner in Chicago stocks his store with hard-to-find jazz, classical, and even heavy-metal titles. He pays close attention to what his customers want, even if the music doesn't appeal to him personally.

Stocking the right inventory is critical, and it's not easy to choose. You should know about the primary music categories, such as pop, classical, and country, and the kinds of people to whom they appeal. Many specialty stores are supported by a small circle of steady clients who come in time after time to find the compact discs they want. This is because the smaller guys have reputations for knowing more about CDs and being more service-oriented than the giant music stores, and this keeps customers coming back.

America's switch to CDs means more than increased sales of new titles. People are also buying their favorite classics on CD. Sometimes, people are interested in the enhanced quality of CD recordings—they sound better and they don't scratch or break like records and cassettes. In other cases, CD versions have additional songs that aren't on the original albums and tapes. As a CD-only store owner, you can sell customers on new releases and recordings they already have—an opportunity you won't find in many other products.

Put Your Ear to the Ground

Entrepreneurs with an ear for hot opportunities are opening compact-disc-only stores around the country. But there's still room for growth in this exciting new industry. CD-only stores have already established a reputation for bringing the personal touch back to music retailing. They're helping millions of music lovers build their CD libraries by offering unusual selections, reasonable prices, and careful attention to customer preferences.

Pool Halls with Panache

Pool has come out of the dark recesses of the nation's dingiest bars to emerge as "pocket billiards"—the same game, but played in elegant, upscale surroundings. Enjoying a veritable renaissance, pool is becoming the entertainment of choice for America's young professionals.

If Steven Foster and Kevin Troy have their way, the pool hall will no longer conjure up images of smoke-filled rooms, tattoos, and beer bellies. Their sophisticated version of the pool hall caters to a more refined clientele—one that gladly pays $8.00 an hour to play billiards, or $30 an hour to delight in the decor of a VIP billiard room reminiscent of an English gentleman's library.

The increasing number of women who are taking part in the sport are a major factor in its newfound popularity. And it was a woman who inspired this pair's interest in opening a billiard club. Foster's wife, Jillian, enjoyed the game but disliked the seedy atmosphere. That set the ball rolling, and in July 1988, the pair opened Jillian's Billiard Club in Boston.

Since the pair opened their 25,000-square-foot billiard club, complete with hardwood floors, brass railings, arched windows, and a café, numerous other upscale pool palaces have popped up. And many entrepreneurs look to Jillian's as a model.

"We have about 3,000 people in here each week," boasts Troy. The partners plan to open establishments in Miami, Cleveland, and New York.

BICYCLE SHOP

High Net Profit Before Taxes:	$150,000
Average Net Profit Before Taxes:	$ 20,000
Minimum Start-up:	$ 25,000
Average Start-up:	$ 35,000

Eighty-eight million Americans can't be wrong—biking is back in style. Since 1983, when 72 million Americans considered themselves bikers, another 16 million have discovered the joys of two-wheeling, according to the Bicycle Federation of America in Washington, D.C. And more and more of these cyclists are taking their recreation seriously.

No longer do folks go to the bike shop for a plain old bike. Of the 10.9 million bicycles reported sold in 1988 by the Bicycle Market Research Institute in Boston, consumers had to choose between mountain bikes, racing bikes, touring bikes, BMX bikes, and beach cruisers. With that decision made, they faced a myriad of brands: Schwinn, Univega, Peugeot, Raleigh, Trek, Bridgestone, Huffy, Bianchi, Centurion, and more. Then there's yet another matter to consider: accessories. These days, it's nearly impossible to leave the store without an air pump, gloves, helmet, shoes, shorts, and water bottle—all of which are available in a staggering array of shapes, sizes, and features.

All this adds up to a $3.1-billion industry. And that fact isn't lost on America's bike retailers, who are enjoying strong sales and a promising future in a market that seems anything but cyclical.

Bicycle Basics

The good news about bicycle sales is that cheap, no-frills models are not the hottest sellers. More expensive mountain bikes, imported racing models, and classic beach cruisers are taking the market by storm. Upscale models are in, and that means more attractive revenues for retailers.

But today's retailers don't profit from bikes alone. Accessories are as hot—if not hotter—than the bikes themselves. And considering that biking enthusiasts will drop $70 on a simple pair of cycling shorts or $150 on a pair of cleats, it's no wonder that accessories retailers are rejoicing in the current cycling craze.

The owner of a San Francisco bike shop estimates that 50 percent of his sales come from accessories. Happily, the profit margin on accessories is higher than on bikes. A typical customer might spend $1,000 on a bike, and another $200 to $300 on clothing, helmets, shoes, speedometers, tires, water bottles, travel bags, bike racks, gloves, air pumps, repair kits, and so on. The abundance of must-have accessories has fueled retail sales, bringing most shops to an average of $300,000 to $400,000 a year in gross sales, up from about $150,000 just a few years ago.

Many bike shops bring in additional revenue by doing bicycle repairs. Consumers who spend $1,000 and more on fancy bikes want to keep their equipment in top shape. Not only are the repairs themselves profitable, but they also give customers an excuse to visit your shop. Once they're there, customers will certainly spot new clothing and accessories that they can't live without.

For Adult Viewing

It's important to remember that today's bike stores are not for kids only. Adults are fueling the latest cycling craze, and it's their tastes you're trying to cater to. Of course, that doesn't mean you shouldn't stock children's bikes and accessories. Both cycling and noncycling parents are interested in quality gear for their children, and they'll look to your shop to provide it.

Many biking enthusiasts are disaffected joggers and aerobics enthusiasts who are looking for something that is less likely to injure them. These tend to be white-collar workers, both men and women, who work in professional fields like psychology, law, or teaching. Blue-collar adult participation in biking is less prevalent, although children of blue-collar market segments are enthusiastic about the sport.

Remember, though, that standing out in the market will mean providing superior selection and service. People who want inexpensive bikes will go to discount stores. To be on the cutting edge of the biking craze, you should aim high, not low: top-flight products, excellent service, and plenty of extras will set your business apart from the mass-market merchandisers in your area.

In the Spirit of Things

Catering to true bicycle enthusiasts entails more than just stocking your store and writing up receipts. The most successful operators are enthusiasts themselves. If you're serious about breaking into the bicycle business, read up on the latest equipment. Participate in local bicycle races, or go on a bike-tour vacation. Make your shop a clearinghouse for information on these kinds of events. Find out firsthand what all the excitement is about. Your interest, expertise, and excitement may prove to be the best marketing of all.

FLOWER VENDING

High Net Profit Before Taxes:	$80,000
Average Net Profit Before Taxes:	$17,000
Minimum Start-up:	$ 200
Average Start-up:	$ 1,500

Several years ago, we met a man in Montreal who was netting $80,000 a year on a $100 original investment plus a few minutes of his time each day.

How did he do it? Selling roses in nightclubs and restaurants. Only he didn't do it himself—he had five young women make the rounds for him. Each night, five women stopped by and picked up the night's quota of 200 roses each. Then each woman visited seven nightclubs and restaurants, five nights each week.

They visited every table where a woman was seated and asked their escorts if they would like to buy roses for their ladies—for only $1.00. They sold about 20 roses per stop, or 140 per night. And on Friday and Saturday nights they increased that to between 200 and 250. For each rose they sold, they received $0.25 (25 percent of the sale). The women we spoke to were making over $200 a week and loved their jobs.

Sales amounted to at least 4,000 roses per week. Figuring $0.30 a rose, cost of sales was $1,500. Commissions were $1,000, leaving a profit of $1,500 per week.

One of the women explained that the club and restaurant owners were in favor of the operation. They felt it was an additional service for their patrons. The only payment they received from the women was in roses—a dozen twice each week for decoration.

Second Case History

Here's a variation on the theme. In some cities, we've spotted high-school boys peddling flowers at stoplights in affluent neighborhoods. After doing a little investigation, we discovered that each boy sold thirty to fifty flowers during the week in winter months, and fifty to eighty per night during the summers (when daylight hours are longer). On weekends, each boy could sell between 100 and 150 flowers each day.

Although not as lucrative as the Montreal operation, their gross of $2,600 to $3,000 a week is nothing to sneeze at. The commission paid the boys was, again, 25 percent. The roses were short-stemmed seconds, but instead of one you received two or three. Their cost to the owner of the business was $0.10 to $0.20 each.

Anyone Can Do It

The fellow behind the stoplight operation was a twenty-four-year-old ex-truck driver without a high-school education. No special expertise or experience is necessary in this business. If you want to try it, all you need is a state resale permit (sales tax permit). Look up "Florists, wholesale" in the Yellow Pages. In most major cities all the flower wholesalers are located on one street in one building.

===================== BRIGHT IDEA =====================

RV RENTALS

These days, more and more Americans are spending their vacations exploring the beauties of their own country. And what better vehicle than a motor home to see every detail of the trip while still enjoying the comforts of home? The motor-home business generated more than $500 million in 1987, and entrepreneur Sandra Bate hopes to corner a big chunk of that market in the years to come.

Bate's company, Rent-A-Motor-Home, Inc., supplies rental motor homes to travelers in more than 100 cities throughout the United States and eighteen foreign countries. Based in Las Vegas, the company's 1988 gross sales are estimated at $800,000, and Bate projects the company's income for 1989 will reach $1.5 million. In four years, Bate feels confident of earning $20 million a year.

It all started with a $300 ad in the *Los Angeles Times* back in 1973. Bate sought to rent her motor home while she wasn't using it and was surprised at the number of eager inquiries that a single advertisement sparked. Encouraged by the show of interest, she began wondering if her friends and neighbors would like to rent their own vehicles out as well.

"Back then, there were no other companies renting out motor homes, so we started with very low rates," Bate remembers. "The business was part-time at first, but within six months things got too busy for that. I had to hire four employees to help out. We'd started out with one motor home, and by the end of the first year in business, we were renting sixty units."

In 1979, Bate relocated her business to Las Vegas, Nevada, to take advantage of the tourist trade—as well as lower overhead costs. Five years later, Bate worked with Eastern Airlines to get her business linked up with worldwide travel agents via computer. With System One, clients prepay for motor-home rentals through their travel agents. A rental agreement is signed, deposits are collected, and if necessary, the motor home is equipped with household equipment such as dishes and silverware for $25 per person. The private owners of the motor homes receive 65 percent of Bate's fee.

A Bate Rent-A-Motor-Home representative can meet the client at the airport with the motor home, or bring it to the client's hotel. After a walk through the unit, the representative turns over the keys.

Bate has a fleet of close to 4,000 motor homes. By the end of 1989, she hopes to increase the fleet by 1,300 units, with 800 of them coming from the West Coast.

BED-AND-BREAKFAST INN

High Net Profit Before Taxes:	$100,000
Average Net Profit Before Taxes:	$ 40,000
Minimum Start-up:	$ 75,000
Average Start-up:	$200,000

Established around 3000 B.C., the earliest inns offered little more than a crude meal and cot to weary travelers. Over the centuries, inns gained sophistication and eventually developed into the high-rise hotels we know today. Despite the overwhelming popularity of commercial hotels and motels in today's society, inns are enjoying a resurgence as travelers shy away from the commercial hotels in favor of more homey, rustic bed-and-breakfast inns.

Renovating the Old Inn

According to Phyllis Featherston, president of the National Bed and Breakfast Association in Norwalk, Connecticut, this age-old industry is undergoing a rapid revitalization. Featherston, who publishes a guide to American and Canadian bed-and-breakfast inns, recalls listing only 359 in the guide eight or nine years ago, while the 1989 volume lists close to 1,600.

As more and more tourists and business travelers seek out a unique traveling experience, innkeepers can see occupancy rates average as high as 70 to 80 percent. With most inns charging approximately $55 to $60 a night—and some going as high as $200 a night—innkeepers can bring in decent profits. Depending on the number of rooms you have available and how much you charge, it's possible to bring in upward of $100,000 a year.

Everyone's an Inn-er

"Everybody—the young, the old, the honeymooner, the businessman, and the businesswoman—are potential clients," says Featherston. Innkeepers even rent out rooms to local residents who don't have enough room in their own homes to house out-of-town guests.

Young or old, single or married, male or female, innkeepers are as diverse as their guests. Featherston says she sees quite a few husband-and-wife teams who want to get out of the corporate jungle and into their own businesses. Others consider innkeeping a part-time venture.

How to Start

Innkeeping is attracting more entrepreneurs because it offers good returns on a low investment. Depending on the shape your home is in, you may simply have to buy a few sets of new linens for the room or rooms you'll rent. On the other hand, what can be a low-investment business may turn into thousands of dollars if you have to do major renovations like adding a bathroom, recarpeting, or knocking out a wall. Before you start making changes, check with your city hall to see if there are any zoning requirements concerning inn-keeping in your area.

Once you've turned the guest area into a paying room, you'll be on your way to a rewarding business. But being a good innkeeper means more than just having a nice room. Successful innkeepers are excellent hosts: hardworking, friendly, and warm. Remember, if people want regular rooms and impersonal service, they can go to a regular motel.

Running an inn from your home isn't always easy. For one thing, innkeeping requires a lot of paperwork. It also calls for all the skills and tasks that a regular business does—market-ing, promotions, bookkeeping, and day-to-day operations. Rooms and bathrooms must be kept spotless at all times. You must provide breakfast, which, even if it isn't fancy, had better be edible. And in between, you should find time to converse with guests, provide them with any advice or infor-mation they need, and generally make them feel comfortable (in other words, no screaming fits or afternoon collapses).

Some Considerations

Bed-and-breakfast inns are prospering in all parts of the country. But not every community and not every home is suitable for this type of business. Naturally, people who own homes with rooms that are already ready for renting out have little to lose by starting this type of business. But if starting an inn will mean a major investment for you, consider the marketability of your particular situation. Is your area one that tourists are likely to visit? If you're in a city, is your home near public transportation, local business centers, or tourist attractions? If you're in the country, is yours an area that people come to visit frequently?

Even though bed-and-breakfast rooms can bring in tidy fees, those fees must cover your overhead and salary. If you plan to make this your full-time business, make sure you can bring in enough guests to make your venture fly.

================= BRIGHT IDEA =================

TOUR DU JOUR

Most of us have experienced traditional tours of famous cities. We've hiked to the top of the Statue of Liberty, schlepped the hills of San Francisco to visit Fisherman's Wharf, flocked to Boston's Old North Church, and stood in line to see the White House. But how much did we really learn about a city that way? And didn't we leave feeling like we missed the real story?

Not anymore. Unusual tour services are cropping up in cities across the country. Thanks to a company called Uncommon Boston, you can sign up for a walking tour that stops at sites most bus tours skip. Visiting Chicago? One tour company there guides guests to various gangster haunts.

And then there's Scandal Tours of Washington. Entrepreneur Rick London and a cast of comic actors take tourists through our capital's more notorious sites. The route includes the Watergate and, of course, Gary Hart's town house. Actors from a local theater company impersonate key Washington figures and recount a few choice scandals. All in all, it's a view of Washington you don't get on most other tours—and one that has the public and the press taking note.

Starting a tour company isn't necessarily expensive. London's initial investment was just $1,800. You don't have to own your own bus (or limo, boat, bike, or horse)—usually you can charter the transportation. Advertising will probably make up your biggest expense, and going after publicity is almost a must. Other than that, a little research into the lesser-known aspects of your city will serve you well. Just remember that a good tour is educational, entertaining, and most of all fun.

7

AUTOMOTIVE BUSINESSES

AUTO PAINT AND BODY SHOP

High Net Profit Before Taxes:	$120,000
Average Net Profit Before Taxes:	$ 40,000
Minimum Start-up:	$ 50,000
Average Start-up:	$100,000

While most businesses aren't illegal, few have the law on their sides the way the $19-billion auto-paint-and-body-repair business does. Most states require drivers to carry car insurance. And as a result, people generally use insurance money to make repairs on their cars that would probably go undone if they had to pay for them out of their own pockets.

Add to this the fact that the rising prices of new autos have forced drivers to hold on to their cars longer, and it's apparent why a steadily increasing number of auto owners opt to keep their cars looking good with a new paint job and body work rather than trading them in for newer models.

New Equipment, Higher Volume

Computer equipment, advanced welding techniques, and fast-drying paint booths make today's paint and body shops more sophisticated—and more profitable—than ever. High-tech body shops can turn out many more cars per week than was ever possible in the typical two- or three-man shop. Gross annual revenues of $1 million and more are an increasingly common reality.

Of course, this new technology doesn't come cheap. Setting up a state-of-the-art shop can cost upward of $100,000. You can, however, start out for less by buying used equipment or by purchasing an existing shop. Another option is to concentrate on painting, which cuts down on equipment needs, but also cuts into profits from doing body repair and selling replacement body parts (usually sold at a 20-to-25-percent retail markup).

Quick Management

Regardless of which route the new body-shop owner takes, the most important early steps are hiring trained employees to perform body work and painting, and setting up efficient methods for writing estimates, thus allowing the shop to work at full volume potential. Recently created computer programs can make this process easier by assisting in writing estimates, scheduling jobs, organizing billables, and handling other related functions.

Advertising and public relations can also make a difference. One successful paint-and-body-shop owner stresses quality and honesty above all else. He points out how many people fear being ripped off when they bring their car to any type of car-repair business. To reach the female market—one that's particularly apprehensive about being taken advantage of—he advertises in the food section of the local paper.

Being sloppy won't fly in this business, either. Most shops are now careful to maintain a clean front office. Gone are the days of the grease-stained area with spare parts strewn about and the shop dog asleep on the sofa. Also disappearing are vague estimating procedures that leave many customers feeling overcharged. Most of the better shops provide customers and insurance companies with detailed estimates in writing, something that has become easier, thanks to collision-repair estimating guides.

Don't Forget Your Friendly Insurance Agent

Insurance companies account for a large percentage of the collision-repair work that goes through the typical body and paint shop. These companies monitor the estimating and repair procedure so closely that they sometimes will go so far as to specify the type of welding machine that must be used on a job in order for them to pay for it. Consequently, a shop must strive to maintain good relations with the insurance companies that refer work to them.

=============== BRIGHT IDEA ===============

MOBILE CAR CARE

Getting your car to the shop is such a drag, it's no wonder smart mechanics are reversing the process. Today, mobile-car-care services come to your car. And according to those in the business, that makes all the difference in the world.

"The mobile-services business is something that has a brilliant future, whether it's mobile oil changing, mobile car washing, or mobile locksmithing," says Steve Wiley, president of Gettysburg, Pennsylvania–based Ameri Mobile Services, the parent company of Mobicare mobile car care. "If it's mobile anything, I think it has a bright future."

Mobicare offers consumers a new twist on quick-lube service. "We've given it an extra twist," says Wiley. "We took the quick-lube business, [combined it with] the popular automotive appearance business"—detailing—"and brought it to the customer. People are having their cars cared for while they sleep, while they work, and while they shop."

Wiley was positive about his concept from the very start. A veteran of automotive franchising (he's the man behind Americlean Mobile Power Wash), Wiley is now selling Mobicare franchises at a rapid clip. If the boom continues, he estimates 1989 oil sales at $5 million to $8 million.

Perhaps the hottest commodity on the consumer market these days is convenience. If you can offer customers the chance to avoid making an appointment, driving to the local shop, and leaving the car there for an indeterminate length of time during which they are completely immobilized, you have a strong selling point indeed. And it doesn't necessarily work for oil changes and detailing services only: everything from tires to tune-ups are more appealing when they require less hassle.

MUFFLER SHOP

High Net Profit Before Taxes:	$132,000
Average Net Profit Before Taxes:	$ 80,000
Minimum Start-up:	$ 86,000
Average Start-up:	$145,000

One muffler shop we talked with grossed $348,000 last year and netted the absentee owner $118,000 before taxes. And that's not unusual! A major franchisor claims that their average shop grosses a minimum of $270,000 a year. Even after substantial leasing, royalty, and franchising fees, the franchisee nets 17.3 percent before taxes after a $15,000 salary.

A muffler shop is within reach of the small business owner's budget, thanks to the development of a machine called a pipe bender and standard mufflers that fit different cars. Before these, a muffler shop had to stock as many as 1,900 different tailpipes and 400 different mufflers. The warehousing space required added tremendously to rent and property expenses—not to mention inventory costs. These factors added up to prohibitively high start-up expenses.

Now, thirty expandable-nipple mufflers fit all American cars. Six diameters of straight tailpipe is all that is necessary to complete your inventory.

The pipe bender is exactly that—a simple hydraulic press that bends pipe to any angle or radius necessary. It flares, flanges, and can deform the pipe opening for a slip connection. When a car comes into the shop, the mechanic pulls a card that shows what setting to use on the bender for that particular model car. He makes the setting, activates the bender, and in six to ten minutes the header and tailpipes are ready to install.

What's even more attractive is the cost. You can make tailpipes on your own equipment for a fraction of what it costs to buy them wholesale. Standardized mufflers are also a bargain at about half what original-equipment mufflers cost. By keeping material costs low, you can undercut the competition and still make an excellent profit.

The Market

Mufflers and tailpipes rank third in sales of replacement auto parts, after tires and batteries. The public spends nearly $4 billion annually to replace exhaust systems. Exhaust service lines up right behind tune-up and ignition repair as the second largest segment of the automotive service business.

A muffler lasts only one and a half to four years. In colder climates, because of corrosion from salt used on the streets, they may not even last that long. What more could you ask?

No Real Merchandisers

We found only one or two hard-hitting merchandisers in this field. Low-price promotions, common in tire and battery sales, were few and far between. Almost everyone at the wholesale-distribution level agreed that offering and promoting discount prices on muffler installations was an excellent idea. Distributors directed us to only a handful of shops that were selling this way aggressively. Predictably, those that were had higher gross sales than those that weren't.

If you're prepared to market your services on the basis of price, your prospects in this industry are excellent. Back up your low prices with quality equipment and service, and you're in business for good.

LIMOUSINE SERVICE

High Net Profit Before Taxes:	$164,000
Average Net Profit Before Taxes:	$ 60,000
Minimum Start-up:	$ 31,000
Average Start-up:	$ 90,000

Limousines are not for rich people only. These days, regular folks are hiring limos to whisk them off to their weddings, chauffeur their kids to the prom, and simply as basic transportation.

What's behind this luxury boom? Several factors have led to the increased popularity of limousines. The work force in general has become more affluent and at the same time more aware of the practicality of using limousine services. As taxi services decline in quality, drunk-driving laws get stricter, and traffic congestion worsens, limousines look better and better—even to average consumers.

The prices look better, too. Over the years, prices of the limousines themselves haven't increased much. For this reason, limousine-service owners haven't had to jack up their rates—and in fact more people are getting into the business. Industry insiders compare the effect to the "cheapening" of airline prices over the past twenty years. Prices have not kept pace with inflation, so a $50-an-hour limousine ride that might have seemed outlandish in 1970 seems downright reasonable in 1990.

Limousines Aren't Cheap

Limo prices may not have risen much over the years, but that doesn't make them cheap. Typical prices range from $32,000 to $60,000 and more. Large limousine companies maintain a variety of limos, ranging from the basic formal sedan to superstretch models that accommodate many people. Unless you have some major capital to invest, though, you probably won't have the option of choosing a fleet. For small operators, choosing a vehicle is a major decision.

For small or beginning limousine services, formal, standard, or presidential stretches are the best buys for the money. Many operators have started their businesses with one used limo of this type, but some experts suggest that anyone entering the industry spend the extra money to buy new. Having reliable equipment that meets your specifications is worth the extra cost.

Catering Luxury

There are many kinds of limousine services. The industry, though in many ways an informal one, is quite flexible in terms of the business setups possible. You can cater to corporate executives or casual users—people who rent limos for a night on the town, a wedding, a sports event, or anything else that requires casual use. One of the major uses of limousines is simply carting people to and from the airport. You can also contract with hotels or hustle for overflow business from other limousine services.

Corporate customers can account for as much as 85 percent of a large limousine company's business. For most small operators, though, handling a variety of tasks is more common. Overflow work, for example, can help you break into the business. Often, established companies are looking for contractors to take over work they can't handle. Overflow work can go both ways, too. Down the road, you can enlarge your own service capacity by contracting your overflow work out to other small operators.

══════ BRIGHT IDEA ══════

CAR-POOLING SERVICE

As America's highways become increasingly clogged, more and more people are looking to car pooling as a way to save gas money, reduce congestion, and make commuting a little more pleasant. Yet, finding a person to pool with isn't easy. Car-poolers must have compatible schedules, routes, and personalities for a car pool to work successfully.

For these reasons, car-pooling services are beginning to surface in metropolitan areas. And as rush-hour traffic worsens, demand for this service should only increase.

To start, distribute cards or fliers in large office buildings. Ask clients to list their business and home addresses, as well as the days and times they'd like to carpool. Also get some routine background information—for instance, you might inquire about driving records or whether or not a person smokes. From there, it's just a question of sorting out the information.

You can charge a flat fee of $20 for initial matchups, and a reduced fee of $10 for reassignments. Repeat business is a cinch, since Americans are prone to switch both jobs and homes frequently these days.

A car-pooling service doesn't have to be limited to commuting. You can arrange to match people for interstate or cross-country drives. College campuses are a ripe market for long-distance car-pooling, especially during vacations.

CONSIGNMENT USED-CAR LOT

High Net Profit Before Taxes:	$93,000 plus
Average Net Profit Before Taxes:	$66,000
Minimum Start-up:	$ 9,000
Average Start-up:	$16,000

About 11 million new cars are sold in this country each year. But over 25 million used cars change hands, which means that the market for used cars is more than twice the size of the new-car market.

You can break into the used-car market with no inventory expenses up front. Impossible? We found one operation selling fifty cars per month with an average gross profit of $150 per car. That's $7,500 per month before expenses. The net profit was over $3,500—not bad considering you can start for as little as $9,000.

The trick is to sell on consignment. It works this way: you sell the merchandise and pay for it afterward. People consign their cars to you with the agreement that they will receive a certain amount of money when the vehicle is sold. You act as an independent agent, selling the car at a markup just as you would if you bought it wholesale.

The Consumer Is Wiser

Most consumers realize that the trade-in allowances they're getting on their old cars aren't what they could get on the retail market. All dealers subscribe to regional publications that list the retail and wholesale prices of used cars. In the west, it's called *Kelly's Blue Book*. In the east, the National Auto Dealers Association publishes a similar list.

Suppose the *Blue Book* retail value of your car is $6,000. If you trade it for another car, you will get the wholesale price, which the *Blue Book* says is about $5,200. Now suppose that the car you trade for has a suggested retail price of $9,000—which you pay. That car cost the dealer $7,200, if he or she was a good buyer. In essence, the dealer is making money on your business twice: once on the markup of your new car and again on the markup of your trade-in. This is good news for the dealer, but not the consumer.

You Get the Markup

Because trade-ins are often skimpy, many consumers prefer to sell their cars through used-car lots. A used-car dealer can secure the best selling price (often at or near retail), so that even after paying a salesperson's commission, the consumer comes out ahead. You (the used-car dealer) and the consumer split the markup instead of handing it over to the new-car dealer.

Make Money from Both Ends

In addition to making money on consignment cars, you can do a brisk trade in auctioned cars. Dealers hold weekly or biweekly auctions where they bring cars to sell to each other. The cars at the auction come primarily from new-car dealers who are overstocked on used cars. Sometimes a sports-car dealer will bring in passenger cars that he or she doesn't handle—or vice versa. The trick is, you must be a licensed dealer to attend.

Offer to take customers to an auction with you, with the understanding that you will buy cars for them at a price $175 over cost. The auctioneer gets a commission of $45 per car sold; you get the remaining $130.

Customers can test-drive a car and check it out thoroughly before the auction begins. When the bidding starts, have your customer stand next to you so he or she can indicate when the bidding gets too high.

Creative ways of selling used cars like the ones we've described here are just being discovered around the country. One operator in Pennsylvania has a new twist: he opens his lot only on weekends. He rents a parking lot on a main thoroughfare and puts up a banner-type sign. His clients leave their cars with him on Saturday morning and pick them up Sunday night if they don't sell.

=========== BRIGHT IDEA ===========

USED-TIRE SALES

Who would think that selling used tires could be the basis for a multimillion-dollar operation? Bob Stuber did, and that's exactly what's happened with his business, Quality Used Tires, based in Paradise, California.

When Stuber decided to go into the used-tire business eight years ago, he used some rather unorthodox means to acquire the tires he sold. "We used to drive by at night and pick them out of garbage cans," he admits.

First located on a dirt lot, Stuber's business attracted mostly low-income customers who wanted an inexpensive alternative to new tires. Today, Stuber has taken the used-tire industry out of the back alley and into retail stores throughout Northern California. "Now, the market is very broad," he explains. "We sell used tires for luxury cars like Porsche, Mercedes Benz, and Rolls-Royce."

Quality Used Tires has already sold about one-half-million tires. "Now, some of the big tire companies are showing some interest in selling used tires," says Stuber, who contends, "In the next couple of years, there will be used-tire dealers everywhere."

Stuber himself may contribute to the growth. In 1989, he hopes to add twenty company-owned stores to the seven existing locations. Who knows? As Americans catch on to the advantages of buying safe, used tires, sales of new tires may flatten out.

AUTO DETAILING

High Net Profit Before Taxes:	$60,000
Average Net Profit Before Taxes:	$30,000
Minimum Start-up:	$ 5,000
Average Start-up:	$10,000

Ever wonder who puts the mirrorlike showroom shine on all the cars at the dealership down the street? If you're thinking it's someone who makes paltry wages for backbreaking labor, think again. Small auto detailing or reconditioning companies do this, and some net over $60,000 a year.

Over the past decade, the auto detailing industry has grown up. What was once a little-known (but lucrative) business is now attracting individual consumers as well as dealers, and new shops are popping up in every neighborhood.

Multibillion-Dollar Market

Anyone who parks a car and walks away from it will invariably turn around and take a final look before the car is out of sight. (Test yourself if you don't believe it.) Psychologists who have studied this curious habit know that it comes from pride of possession and it affects all of us.

For the 120-million-plus people who own vehicles—from Cadillacs to clunkers—an automobile is a prized necessity. Manufacturers and dealers know this, and play on pride and ego when making a sale. Cleanliness is part and parcel of this pride. That's why every new or used automobile is prepped by the dealer prior to sale. Most cars will be reconditioned cosmetically at least once during their lifetimes; many will be detailed three or more times.

Down to the Smallest Detail

What do detailers do? They start with a thorough cleaning, inside and out. This is more than a wash—it involves rubbing, polishing, and buffing with rags, brushes, toothbrushes, and cotton swabs. Using the best polishes and waxes, the car is given a showroom finish so that no streak or speck of dust remains.

Detailing does not include bodywork, painting, mechanical repair, or upholstery work. Nor does it usually include vinyl or convertible-top repairs. This work is done by other tradespeople.

Providing detailing services by contract to dealers is a full-time task for many operators. All but the highest-volume dealers, who have their own staff to do the work, will farm it out to independent detailers. The detailer who does the best work at the lowest price per car will get plenty of work.

Changing Competition

When we first investigated this business over a decade ago, the market for consumer detailing was virtually untapped. Today, that isn't the case. Consumers have discovered the advantages of professional detailing with a vengeance. And as a result, detailing operations exist in cities large and small all across the country. Experts estimate that there are more than 7,000 detailers nationwide bringing in gross annual sales of nearly $2.5 billion.

Of course, there's always room at the top. Smart marketing, superior service, lower prices, and crack management can all help you take on the competition successfully. To outdo existing shops, you'll need more cash than you would have ten years ago. While it's still possible to buy yourself some cleaning equipment and call yourself a detailer, staying ahead of the competition may require some more sophisticated marketing and operations.

Look for opportunities in your local market. What have the existing detailers overlooked? What can you offer that they can't? The detailing industry is still growing: you just have to find your own best inroad.

Work Anywhere

One reason detailing requires a relatively low initial investment is that you can do the work almost anywhere. We found one operator working in an alley behind a parking lot grossing $60,000 a year. His office was a portable toolshed, and in the evening he packed his equipment in the trunk of his car and drove away.

We found several shoestring operators making an excellent income working out of their homes, using the garage, driveway, and nearby streets as their work areas. Others set up an answering machine on their home phones and work out of vans or at the customers' locations. This is an excellent, timesaving approach to the executive market.

CAR WASH

High Net Profit Before Taxes:	$250,000
Average Net Profit Before Taxes:	$ 75,000
Minimum Start-up:	$ 50,000
Average Start-up:	$250,000

In 1914, two young fellows in Detroit opened the world's first car wash: the Automated Laundry. The cars had to be left all day, since they were pushed through the system manually, and even brass parts were removed for polishing by hand.

Twenty-five years later the first crude "automatic" conveyor car wash was opened in Hollywood, California. On busy days as many as forty men splashed in the tunnel soaping, scrubbing, wiping, and drying cars as they were pulled through.

Today, there are over 20,000 automatic car washes, many of which can completely wash and dry a car in less than thirty seconds, without it being touched by human hands. Some car washes handle 20,000 cars per month and net over $200,000 a year before income taxes. Net profits of $50,000 to $75,000 are common.

Your out-of-pocket cash investment needn't be exorbitant. It is possible to set up a fully equipped, four-bay, self-service car wash for $140,000, excluding land costs. Larger, full-service operations in prime locations require investments of $100,000 to $300,000 down, with loans in the $400,000-to-$1-million range.

What Happens When It Rains?

That seems to be the first question that prospective car-wash owners ask. If your part of the country has 250 rain-free days a year, you're in a good position to do business. And remember that night or morning rains don't necessarily hurt business. In fact, the day after a heavy rain, business is usually better than normal in car washes because autos get muddy and sloppy driving around.

Car washes in northern climates do much more business during the winter because car owners are concerned with keeping their cars free of the corrosive road salts used for melting snow and ice.

Nationwide, the car-wash industry does less business during June, July, and August, because people wash their own cars more during these warm months. On the other hand, Southern California—which usually has fewer than twenty rainy days per year—grosses more per car than any other part of the nation. Buying attitudes are different in different parts of the country, a factor you must consider in your area.

One thing is certain: car washes are more popular than ever. Like so many other household chores, washing the car is becoming just too much work for busy professionals. Given a choice between spending a Saturday afternoon relaxing or being up to their armpits in soap, most working people will opt for a day of rest. And that spells good news for the car-wash industry—both currently and for the future.

The Choice: To Buy or to Build?

You have to be more careful if you are going to buy an existing car wash. It is very important to unearth the real reason that the previous owner is selling. After about five years the maintenance costs for car-wash equipment can start getting high. Perhaps the owner foresees some large expenditures for replacing major components.

On the other hand, maybe your area is experiencing a shift in demographics. If people are leaving in droves, yours is not the right neighborhood for a car wash—or any new business for that matter. The owner may anticipate radical changes in your area's population: check into this yourself before you set up shop.

Bear in mind that car-wash books can easily be manipulated to hide high maintenance costs and to reflect higher earnings than those actually received. If there isn't a water reclamation system, sometimes you can correlate water usage (available from the manufacturer) with gallonage on the water bills and arrive at the number of cars being washed. If your figure is much lower than that claimed by the owner or shown in the books, something is wrong, because water usage should go up slightly as the equipment wears.

====== BRIGHT IDEA ======

AUTO AUDITS

For many used-car buyers, shopping for a vehicle is one big gamble. But Edison, New Jersey, entrepreneurs Wendy Mandell and Lee Geller believe it doesn't have to be so. As president and executive vice-president of Car Checkers of America, Mandell and Geller perform used-vehicle inspections and appraisals for people buying used cars.

For $49.95, Geller or one of his technicians will inspect more than 275 items on a used car before the purchase is made and will give the customer a written evaluation and recommendations. "If the car meets our qualifications, we can also [guarantee] it for up to two years or 40,000 miles through an insurance company," says Geller.

Former used-car wholesalers, Mandell and Geller thought of the idea for their business when Geller sold a car to one of his neighbors. "I knew the car needed new brakes," he says, "so I had our mechanic put them in and encouraged my neighbor to have her mechanic inspect the car. He said the car needed new brakes and charged her $175 to put them in." That's when Mandell and Geller decided there was a need for a nonbiased service to do vehicle inspections.

First-year sales exceeded $100,000, prompting Mandell and Geller to move from their home-based office to commercial space. They're so optimistic about the market for their services that they've started franchising the business.

QUICK OIL-CHANGE SHOP

High Net Profit Before Taxes:	$ 45,000 plus
Average Net Profit Before Taxes:	$ 31,000
Minimum Start-up:	$ 80,000
Average Start-up:	$100,000

Wave good-bye to the service station. Today's gas stations may have a large selection of snacks and cosmetics, but many don't offer the kinds of basic maintenance services they used to. Self-service pumps and minimarkets have replaced the old service station of yore.

Why the Change?

Several things encouraged the demise of the service station: high oil prices, franchise laws, specialization, public buying attitudes, and the realization that marketing today is much different from what it was in the forties and fifties. The main reason is simply that the oil companies are not interested in repair work because they don't make any money on it. Until recently, it was a necessary evil of running a gas station.

When service stations convert repair bays to self-serve islands, their sales volume can increase by ten times. That in itself is a pretty strong argument against the old system.

What About Changing Your Oil?

Since gas stations no longer provide repair services, where do you go to have your car repaired? The answer is, to specialists: tire dealers, brake shops, tune-up shops, transmission shops, diagnostic multirepair centers, and single-purpose service facilities.

A car needs an oil change every 3,000 to 6,000 miles. Several years ago, an auto repairman realized that a person who wanted a simple oil change either had to leave his or her car at a repair shop or wait from a half hour to three hours for the work to be done.

He reasoned that a shop doing only oil changes could, with two workers, do the job in less than ten minutes and at the same time do a grease job, replace the oil filter, check and add rear-end lubricant, transmission, power steering, and brake fluid, blow out the air filter, check the radiator level, clean battery terminals, and add water.

Today, this man owns a chain of quick oil-change shops—and a host of smart competitors. Most shops handle 100 to 200 cars per week at $15.95 each minimum. Average gross sales per shop are about $1,800 per week. The average net for an absentee owner is over $500 per week. The average owner-operated shop should net $36,000 before taxes annually.

The Angle

If you buy your oil, transmission fluid, and other oil products in quart cans, you won't be able to sell your services at $15.95. The angle is to purchase oil products in bulk—fifty-five-gallon drums. The cost per quart drops by one third.

The oil is hydraulically pumped directly to the crankcase through a metering gun. The same is done with rear-end grease, automatic- and standard-transmission lubricants, power-steering fluid, and filtering grease. Instead of taking several minutes to fill a crankcase from individual cans, five quarts of oil can be pumped in within a minute.

Why People Buy This Service

Speed, convenience, and expertise are what ensure the success of this business. Everyone is anxious to make auto maintenance a less time-consuming and complicated affair. Even if your local gas station provides oil-change services, you can still crack the market with reliable, fast service.

THIRTY-MINUTE TUNE-UP SHOP

High Net Profit Before Taxes:	$108,000 plus
Average Net Profit Before Taxes:	$ 64,000
Minimum Start-up:	$ 43,000
Average Start-up:	$ 56,000

Like the quick oil-change operation, the thirty-minute tune-up shop proves that specialization is the word of the day in automotive repairs. Faced with a confusing maze of technology, people prefer doing business with someone they feel knows everything about their problem. So if someone's car starts running erratically, he or she will probably visit a shop that does tune-ups only, confident that the tune-up specialists will know how to handle the problem quickly and reliably.

Specialization offers some special benefits for you, too. The absentee owner or chain operator must have rigid control over every aspect of his or her business. This is easier to do when one product or service is offered. You can focus on making your operations efficient and tight instead of trying to figure out where your profit is coming from and where your expenses are going.

The Universal Tune-up

All cars need regular tune-ups to keep them gas efficient and in good running order. Since people are keeping their cars longer these days, proper maintenance is a must. Yet few people have the time or the expertise to do their own car maintenance. That's where your tune-up business comes in.

As a tune-up specialist, you can offer customers two main benefits: quality service and convenience. Providing quality service is a given—you won't last long in the business without good work. But the convenience angle is also critical. Few things are more tedious than bringing a car in for repairs. If your service can complete the job quickly, without taking up the customer's entire day, you'll gather a loyal following in short order.

As a tune-up specialist, you may also offer your clients a third benefit: economy. A well-managed tune-up shop should be able to do a tune-up in less time than a general repair shop. As a result, you may be able to charge less and still turn a nice profit. Pay special attention to keeping your operations lean and mean. Low prices can be as much of an incentive as convenience.

What's in a Tune-up?

A tune-up involves a complete electronic check of the ignition system. All poorly operating parts are replaced. The entire system and all parts are adjusted to peak operating efficiency as shown by both engine analyzer and in some cases an optional dyno test at speed. All diagnosed difficulties that are not part of the basic service are explained verbally to the customer and put in writing on the customer's receipt. In turn, customers can get these repairs elsewhere.

All tune-ups include engine diagnosis, chemical carburetor cleaning and adjustment, timing set, check and cleaning of smog control valve, and replacement of the following parts when necessary: plugs, points, condenser, rotor, air filter, fuel filter, distributor cap, and spark-plug wires. Some shops also include complete carburetor disassembly and overhaul, if necessary.

Equipment Needs Are Simple

Tune-up shops need only one major piece of equipment: an electronic engine analyzer. It is mounted on a test stand that rolls up to the car. The mechanic clips some wires to the ignition system, watches meters and oscilloscope displays, and pushes a few buttons. In about five minutes, he can tell you the condition of every part of your ignition system. Electronic analyzers are impressive to the customer and eliminate the guesswork in tuning an engine. They are essential to any state-of-the-art tune-up shop.

You may also want to buy a dynamometer. A dynamometer consists of two rollers placed on the floor and hooked to two meters. You can drive the car onto these rollers and run it at highway speeds under load without taking it out of the shop. A dynamometer is especially useful for tuning carburetors. Since many new cars are fuel-injected and don't have carburetors, you may decide the $3,400 to $7,500 investment for this equipment isn't worthwhile.

In addition, you'll need battery chargers, hand tools, a vacuum gauge, an air-conditioning charging station, a circuit tester, shop battery and cable clamps, a battery hydrometer, and miscellaneous items such as safety goggles and distributor tools.

Altogether, plan to spend between $22,000 and $35,000 for equipment. Though this may sound like a lot of equipment, remember that good, high-tech equipment will help streamline your operations and increase your effectiveness. In today's environment, it just doesn't make sense to skimp in this department.

What's an Average Day?

Typical hours for a tune-up shop are 7:30 A.M. to 6 or 7 P.M. To make your services more convenient, you may want to stay open in the evenings or on weekends. Some shops maintain a flexible schedule to accommodate a wide range of customers. For instance, consider working from 10 A.M. to 9

P.M. just one day a week. That way, you won't have to hire a second shift of mechanics and you can still attract working people who don't have time to come in during regular business hours.

After your first six months or a year, twelve cars per day is the average traffic on weekdays, and twenty on Saturdays. Some shops consistently average fifteen cars per day during the week and thirty on Saturday.

Remember, though, that no single location can handle an indefinite number of cars, even if it's open seven days a week. Some jobs will take considerable time; some of your mechanics will be less motivated than others; problems will creep in with corresponding delays; just writing up payments may take more time than you think. Opening additional locations is a smart down-the-road move for any tune-up-shop operator. You'll find that two locations may live almost as cheaply as one—on twice as much revenue.

8

PUBLISHING

DESKTOP PUBLISHING

High Net Profit Before Taxes:	$129,000
Average Net Profit Before Taxes:	$ 43,000
Minimum Start-up:	$ 15,000
Average Start-up:	$ 35,000

Producing professional-looking documents used to be expensive. Now, anyone with a personal computer and the right software can look good in print. Desktop publishing is the fastest growing of all home-based computer businesses. And the boom is far from reaching its peak.

The Desktop Revolution

What is desktop publishing and what can it do? With powerful new personal computers, advanced software, and high-quality laser printers, beginning publishers can produce near-typeset-quality pages for a fraction of what traditional typesetting costs. A desktop page costs about a penny to produce; typesetting costs about $20 per page.

Thanks to desktop publishing, professional-looking books, newsletters, ads, annual reports, and brochures are accessible to all kinds of businesses—from start-up firms to major corporations. The result? "Desktop publishing has raised expectations," says one desktop newsletter publisher. "It has also raised the stakes on what things should look like. People expect [a publication] to look professional now, even when it's just a little company-produced newsletter."

Opportunities Abound

These higher expectations mean a raft of interesting opportunities for desktop publishers in the years to come. Entrepreneurs are breaking into this business on all levels. Some are becoming publishers—writing, editing, designing, and producing their own books or periodicals. Others are catering to the design and production end by providing specialized graphics or output services for desktop clients. Still others work on a consulting basis, setting up in-house programs and training employees to use the systems most advantageously. Even copy-shop owners are riding the wave: many have installed desktop equipment to provide customers with low-cost artwork for ads, fliers, and so on.

You can find your own angle by taking stock of your current skills. Are you a closet author, ready to start producing your own newsletter, magazine, or series of books? Do you have a flair for graphic design? Are you a technical whiz interested in finding a new field of expertise? Can you combine desktop-publishing services with another business idea—for instance, using it in an advertising agency or printing plant? There is no one way to get into the desktop-publishing business. Your imagination is your only limit.

A Word about Equipment

In recent years, there has been a proliferation of desktop-publishing equipment as never before. That's good news to you, the aspiring publisher, since it means you'll be able to choose from a wide range of brands, features, and prices. But it also means that your choice can be complicated and confusing.

Though your decision will be largely individual, we can offer these words of advice: don't skimp on equipment and do as much research as possible before you buy. A bargain system may be adequate for your first few months in business, but will it still work when your work load doubles? Will clients be satisfied with the output? If you're undecided about which system to buy, try out a number of them on a rental basis. Many instant print shops have desktop-publishing stations set up for clients. Find one that has the system you're considering, and spend a few hours—or a few days—getting to know the equipment. You'll be in a better position to evaluate after you've had some experience.

Be Creative

If you're intrigued by the idea of desktop publishing, but have no idea where to start, consider taking a class on the subject at a local community college or night school. You'll get a feeling for what the computers can do and pick up essential skills for your new business.

In this section, we mentioned a few applications for desktop publishing in today's market, but we've been far from comprehensive. This field has just begun to grow, and we believe there's plenty of room for creative ideas. Keep your eyes peeled. A new opportunity could be just bytes away.

COMMERCIAL FREE-LANCE WRITING

High Net Profit Before Taxes:	Variable
Average Net Profit Before Taxes:	Variable
Minimum Start-up:	$3,000
Average Start-up:	$5,000

One of the hottest-selling products in today's economy isn't even tangible: it's information. People have a lot to learn, and they're learning from magazines, books, manuals, brochures, newsletters, advertisements, radio and television broadcasts, product packages—the list is virtually endless. And so is the need for people to gather, organize, and present that information. Professional writing is a viable and growing field, and it should continue to grow well into the future.

The Write Stuff

Most people think of professional writing as a make-it-or-break-it kind of business. Either you're raking in the bucks on your latest steamy best-seller, or you starve waiting for your big break. Yet in reality most writers fall somewhere in between. While a relatively small percentage of writers actually make millionaire status, the rest aren't necessarily starving. Many make a decent living writing books, articles, advertising copy, technical manuscripts, and so on.

Another myth surrounding the writing business is that you need genius-level talent to succeed. That isn't true. While you must be able to write clear, concise, informative copy, you don't have to be Charles Dickens. Like any other business, writing depends as much on marketing ability as it does on technical skill. Your salesmanship and professional follow-through will be critical factors in your success.

Many Potential Markets

Though there are scores of potential markets for free-lance writers, the nonfiction-narrative market is probably the largest. This includes articles, ad copy, book reviews, and so on. Who will buy nonfiction?

First, publications. These consist of magazines and newspapers that are published all over the country. In addition to major-market consumer magazines like *Harper's* or *People*, a number of lesser-known trade magazines represent promising outlets. Additionally, local newspapers pay for stories from free-lancers if they are pitched and presented properly. Indeed, a newspaper editor's major problem is filling the paper with newsworthy items or articles of general interest.

Advertising and public-relations agencies have an ongoing need for copywriters who can turn out snappy copy fast. While many have copywriters on staff, many others also use material from well-developed free-lance sources. Ad and commercial copy and press releases are the principal forms of writing produced for these sources. Additionally, articles intended for publication under the byline of a PR firm's client are sometimes commissioned by the firm and assigned to ghostwriters.

The corporate market is another avenue to consider. Many major, and for that matter minor, companies are commissioning company histories. In addition to this specialized avenue of writing, corporations are using freelancers to produce company newsletters as well as company-produced videotapes, newsletters, or trade publications that are made available to corporate clients or consumers.

The federal government represents a market all its own. You have seen government publications on everything from how to wash clothes to the state of the U.S. cattle industry. Somebody has to write these pamphlets and books. You can bid on various projects as a prime contractor, or you can be a subcontractor to a corporation that has a contract to produce a written document.

Another way of taking part in federal contracting is to write proposals for people who wish to obtain contracts. Additionally, writing proposals for nonprofit agencies seeking grants from the government or from private-sector foundations represents another way of selling writing services.

The field of technical writing is virtually exploding with potential for the free-lancer. For instance, computer software companies and their clients represent an opportunity to do everything from document computer programs to describing what a piece of scientific equipment looks like.

You may also wish to pursue the following options: speech writing for corporate and political clients; ghostwriting books; writing manuals and presentations for seminars; writing greeting-card copy; scriptwriting for independent video-production houses; producing your own newsletter.

Here's the one you've been waiting for, if you're like most writers: writing nonfiction books. Breaking into book publishing is much more difficult than, say, getting your first trade-magazine article published. You'll need to establish a track record, make some contacts, and develop some expertise. But it's not out of the question, especially as a down-the-road goal.

Just Do It

When asked what separates amateur writers from professionals, one famous author answered, "Writers write." That may sound redundant, yet we've all encountered self-pro-claimed writers who haven't written a word, let alone published anything. If you're serious about becoming a professional writer, the first order of business is to write and sell your work.

Start small. Don't pitch a story to the *New Yorker* or go after a big advertising account right out of the box. Look for a story of local interest to sell to your community newspaper ("New Business Sets Up Shop Downtown," "Local Fireman Wins National Award"). Or offer to produce a brochure for a small business in your community. Small projects like these may not make you immediately and insanely wealthy, but they may pave the way to bigger and better things. And since free-lance writing is a low-investment business to start (many start with just a typewriter, a phone, and a desk), you can keep your regular job until your new business takes off.

The income you make as a free-lance writer will vary depending on the type and volume of work you do. Some journalists make as little as $10,000 a year working full-time. On the other hand, advertising copywriters can make more than $100,000 a year working from home. Whatever your specialty, you'll probably find that personal rewards are as substantial as the financial benefits.

WHO'S WHO DIRECTORY PUBLISHING

High Net Profit Before Taxes:	$173,000
Average Net Profit Before Taxes:	$ 98,000
Minimum Start-up:	$ 45,000
Average Start-up:	$ 72,000

How would you like to see your name in *Who's Who in America*? Silly question! Who wouldn't like that kind of recognition? In fact, most people would love to be in a Who's Who directory in their own hometown—even if that town is Tree-in-the-Middle-of-the-Road, Texas.

But alas, most of us aren't listed in a Who's Who. And that means millions of Americans going unrecognized. In some cities, social registers take up some of the slack. But they list only the most prominent local people, including politicians and industry leaders. The majority of successful businesspeople, executives, clergy, civil leaders, etc. are left out.

So Where's the Profit?

At this point, you are probably wondering how one makes money in this business. Well, ask yourself this: if you were listed in a Who's Who, wouldn't you want a copy? And your parents would want a copy—and probably your grandparents, too. Even if the publisher asked $35 or more for a copy, you wouldn't give it a second thought.

Some publishers of local Who's Who directories charge as much as $50 a copy. Experience has shown that sales come in from as many as 80 percent of the people listed. For 10,000 people listed, it's possible to sell 8,000 copies. At $35 per copy, this is a gross of $280,000; net profit before taxes will be almost 50 percent.

Profit Margin Astounding

In addition, the higher the volume or number of listings, the lower your cost. With 50,000 listings, net profit may reach 70 percent of the gross.

It is a simple business to start and operate. All biographies are written by the people listed (they fill out a form) and collected by mail. After your book is printed, all sales are made by mail. All you need is a few form letters and a mailing list.

To start, check with your local library or the editor of your newspaper to see if any book is being published or has been published in your city recently. If there is a book listing only upper-class social names, go ahead. You are interested in everyone.

Trademark Infringement

You probably won't want to use the title *Who's Who* for your book. You could run the risk of trademark infringement—a risk that's not worth the trouble, especially considering the hundreds of alternatives that are just as effective for your purposes.

The Blue Book of Grover County will provide as much class as *Who's Who*. And since the words "who is who" are conversational, and outside trademark protection, you can use the words descriptively in your letters soliciting biographies.

Who to List?

You'll need mailing lists of everyone you wish to list in your book. There are mailing-list brokers and compilers in practically every city. If you don't have one in your area, go to the nearest big city. The brokers there will have a list for your town or county.

You may have to rent several lists to get the names you want. The easiest list to obtain is that of all business owners. These people will comprise the majority of your listings. Doctors, lawyers, and other professionals will be listed in the telephone directories. We doubt that you will be able to find a list of religious leaders, but phone calls will do the trick.

If there is a military base in your area, you will want to include the brass. You will probably have to make a trip to see the commanding officer. Before you go, decide how far down the ranks you want to list.

A list of top company executives may be harder to acquire, though it is readily available in many cities. Most politicians have business interests on the side, so you will get them in the business owners' list. The city and county offices can provide a list of their appointed and elected officials to use as a cross-reference. Don't leave any out. These are your community leaders.

Federal, state, and local civil-service executives should also be included; a list of these people may be obtained from their respective offices.

=== BRIGHT IDEA ===

PUBLISH GREETING CARDS

While you'd have to go far to catch up with the likes of Hallmark, it's not impossible to break into the greeting-card business. In fact, this business may be more accessible than you think.

Whatever else we can say about the eighties, one fact is almost indisputable: stationery improved. Ho-hum graphics, sappy greetings, and cheap paper gave way to clever sentiments, eye-catching illustration, and luxuries like hand printing and exotic paper. Moreover, people are willing to pay for quality. Hand-screened cards sell for as much as $3.50 each.

Many greeting-card entrepreneurs get into the business through art. And indeed, printing one's drawings, paintings, or cartoons on greeting cards is one good way to popularize them. But you don't have to be an artist to be a success in this business. Local talent abounds. If you can coordinate the business end—printing, marketing, distribution, etc.— you can hire artists to do the creative work.

The best strategy for new entrepreneurs seems to be finding an angle. Make your cards smaller, bigger, more elegant, friendlier, funnier, raunchier. We've seen successful ethnic cards, cards for pets(!), foreign-language cards. Using your imagination, wit, and salesmanship, you may find that a wealthy future is in the cards for you.

RENTAL-LIST PUBLISHING

High Net Profit Before Taxes:	$35,000
Average Net Profit Before Taxes:	$28,000
Minimum Start-up:	$17,000
Average Start-up:	$22,500

Almost one third of the people who currently live in rental units will move within the next year. These millions of tenants can provide a lucrative market for an apartment- and home-finding service.

In most states, you don't need to be a real-estate broker to start this kind of service. And better yet, you can end up making more money than the average real-estate salesperson. As long as you know how to present yourself properly, you probably won't have to meet any special requirements or undergo any additional schooling.

If a landlord lists a property with a real-estate broker, he or she pays anywhere from $50 to one month's rent as a finder's fee. With the service we outline here, the landlord doesn't pay a cent.

This service is ideal for prospective tenants who are too busy to shop for a suitable rental—or for those who are looking for an unusual place, have special circumstances that make renting difficult, or are just plain lazy.

How Does It Work?

Let's assume that a couple is looking for new lodgings in your area. They need an apartment with two bedrooms and two baths, since they have a nine-year-old son. In addition, they'd like a garage. And since they are professionals with large wardrobes, lots of closet space is essential.

Immediately, they have two problems. Even though their son is a quiet boy, many places post a straight-out no-children edict. Also—depending on the area—garages may be scarce. As a result, apartment hunting turns out to be a tedious chore, requiring hours and hours of telephoning prospective landlords and driving around to locations.

But suppose they could sit down and scan a list that shows every apartment and house available for rent in the area—a list that not only shows the location, but also every detail they need to know about a place without having to go look at it. A list like this one could save the couple a lot of time and effort—as well as gas and phone calls.

Most landlords leave out important details, requirements, and restrictions when they place ads because extra words cost money. In some cases, they have additional units for rent, but don't list them all in the newspaper ad. Some landlords are difficult to reach as well, making it difficult to find out the information renters need to know.

These are the limitations of regular newspaper advertising. Your service, however, will be designed to provide a compilation on every apartment and home available for rent on any given day, a listing that includes every detail about the rental unit. The rental seeker pays you $25 to $35 once for the opportunity to come by your office every day for up to two years and pick up your updated listing bulletin.

How to Obtain Listings

Most of your listings can be obtained simply by calling each new advertiser every day—apartment managers, private landlords, and real-estate agents. To start, this means a couple of days of steady calling to build up your list. But after this original telephone bout, daily updating should be relatively easy.

Contact every real-estate broker in your area. Many don't advertise rental listings, relying instead on signs and their office location to draw prospective tenants. But once brokers realize you will be advertising their listings for free, they will be eager to cooperate with you. This is true of landlords as well.

Next, if the landlord or broker has a vacancy, ask all of the questions on your listing form. Since you guarantee up-to-the-minute information to prospective tenants, you will have to call periodically to check on whether the unit is still available. Ask clients, landlords, and brokers to call you if they rent a unit so you can remove that listing from your list. A quick phone call from them can save you time.

Low Investment, High Return

Let's turn to the profit picture. In a city of 100,000 people we found not one, but three of these services operating successfully, with annual grosses of $42,814 to $90,682. The one with the lowest gross still netted the absentee owner $12,140 last year. The highest-grossing operation netted the owner over $46,000 in this city; he is doing equally well in three other cities.

The service is currently available in many cities, but we feel it could stand some additional competition. Try covering an area of at least 10,000 rental units per rental service. The chamber of commerce in your city will supply the statistics you need. Just ask them how many rental units there are in the city. A quick scan of the classified ads will let you know how many rental services are operating.

The most appealing part of this business is the ease with which you can set up operations. Your total cash outlay could be as little as $900.

======= BRIGHT IDEA =======

SELF-PUBLISHING

You don't have to be rich or famous to start your own publishing company. If you have a good, marketable idea for a book, you can publish it yourself for about $12,000—and reap the profits for years to come.

Santa Barbara, California, publisher Dan Poynter launched his company, Para Publishing, with the release of a how-to book on parachuting. After years of designing parachutes, Poynter knew the industry well enough to know that no comprehensive book was available on the topic. That book was such a hit that he decided to write additional books— first on hang gliding, and eventually on self-publishing books.

According to Poynter, you can learn just about everything you need to know about publishing along the way. "We try to impress upon people that you can work with other people," he says. "In fact, it's usually a good idea." Bringing writers, editors, or technical experts into the production of your book will enhance its quality and take some of the pressure off you.

Before you set up your typewriter and quit your job, however, Poynter stresses that finding a marketable idea is crucial. A little research can go a long way. Find out who your target market is before you get started, as well as what books are already available and how you can reach your intended audience. A good idea may lead to a glutted market. On the other hand, a seemingly banal subject could have real potential.

"I tell people to write what they know," says Poynter. One man called Poynter to ask for a hot topic in publishing. When he suggested writing about what he knew, the man said, "I'm in real estate: who wants to know about that?" In fact, Poynter notes, hundreds of thousands of real-estate agents around the country want to know about real-estate trends. And so do millions of home buyers. Good subjects abound, Poynter contends—all you have to do is ferret them out.

Free Classified Newspaper Publishing

High Net Profit Before Taxes:	$300,000
Average Net Profit Before Taxes:	$190,000
Minimum Start-up:	$ 61,000
Average Start-up:	$ 90,000

Where do you sell a perfectly good used dishwasher? How do you advertise a roomful of baby furniture? And conversely, where do you look if you're in the market for these items?

In many communities, the answer is in the classifieds. Not the classified section of the regular newspaper, mind you—those ads can cost more than the item for sale. Free classified newspapers fill the gap between time-consuming flea markets and garage sales and daily newspaper ads.

Sell Free Ads!

You can charge a modest fee for advertisements in your paper, or you can do what scores of other successful free papers do: sell ads for free—unless the ad sells. Give four to six short exclusive listings in consecutive issues to each individual who has something for sale. Advertisers feel they're getting something for nothing as well as a convenient way to sell their items. And you get higher profits than you might under other arrangements.

When the item sells, you collect a commission based on the advertised price of the item—not the selling price, which is often bargained down. The commission is payable if an individual decides not to sell and cancels the ad early, or if a person moves or disconnects the phone. An "exclusive" means that if the item is sold or traded in any other way, even through another paper, you still collect.

Papers that operate this way carry from 3,000 to 10,000 listings an issue. Commissions charged are typically 10 percent of the first $100, 5 percent of the second $100, and 1 percent of anything over $200. Usually, the minimum charge is $1.00 to $2.00. A minority of publishers have a maximum commission of $25 to $30.

Many listings are for inexpensive items, but there are also many for big-ticket articles like camera and stereo gear or cars, recreational vehicles, boats, and mobile homes. Prices may be as high as $10,000.

A Unique Approach

The trader approach is entirely different from that used by weekly or monthly throwaways or "shoppers," which are free papers that rely on hard-to-get display ads for profit. These are heavily distributed in limited target areas, usually by bulk mail or delivery people.

Shoppers have been around since the twenties, and under ideal marketing conditions can compete successfully on a price basis with other media—and other shoppers—due to lower operating overheads. But stiff competition means that the failure rate is high.

As the publisher of a trader, you should arrange for a local newspaper distributor to distribute your newspaper. Large-circulation dailies often franchise distribution rights to such companies, which handle all the work involved for a commission on each copy sold. Even if you pay half the newsstand sales volume to such a company, it may be worthwhile in the long run.

Profits Fantastic

We found one classified-only trader in Virginia who grosses nearly $1 million a year and nets an almost unbelievable $235,000 per year! That's a margin of 24 percent—which is remarkable for a publishing operation, where 10-to-15-percent margins are more common.

The Virginia operation is a twenty-eight-page weekly crammed with over 10,000 listings. Its circulation is 20,000 in a market area of about 1.5 million people.

Your operation can produce the same kind of margin after a year or two of operation—depending on market area, frequency of issue, production costs, and other variables.

The average item for sale lists for $300. Of course, there are many low-priced articles, but the average price goes up when you factor in big-ticket items. An average commission of $16 per sale is realistic.

Our research indicates that 26 percent of the items listed in a trader are sold through the paper. This is a higher batting average than that of a typical newspaper classified section, because more of your readers are looking for a specific item.

A salable item is likely to sell in the first three weeks. About 30 percent of the listings are replaced weekly. So in a given month, revenue will come from a combination of current and prior listings. It works out to about $43,000 a month, assuming commissions are collected from 80 percent of the sellers.

Some Ads Are Prepaid

Some categories of advertising are not feasible on a commission basis: business investments, business property or houses for sale or for rent, help or work wanted, swaps, general notices, and the like. People will phone in with requests to run ads like these, especially as the popularity of your publication builds. Accept the ads and run them on a prepaid basis, charging $1.00 per column line (minimum four lines).

Prepaid advertising linage can generate over 10 percent of net income. The Virginia operation brings in $24,000 to $26,000 per year from prepaid advertising.

Another Revenue Source

Newsstand sales of each issue are a secondary source of revenue. Price per copy is set according to the market, the competition, and the distribution costs. The Virginia paper costs $0.50 an issue on the newsstand, but it has been in existence for ten years and is quite popular. Most sell out within a short time after they hit the streets. The price for a smaller paper, especially a new one, might be $0.35.

Most publishers price issues to cover a good part of the production costs. The best you can expect is a break-even situation. A weekly with a circulation of 20,000, priced at $0.45 an issue, would generate $421,000 a year—slightly less than printing costs, assuming only 10 percent return unsold from the news racks.

NEWSLETTER PUBLISHING

High Net Profit Before Taxes:	$128,400
Average Net Profit Before Taxes:	$ 73,800
Minimum Start-up:	$ 2,625
Average Start-up:	$ 9,888

Newsletters represent one of the fastest-growing segments of the communications industry. Why? These days, people are required to process a lot of information. On the job, they read technical publications, how-to manuals, policy handbooks, memos, and reports. At home, they read up on current events, hobbies, fashion, gossip, parenting, careers, trends, or literature. With all this reading, who has time for a life?

Newsletters help keep information manageable. Instead of scanning a dozen trade publications, an executive might read a newsletter that summarizes important information in a brief four pages. A newsletter can also deliver hard-to-find information—the latest about an obscure hobby or highly specialized field. Newsletters tend to be current; since they're fast to produce, they can convey information sooner than most magazines or books can. In short, newsletters are the information form for the nineties—quick, precise, and digestible.

That does not mean, however, that newsletters are no-risk ventures. On the contrary, newsletters have a high mortality rate. Low start-up costs attract a lot of would-be publishers. But it takes advertising and marketing savvy to make a newsletter work. Your choice of topic, methods of advertising, and management skills will all determine the success or failure of your venture.

What Is a Newsletter?

A newsletter is a specialized information service concentrating on in-depth coverage of one topic. The newsletter publisher markets his product to subscribers for whom the newsletter's information is particularly valuable. Inside information is one of the hallmarks of the newsletter trade, and timeliness is of the essence: old news has no value.

Most newsletters are short—two to eight pages are standard. The information is concentrated. There are usually no pictures, no clever graphics, and no advertisements. Subscribers pay for solid information, not professional packaging.

Newsletter subscriptions often cost more than magazines. This is because subscriptions are the sole source of revenue for newsletters, while magazines make money from advertisements. People are willing to pay more for newsletters for reasons we've already covered: they're concise, easy to understand, and focused on a specialized topic. In putting your newsletter together, keep the following questions in mind:

—Is this information intrinsically valuable? For instance, business owners might pay $100 a year to get inside tips on avoiding lawsuits. They probably wouldn't pay that much for monthly tips on keeping the office tidy.

—Does this newsletter provide information subscribers can't get elsewhere? Do you have exclusive interviews? Hard-to-find statistics?

—How does this newsletter save subscribers time and money? One way to gauge this is to calculate the research time you spend putting the newsletter together. If you spend fifty hours combing periodicals and books for each issue, you're providing a timesaving service to readers. Follow up by asking yourself how this information will benefit readers.

To Market, to Market

Once you've found a good topic and a usable format, the next critical issue is marketing. And it *is* critical. Without proper marketing, the most brilliantly conceived newsletter won't get off the ground.

How will you reach your target market? One good way is direct mail. The direct-mail industry probably knows more about you—and every other consumer—than your own mother does. Today's mailing lists are highly specific. You can select subscribers to particular magazines, people who have purchased certain products, consumers in various age groups and income brackets, men only, women only, residents of a certain geographical area. This kind of specificity costs money, however. To start, you'll need a list with about

30,000 prospects. A mailing this size will cost you $10,000 or more and yield about 3,000 subscribers.

Direct mail is not the only option. Take out ads in trade magazines. Speak at industry seminars and hand out free copies to students. Rent a booth at a trade show. Network. In some cases, your market may be hard to reach via conventional media. It's your job to devise a way to reach them, and to make sure that your methods are cost-effective.

Getting Help

By and large, newsletter staffs are small. You'll probably end up doing a lot of the work yourself, especially if your budget is tight. But don't rule out the possibility of hiring help. Many skills go into producing a successful newsletter— from writing and researching to marketing, design, and administration. Few people excel in all these areas. If you're weak at any of these tasks, get help.

Hiring consultants and free-lancers is a good option. Get a professional graphic designer to plan the layout of your newsletter, then follow his or her format on subsequent issues. Or hire a consultant to set up templates on your computer so you can plug in new stories for future issues. Can't crank out enough copy? Contract with a free-lance writer. Help is available in almost every aspect of your business— from bookkeeping to marketing to printing and production.

9

OUT OF THE
ORDINARY

———

================= BRIGHT IDEA =================

PUTTING ON THE SQUEEZE

When Grant Peck and Michael Delaney started shopping for
an interesting new business, their fancies turned to
thoughts of orange juice. What's new and interesting about
orange juice? Nothing, unless it's fresh-squeezed, un-
pasteurized, and lasts fourteen days—like Colorado-based
J. S. Grant's does.

Peck and Delaney developed an interest in fresh-squeezed
juice while working at a Colorado health-food-restaurant
chain. After a little investigating, they discovered that in
1986 orange juice represented $3 billion in annual sales, and
the overall juice industry was doing $9.3 billion a year. They
noticed a trend away from frozen concentrates toward ready-
to-serve products. "People want convenience," Peck says.
"There's been a 30-percent increase in the ready-to-serve
market." At the same time, they witnessed the advent of
"healthy sodas" like Hansen's natural and fruit-juice Crush.
The evidence was in: the time was ripe for a fresh-juice
business.

278

Starting a new juice business is not without its obstacles. One of the biggest drawbacks to fresh juice is its traditionally short shelf life. Peck and Delaney developed a method of sanitation and temperature control that enables them to preserve the juice for fourteen days. The result? J. S. Grant has grown into a multimillion-dollar business in only three short years.

"People are moving away from soda and toward more nutritious products," Peck reports. In response, J. S. Grant has expanded into new flavors (grapefruit, apple, orange/cranberry, apple/cranberry, and lemonade) and hopes to set up nationwide distribution. If these ambitious partners have their way, fruit juice may become the new toast of the beverage industry.

MAIL ORDER

High Net Profit Before Taxes:	$337,500
Average Net Profit Before Taxes:	$ 42,000
Minimum Start-up:	$ 6,000
Average Start-up:	$ 40,000

There's no place like home—especially for shopping. In the past decade, mail order has become an absolute mania for American consumers, making this a $117-billion industry. Thanks to this burgeoning business, you can now shop for everything from Virginia ham to discount panty hose from your living-room sofa. For working people, rural residents, and just plain couch potatoes, mail order is the only way to shop.

Taking the First Steps

Choosing the right type of mail-order business is your first step. While many successful catalogs offer fashion, furniture, and houseware items, you needn't stick to this standard. Today, just about anything can be sold by mail order. And according to experts, it's the untapped markets that are the most lucrative.

One Greensboro, North Carolina, entrepreneur, for example, started a specialty mail-order business selling computerized lists of hard-to-find tableware. Another specializes in photo-related products. Gifts are another popular mail-order item, as are baby products, imported goods, specialty foods, and handmade items.

Which specialty is right for you? Of course, you should pay attention to your own personal tastes. If you specialize in a product that you're enthusiastic about, your work will be easier, more enjoyable, and probably more successful. But also consider who your market will be, and how you will reach that market. Is there a need for the products you want to sell? Is there an easy way to reach them (for instance, through the subscriber list of a trade magazine or the customer list of another catalog)?

"I could have started a hundred businesses, and I would have failed at every one of them if the market wasn't there for the product I wanted to supply," says one mail-order veteran.

Choosing Products and Suppliers

Once you've focused on a theme, your next step is finding suppliers. Trade shows designed for the exhibition of specialized merchandise are an excellent source of products for your catalog. They're also a good place to scout out new trends in your field. Most large cities host trade shows for specific industries such as giftware, crafts, sportswear, or high fashion. The shows are listed periodically during the year—so watch the trade publications carefully to be aware of where and when the shows will be held.

Another good source for catalogers are trade publications themselves. Classified ads contain ad after ad of suppliers, importers, and manufacturers selling the merchandise you're seeking. There are probably more of these publications than you're aware of, so consult your local librarian for a list of trade publications related to your field.

Additional ideas for locating merchandise: visit gift buildings (located in major cities like New York and Los Angeles) or contact your trade association. Before you visit a gift building, find out the requirements of attending. You may need business cards, copies of your catalog, or a wholesale license to shop there.

Getting It in the Mail

Your business can depend on the quality of your catalog, so be prepared to put some thought into design and production. This doesn't mean you have to spend huge sums of money to get a slick, glossy, four-color catalog. In some cases, black-and-white brochures or even simple listings without pictures are adequate. Your requirements will depend on what you're selling. Office supplies, for example, require less dramatic presentation than gifts or exotic lingerie.

Start collecting various catalogs for ideas. Look for type styles, copy, photography, graphics, sizes, and layouts that are particularly effective. You can incorporate many of these ideas into your own work. If you feel you need extra help with design or copywriting, don't hesitate to hire experts. The Direct Marketing Association and the classified section of *Catalog Age* magazine are two sources to check. You can also enlist the help of a mailing house to get your catalogs addressed, sorted, and mailed. Check your Yellow Pages for local companies that provide these services.

Building a Customer Base

You can develop a sizable customer base by following several simple strategies. The simplest is to take names, addresses, and phone numbers from every contact you make and every person who inquires about your services. When you're ready to mail, make sure these people are on your mailing list.

Chances are, inquiries won't be enough to get your business off the ground, however. Experts suggest an initial mailing of at least 100,000 names—far more than you're likely to get without advertising or renting lists. You can take out display ads in magazines to bring in an initial response. This costs relatively little and can elicit a large response.

Additionally, you can rent established mailing lists from publications, mail-order companies, and list compilers. The number and variety of mailing lists available can be overwhelming, so consider hiring a list broker to help you make the right selections. A list broker can provide valuable information about the mailing and marketing, and won't cost you anything (their commissions are paid by the list owners).

There are a host of regulations regarding the mail-order business. As a new operator, you are responsible for meeting these regulations. Check with the post office as well as your state and local governments for requirements in your area.

=================== BRIGHT IDEA ===================

WILD ABOUT WATER

Water isn't just water anymore. We can no longer assume that the liquid flowing out of our sink taps at home or work is good, let alone safe to drink. Every day we are bombarded with news about leaking septic tanks, carelessly treated waste water, and other toxic pollutants that threaten to wipe out a significant portion of our drinking-water supply. That's why so many health-conscious Americans are turning to commercially bottled water to quench their thirst.

To fill the consumer's demand for pure, natural water, companies both big and small are rushing to the nearest natural spring and putting it in bottles. Between 1975 and 1985, sales of bottled water increased by a whopping 300 percent. According to the Beverage Market Corp., preliminary statistics for bottled-water sales will exceed $2 billion in 1988. On the average, for 1988, Americans are expected to have consumed 7.2 gallons of nonsparkling and sparkling water per capita in 1988.

Commercial water bottling is a huge undertaking, as many entrepreneurs have found. You have to find a source, test it, make sure it produces enough water, get it approved for public consumption, and then buy the rights to use it. Add to that packaging, bottling, distributing, and marketing. And, of course, the water has to taste good. Sound daunting? Maybe, but the bottled-water industry shows promising growth for those who have a thirst for a good, clean, profitable business.

Though some water companies have national distribution, most reach a regional clientele. Local flavor can be a strong marketing point, as evidenced by Artesia Waters, Inc., in San Antonio, Texas. Once owner Rick Scoville discovered a potable source, he knew he had a winner on his hands.

Texans, he figured, would rather drink pure Texas water than Perrier water from France. And he was right: he projects 1989 sales at $4 million to $6 million.

EVENT PLANNING

High Net Profit Before Taxes:	$76,500
Average Net Profit Before Taxes:	$49,000
Minimum Start-up:	$ 5,000
Average Start-up:	$10,000

Do you have what it takes to party professionally? If you're detail-oriented, organized, creative, and know how to have fun, you're the ideal candidate for an event-planning business.

Event planning is an especially attractive opportunity. It requires very little start-up capital—many successful planners start from home with just a typewriter, some stationery, and a telephone. Yet top-notch event planners bring in top dollar. Gross annual revenues can go as high as $180,000 for a small operation: we even found a one-person planning business that grossed nearly $300,000 in a single year.

From Weddings to Workplace

Event planners handle every kind of occasion—weddings, conventions, parties, class reunions, trade shows, and fundraisers, to name just a few. Planners handle everything from travel arrangements to entertainment. Typical duties might include booking celebrities, designing exhibits, negotiating with the caterer, and coordinating awards dinners.

"We combine a lot of different resources and services," says one successful planner. "We are not a professional fundraising organization, not a travel agency, not a public-relations agency; nonetheless, we do have expertise in these fields."

Getting Organized

Good event planning is one part creativity and two parts pragmatism. To be effective, you must be able to provide interesting ideas and the follow-up necessary to see that everything comes off without a hitch.

Planning for profits requires a good measure of professionalism. Typical planner's fees are $35 to $100 an hour. In return for this kind of money, clients expect results. You must know how to determine the clients' goals, translate those ideas into a well-run affair, and stay within the prescribed budget (at all costs!).

Seasoned planners stress that although event planning calls for enthusiasm and creativity, it isn't all fun and games. A good planner needs a thorough understanding of budgeting, costs, site selection, marketing, and promotion—not just for getting client parties off the ground, but for getting their businesses started as well.

People Skills a Must

Personality plays a major role in this business. For one thing, you must be levelheaded. Last-minute glitches are almost routine in this business. Your competence will be measured in part by your ability to handle these glitches with grace. For instance, what if your keynote speaker calls from the airport and says she missed her plane? You may be faced with an angry audience—unless you have arranged for a backup speaker.

Maintaining good relationships with suppliers and others in the service industry (hotels, caterers, delivery services, etc.) helps create a steady flow of referrals, which is crucial because traditional advertising media have proven largely ineffective for this industry.

Learning the Trade

Many event planners gain experience on the job—planning weekly meetings or annual parties—before launching their own businesses. If you're a novice, consider joining one of the forty-two local chapters of Meeting Planners International, based in Dallas. The association publishes a monthly magazine, *The Meeting Manager*. Meeting planners with three or more years of experience can take an exam given by the Convention Liaison Council in Washington, D.C., to qualify as certified meeting planners.

Reading about planning, however, will not replace hands-on experience. Learning the basics of this business—by doing legwork for a supplier in the hospitality industry, for example—is the first step toward conquering the organizational challenges and reaping the financial rewards of being a professional event planner.

================ BRIGHT IDEA ================

CABOOSE CONCEPT FINISHES FIRST

Ever wonder what happened to all those wonderful red cabooses that followed every train? Regulations no longer require them, so many are moldering away, forgotten, in train yards. Not everyone, however, is willing to let old cabooses become junk metal.

Ron Lundeen and Ray Lindstrom, two Phoenix entrepreneurs, discovered that these relics can be successfully converted into unusual and luxurious office suites or home add-ons. In 1987, they started the Custom Caboose Company, and as far as they know, they are the first and only customized-caboose-office makers around.

"Ron's the train buff," explains Lindstrom. "He has an extensive collection of toy trains from forty and fifty years ago." Lundeen decided to buy a real caboose, gut it completely, and rebuild it into an office for himself. "I watched him build it," says Lindstrom, "and when it was completed, I thought it was so beautiful, I said, 'Ron, I think we've got a business here!'" The two decided to offer custom-designed cabooses cum offices to the public, using Lundeen's office as a prototype.

It took about four months from the time Lundeen purchased his 1926 Santa Fe caboose in California until the final touches were put on the interior decoration. The process was not without its hitches. For example, moving the twenty-five-ton car from the rails to the industrial park two blocks away where Lundeen planned to put his office took all day, twenty people, and an eighty-ton crane to accomplish. Another obstacle was finding a toilet and sink small enough to fit in the original caboose bathroom (that search took six months).

The finished office combines the height of modern conveniences with faithful restoration of the caboose's original decor. Along with elegant office furniture, Lundeen's office/prototype also features a microwave, refrigerator, wet bar, and personal computer, as well as air-conditioning and heating. A television, stereo, and security system are also included in the package price. A package price of $99,000 includes the car, complete interior and exterior restoration, and delivery to the nearest rail siding.

PRIVATE INVESTIGATING

High Net Profit Before Taxes:	$120,000
Average Net Profit Before Taxes:	$ 75,000
Minimum Start-up:	$ 6,500
Average Start-up:	$ 20,000

Though television shows don't necessarily portray the real life-style or job functions of the contemporary PI, they are one of the reasons this industry is growing at a fast pace.

According to Ralph Thomas, founder and director of the National Association of Investigative Specialists, the number of investigators in the United States is growing at a rate of 10 to 15 percent annually. Today, Thomas estimates that there are about 26,000 PI agencies throughout the United States. And with the average agency employing 2.5 investigators, that adds up to over 65,000 PIs in the nation. But that doesn't mean competition is getting stiff. Thomas says, "There's still plenty of business for everyone."

Hot on the Trail

All that business means that PIs are bringing in big profits with their investigative talents. Thomas claims that today's average agency grosses about $75,000 to $100,000. And since overhead is low in this business, an independent PI can bring in net profits of approximately 75 percent.

One reason for this growth is a new diversity in the types

of cases PIs are taking on. Once hired mainly to spy on erring spouses, private investigators now locate missing persons, investigate insurance-fraud cases, find missing heirs, track down people who have skipped out on loans, do background checks on prospective employees, find people's hidden assets, and screen potential tenants. And, of course, they still spy on erring spouses.

Clients come in both the individual and corporate varieties. Private citizens often use PIs to locate lost loved ones. And insurance companies, banks, blue-chip companies, lawyers, and doctors are all-starting to clue in to the fact that PIs can save them a lot of time and money. This expanding corporate market translates into big profits for PIs.

Sometimes, a PI doesn't even need a client to solve a case and make a profit. PIs can check courthouse records to look at files of missing heirs and unclaimed property that, according to the federal government, amounts to more than $25 billion in unclaimed assets. The investigator then finds the missing heir or property owner, notifies them that they may be entitled to the assets, and charges them a finder's fee of up to 50 percent of the property value.

You Won't Look Like Magnum

Forget the image of a gun-toting PI pounding the pavement and knocking on doors to get information. Today's PI is more likely to wield a phone or a personal computer, and spends his or her hours at the county courthouse.

Knowing how to find a missing person (or someone who's skipped bail) is a definite skill. Checking public records, following up on leads, and sometimes playing a fictional part are just a few of the seasoned investigator's techniques. For most detective work, you needn't be big, burly, and a good shot to succeed. Curiosity, perseverance, and tenacity are far more important. In some areas, you will need a license to be a private investigator. Check with your state and local governments for any licensing requirements.

A PI's Work Is Never Done

The concept of 9-to-5 simply isn't part of a PI's vocabulary. Following a subject can easily take you into the wee hours of the morning, as well as into another state. As a PI, you control your own hours, but you also must work whenever you're needed—often during everyone else's off hours.

Still, the work can be fun and exciting. Solving a case can be a real kick even for seasoned professionals. "You can hear one of our investigators a mile away when they find someone," says one successful agency owner. "They get so excited."

IMPORT AND EXPORT

(Due to the wide range of variations in import and export businesses, profit and start-up figures are not available.)

The world market is simply too vast to be ignored. Foreign businesses are anxious to tap into the American market. And increasingly, American companies are interested in doing business abroad. Imports and exports account for billions of dollars in sales every year. Yet hundreds of thousands of companies that could export goods and services don't—a huge potential market.

Importing and exporting is not a typical business. It involves dealing with such intangibles as your services as an intermediary, your knowledge of markets, banking, and shipping, and your ability to match producers with purchasers. This may sound complex, but with the right combination of research, resources, and study, you can learn the ins and outs of this business. Your success will be directly proportional to your skill as a salesperson and your perseverance in initiating contacts.

What Is the Import-Export Business?

The owner of a men's clothing store may purchase some suits from Korea—thereby importing goods—but he is not in the import business. He is in the retail clothing business and just happens to be purchasing foreign goods.

Likewise, a ladies' earring manufacturer that sells merchandise to a department store in Bonn, West Germany, is not in the export business, either. It is an earring-manufacturing business with a European customer.

The business of import and export consists of matching buyers in one country with sellers in another. Generally speaking, exporting goods from the United States is usually more profitable than importing. Moreover, it usually entails fewer capital-investment and risk problems and requires less selling. Unless you have a specific opportunity in mind, exporting is the safer bet to start. You can always start importing as well down the road.

Help at Every Turn

If you decide to become an exporter, there's plenty of help to be had. The U.S. government is eager to help American companies export their goods and services and has a wealth of information and advice for would-be exporters. Call the U.S. Department of Commerce for more information.

The same is true of foreign governments. Their interest in getting goods in their countries exported to the United States is keen. They may be able to supply you with information, advice, and even leads. Freight companies are another good source of information and advice. After all, your success could mean additional business for them.

Money to Be Made

Importing and exporting is a tricky business. While you can be successful in this field, it won't happen without a good deal of dedication, considerable time, and expert selling. Until you develop a network of contacts, breaking through can be tough. Good opportunities certainly exist, but you must be able to put the right components together.

The most knowledgeable field officers we interviewed estimated that small exporters and importers were netting $40,000 and up per year, after they'd become established. A handful of top-notch dealers were netting medium six-figure incomes. You can make a nice sum of money in this business with a small cash investment. Your biggest expenditure will probably be in time, effort, and getting a good grasp of the techniques of international trading.

LARGE-SIZE JEWELRY

Here's an idea for people who think there's no room for improvement in the jewelry business. Sizzle Marketing and Promotions, Inc., in Warwick, Rhode Island, recently introduced three lines of fashion jewelry designed specifically with the large-size woman in mind. According to Sizzle's president Lisa Weingeroff, large women have a difficult time finding jewelry that fits.

"Chokers literally choke these women," Weingeroff says. "And regular costume earrings will not fit because either the posts are not long enough or the clips are not big enough."

The three jewelry lines include the moderately priced Plus-Size Jewelry (tm), the high-fashion Lisa-Michael (tm) collection and the Kenneth Jay Lane Plus-Size Jewelry (tm) collection. Kenneth Jay Lane's claim to fame is having designed First Lady Barbara Bush's 12-millimeter, triple-strand, faux pearl necklace. Sizzle is marketing the Plus-Size Jewelry Collection through wholesalers and BBW (Big Beautiful Woman).

PAPER COLLECTING AND RECYCLING

High Net Profit Before Taxes:	$60,000
Average Net Profit Before Taxes:	$38,000
Minimum Start-up:	$13,000
Average Start-up:	$23,000

While the throwaway society is busy tossing out its cardboard boxes, newspapers, and other paper goods, you can capitalize on its wastefulness.

We followed one entrepreneur around as he dug through piles of discarded waste at various industrial and business locations. We felt sorry for him—until we discovered how much money he was making. By gathering only certain grades of wastepaper and cardboard, he could sell it by the ton to recycling plants. He grossed over $120,000 in a year.

Another paper recycler we found quit his job as a produce clerk, began a collection route, and grossed $65,000 his first year, with a net after tax of $20,000. Both started with no more than an old pickup truck and some inside knowledge about the market and supply sources.

Paper Is Everywhere

The bureaucratic and manufacturing explosions of the twentieth century, along with the increasing scarcity of natural resources, have created the perfect conditions for this business. The prices paid for reusable paper have risen tremendously during the past few years. A large office can go through a veritable forest of paper goods in a single work week.

The Market Is Waiting

The age-old, relatively simple process of paper manufacturing is capital- and labor-intensive, and each step of the manufacturing process adds to the cost. This process goes like this: trees are cut down and mashed to pulp. The pulp is put into gigantic blenders with water and other chemicals and beaten to a gooey dough. The dough is spread out on huge screens to dry, and the result is paper.

The only way to get cheaper paper is to cut back somewhere along the way—and that's where recycling comes in. A paper mill using recycled paper eliminates the capital costs of felling and replanting trees, pulverizing trees into a pulp, and shipping the pulp to the mills. By using recycled paper waste, a manufacturer can cut the cost of a ream of standard twenty-pound bond paper as much as 45 percent.

You can make money helping others solve their waste-disposal problems. A savvy paper recycler can set up accounts with local businesses and government agencies to haul away paper trash for a percentage of the take.

For example, a 110-store chain in the northeast threw out 250 tons of corrugated containers each week. It cost $2 million a year to dispose of it until a paper recycler offered to take it away, splitting the gross sixty–forty. The management of the chain store quickly saw the advantage: it earned

$390,000 from its paper refuse, while the knowledgeable recycler pocketed a gross of $585,000 from this account alone.

Promotion Comes Naturally

Obtaining free publicity is a snap in this business. Radio and television stations are required by law to devote a certain amount of airtime to public service. Recycling is an ideal topic for editors looking for "meaty" stories. Remember, recycling is not only the business of the future, it's a community service. You're saving trees. You're helping to keep the environment clean. You're putting money not just in the taxpayer's pocket, but in your own at the same time.

=========================== BRIGHT IDEA ===========================

MONOGRAMMING SERVICE

For those of you who think of monogramming as just so many towels, this burgeoning industry has some news for you. Monogramming provides a lucrative, creative opportunity to make profits from your home with a modest initial investment.

Of course, monogramming still adds a special touch to shirts, towels, baby blankets, gym bags, and scores of other items. But there are dozens of uses for monogramming that most of us take for granted. For instance, military stripes and name tags must be monogrammed. Work uniforms and team uniforms require personalization. Wholesale accounts from makers and distributors of these garments can bring in sizable profits. One monogramming franchise landed a telecommunications account worth $80,000.

What if you can't sew a stitch? Modern monogramming equipment is computerized. And while it does require some training to use properly, it doesn't require extensive sewing experience.

Starting a successful monogramming business will depend partly on your local market and your marketing abilities. List potential customers before you start up to get a feeling for what your community needs. Also, consider offering auxiliary services like alterations, dry cleaning, and silk screening to boost profits.

════════════ BRIGHT IDEA ════════════

PIGS BY THE TAIL

On the bright side, he won't chew your furniture or bark at the neighbors. And there's something about the pitter patter of cloven hooves on your linoleum. It's a pet. It's a business. It's—a Chinese potbelly miniature pig.

Granted, pigs aren't the commonest of pets. But according to breeder Kiyoko Hancock, they make ideal companions. "The gentle pigs can walk on a leash, heel, do tricks, and certainly behave in public," she says.

They sell pretty well, too. Hancock has turned her porcine penchant into a full-time breeding business. Since February 1988, she has bred and sold forty of the snub-nosed creatures at her eight-acre gentleman's ranch in Pescadero, California. A single piglet sells for between $1,500 and $2,500; a breeding female can fetch up to $10,000.

Hancock is doing her part to make the pigs more popular as well. Her experiences with her own pig, Arnold, inspired her to write and publish her own children's book, *Pig Tales, the Adventures of Arnold, the Chinese Potbelly Miniature Pig*. Additionally, she has written two other children's books and a newsletter called *Pig Tales*.

SWAP-MEET PROMOTING

High Net Profit Before Taxes:	$148,000
Average Net Profit Before Taxes:	$124,000
Minimum Start-up:	$ 13,000
Average Start-up:	$ 16,000

For millions of Americans, swap meets and flea markets are the last of the truly great shopping experiences. Nowhere else is the merchandise so diverse, so unexpected—and so cheap. As malls become increasingly homogenized (sometimes you can scarcely tell one from the next) and retail goods become more and more exorbitant, the idea of finding a vintage dress for $0.79 or a toaster oven for $5.00 is a real joy.

Swap meets (or flea markets) are gatherings of small-time merchants and amateur sellers. Depending on the meet, about 20 to 30 percent of the vendors are people who just want to empty their garages, basements, attics, and homes of items they no longer use but are still usable.

The rest of the vendors are either part-time merchants who buy seconds or closeout, distressed, auctioned, or surplus merchandise—or people who are marketing their own handicrafts. The swap-meet selection is so endless and varied that many people attend for sheer entertainment—not that they don't wind up bringing home their share of the booty.

You can see bargains at a swap meet that you won't find anywhere else. Some of the merchants buy regular products at normal wholesale prices, but maintain a low markup because their overhead is so low. We found one dealer retailing a $1.25 can of spray paint for $0.50—and he was making $0.20.

$1.5-Million Profit

The most successful operator we found was grossing over $1.4 million per year on space rentals and admissions fees. He was grossing another $850,000 on food and snack-shop sales. After all wages and state and federal taxes were paid, the gross profit on space and admissions came to an excess of $1,270,000. The gross profit after product cost and wages on food sales topped $630,000 per year.

There are few businesses that can show gross profits of 83 percent like this! And such profits are not unusual. Expenses you must subtract to ascertain the net profit before taxes include insurance, maintenance products and labor, phone utilities, office supplies, printing, legal, accounting, advertising, and depreciation.

In this swap meet, the hidden expenses add up to a scant $50,000 a year. After subtracting 100 percent of the absentee ownership's management salaries, the net profit before taxes is still over $1.5 million a year.

The Story Behind the Name

The term "swap meet" was originated to ward off business-license inspectors and sales-tax collectors. After a while, many cities decided that strict enforcement of license laws would close any swap meet down. They decided instead to extract a large license from the promoters to cover all the merchants participating. The policy varies, however, from city to city. Some cities don't bother to ask for additional fees.

Get Started Now

We found one small operator who holds his meet each Sunday in the small packaging lot (100 by 120 feet) of a manufacturer next to a main thoroughfare. His only advertising is 10,000 handbills he distributed on cars and tacked to poles in the area. The first few weeks he barely broke even, but after three months he was operating on Saturday and Sunday, with sixty spaces rented at $4.00 each—and was netting $365 from rentals and over $100 from the sale of cold drinks, a one-worker operation.

His start-up expenses were rent, $35 a day; insurance for three months, $125; initial printing of handbills, $135; cloth banner signs, $38; cleanup brooms, $12; and chalk marker for spaces, $8.00. After the first week, he cut his handbill distribution to 5,000 pieces, which reduced his weekly operating expenses to $105, not including the setup costs for the cold-drink stand. Since he operated outside the city limits, he didn't need a business license.

Negotiate with Drive-in Theaters

Drive-in theaters are the most common sites for swap meets. So unless you already own a drive-in theater, you'll have to negotiate a rental arrangement with the owner. Your key arguments are that a hefty portion of a drive-in's profit comes from snack-shop sales (the profit margin will be almost as high as that obtained while showing a film), and that a drive-in stands useless during the daylight hours, drawing no income. This should make any owner open to suggestions for making daytime profits.

Of course, the drive-in owner could promote his or her own swap meet. But most are reluctant, feeling it will require a substantial investment to get a meet rolling in a new area—not to mention the investment in time and trouble. If you agree to finance, organize, and promote the operation, the owner has nothing to lose and everything to gain. You can offer to split all the profits from food sales, rentals, and admissions. All the owner has to do is make the property available. Or you can take all the income from rentals and admissions while the owner takes all the income from food sales—each of you handling expenses related to his or her division. You provide the promotion and the owner the property.

Before you start, get a lawyer to draw up a solid contract to protect your long-range investment. Less promotion will be needed once the meet is established.

Location

Lower-income areas full of bargain hunters are a good choice. However, this rule doesn't always apply. The Rose Bowl Swap Meet is among the largest in the country: it's located just a stone's throw from stately Pasadena homes.

Swap meets work best in cities with at least 250,000 people. Get the biggest lot you can find so you'll have room to grow (there's really no disadvantage to having a big lot). Allow plenty of space for vendors to park their cars and display their wares. If your meet is small to start out with, cluster all the vendors in one space and use the rest for customer parking. As your meet grows, you may fill your entire lot with vendors and have to let customers fend for their own parking.

========= BRIGHT IDEA =========

BREW YOUR OWN BEER

Today's upscale consumers are making an important discovery: you can't wash down gourmet pizza or hand-cut potato chips with a regular old brewski. Boutique beer is in—and for brew-minded entrepreneurs, this trend couldn't be cooler.

Deregulation of the brewing industry in the late seventies and early eighties gave today's microbrewers the chance to make their marks on America's beer industry. Using time-tested techniques, quality ingredients, and a good measure of individuality, small breweries like Anchor Steam in San Francisco and Dock Street in Philadelphia are turning out products with character and taste.

Starting a brewery isn't a cheap proposition. Industry experts estimate start-up costs at about $2 million. But consumer interest is growing, and the future looks bright for new ventures. Variations on the theme are also an option; for instance, brewpubs are opening up around the country. These establishments brew their own house beer downstairs and sell it upstairs in a publike atmosphere. Start-up costs for these ventures are considerably less than for a real brewery (figure about $300,000), but the appeal is much the same.

As Americans continue turning on to upscale beer—both the boutique and the imported varieties—this market should continue to grow. In this business, as one successful microbrewer points out, even mistakes are enjoyable—down to the very last drop.

ART-SHOW PROMOTING

High Net Profit Before Taxes:	$118,000
Average Net Profit Before Taxes:	$ 90,000
Minimum Start-up:	$ 11,000
Average Start-up:	$ 14,000

You don't have to know the difference between a Renoir and a Picasso. In fact, you don't need to know about art at all to put on a successful art show. Not only that, but it pays far better to be a promoter than it does to be an artist.

One operator we contacted held his first art shows in parking lots on Saturdays and Sundays. He netted over $30,000 a year from his two-day-a-week enterprise, and his cash outlay at any one time never exceeded $500.

His expenses included rent for his location (the parking lot of a fancy dinner restaurant next door) at $100 per weekend, liability insurance to protect him and the lot owner, and a small amount of promotional printing.

He attracted an average of 54 artists a day and has had as many as 100 on hand to display their wares. Each craftsman paid him $4.00 per day for a display area about the size of one parking space, ten by twenty feet. In addition, they agreed to pay him 10 percent of the price of any art object or painting they sold that day. Art galleries, by the way, charge a minimum commission of 20 percent, and often as high as 50 percent.

On the average day, sales totaled $2,000; they reached $5,000 a few times. Our promoter's average weekly gross was about $732, with a net of $600 after expenses.

Subsequently, a bank bought the parking lot that our operator was using, forcing him to use a smaller parking lot across the street. This move reduced the number of displays that he could accommodate. Nevertheless, he continued to fill up each weekend.

Second Case History

This story is not unique. In a pleasure-boat harbor, another promoter has been operating with comparable success. The area is an exclusive high-rent district catering to the wealthy and the young jet-set crowd. It is also something of a tourist attraction, with many unusual restaurants and a beautiful marina. It is, in short, the ideal setting for an art sale.

This promoter sets up his show in the parking lot of a medical center that's closed on weekends. He averages twenty-six artists per day, and total art sales are about $2,000 a day. His weekly gross on commissions is $556. His rent for the parking lot is only $100 per week, which means he maintains a healthy net.

Expenses Are Negligible

Most property owners will request that you take out insurance on the property you will be using—these costs will vary from area to area and company to company. Besides a month's rent in advance, some incidental printing costs, and a business license, this is your only expense.

Many promoters don't allow the display of manufactured arts and crafts—they feel these cheapen the overall effect. This business is oriented toward customers with taste. The higher the quality of art displayed, the higher the gross sales are.

=================== BRIGHT IDEA ===================

EVERYDAY ODDITIES

Dreaming up a new and useful product is a difficult—and risky—proposition. There are no guarantees that the public will like, or even understand, your new invention. So many new entrepreneurs are getting into business with jazzed-up versions of old standbys.

For instance, consider the case of Adrian and Toody Maher of Fun Products, Inc., in Berkeley, California. They took the basic telephone and turned it into a work of art. "There are approximately 2.2 phones per household in America," says Toody. "That's a large market, and everybody wants a unique phone."

Indeed, Fun Phones put ordinary units to shame. They're made of see-through Lexan plastic with multicolored component parts and five orange-and-green neon lights that flash when the phone rings. Even the cords feature multicolored stripes and patterns.

Who needs a decorator phone? No one. But with $8.5 million in annual sales, Fun Products is demonstrating that form can be as marketable as function—a lesson the Mahers learned as distributors of the Swatch Watch. "With Fun Products, we want to accomplish the same goal by moving through the house redesigning products whose designs are taken for granted," says Toody. "We believe that people should be able to have fun with the products they use."

FINDING PRODUCTS FOR FLEA MARKETS

High Net Profit Before Taxes:	$35,000
Average Net Profit Before Taxes:	$10,000
Minimum Start-up:	$ 100
Average Start-up:	$ 500

What sells at the nation's 2,000-plus flea markets and swap meets? Goods of all kinds—from antiques and collectibles to clothing and jewelry. We talked to vendors making $600 in a single week, and they only worked four days a week to make it.

You don't have to sell every useful item in your home to cash in on the flea-market boom. Gather your own inventory and become a flea-market regular. On average, regular flea-market sellers net $100 a day and more for their trouble.

Antiques Sell Best

Antique dealers can net $300 to $500 a day selling at swap meets and flea markets. The market is there if the goods are worthwhile. You can spend two days a week selling at meets and markets and the rest of the week collecting and buying items to sell.

Jeans, dresses, blouses, and shirts are second highest in the profit category. Most vendors claimed daily profits in the $100-to-$300 range. Jewelry dealers came in third with estimated sales of $100 to $200 a day. Costume jewelry seemed to outsell the more expensive items. Other items we spotted: new (probably homemade) furniture, auto parts, sunglasses, and athletic shoes.

$30,000 Annually Working Four Days a Week

Those selling cast-off and collected items were usually more amateurish in their display and sales efforts. They weren't making much money. Nevertheless, we found an occasional hustler who was pulling steady high profits on junk items.

One engineer who had been laid off claimed he had found a new niche and would never return to engineering. He told us that making $600 per week in less than four days was a lot better than he was doing in an office.

Anyone can make money at a flea market or swap meet, provided that he or she has the right products at the right prices.

Stay away from electrically powered items such as radios, phonographs, irons, and toasters. They don't sell well, and you'll have to demonstrate that they work before you can sell them, which takes too much time. Besides, unless you get them for nothing, you won't make much money per piece. The exception is items that have an antique look. You can pick them up for next to nothing and make a nice profit.

If you buy anything new or as a closeout, try to get it at 75 to 90 percent off regular or current lowest retail price. Remember, you must sell the item for at least 20 percent below the lowest retail price to have a fast turnover.

Your Products Must Be Cheap or Unusual

Most regular flea-market customers are price-conscious bargain hunters. The rest are looking for something special or unique. Therefore, you must offer easily recognized cheap prices or you must stock unusual items.

How unusual? At one flea market, we saw one vendor selling globs of clear Plexiglas that had apparently been miscast in a plastics factory. Each time we checked, a crowd was examining and buying these defective scraps of plastic. Apparently, no item is too unusual.

IN THE SWING

At first, professional carpenter Bob Beardon thought building swing sets was child's play. After a quick tour of the local stores, Beardon and his wife, Nancy, realized that commercially available sets weren't what they wanted. So Bob constructed a simple A-frame swing set himself using seasoned pine boards and a few nuts and bolts.

As the local kids discovered the swing set, requests started pouring in from friends and neighbors. Bob found himself building similar sets around the neighborhood. Then he and Nancy realized that there might be a commercial market for their product. After discussing the idea with Nancy's sister Jean and her husband, Charlie Schappet, the four became business partners and Woodset, Inc., was born.

Woodset is part of the growing business of building children's play structures. Whether they're sold through retail outlets or custom-constructed on-site, quality wooden swing sets, slides, and jungle gyms are becoming the play sets of choice for safety- and quality-conscious parents. Woodset's success is proof of the trend: they employ fifty-five people and sell 3,000 swing sets and additions each year.

Partner Jean Schappet stresses, though, that run-of-the-mill products won't fly in the upscale market. "All of us are genuinely interested in the safety of our children and in providing challenging play equipment that suits a growing child's needs," she says. In addition to maintaining high standards, Woodset puts a strong emphasis on innovation. "When we founded this firm, we had a vision of giving children the safest, most durable, and most fascinating play sets possible," Schappet continues. "We have come a long way in that direction, but there are still improvements we can make in both the product and the business."

CRAFT BUSINESSES

High Net Profit Before Taxes:	$39,000 plus
Average Net Profit Before Taxes:	$29,000
Minimum Start-up:	$ 4,300
Average Start-up:	$ 9,500

Even if you have no artistic ability or special knowledge, you can join the entrepreneurs who transformed simple craft making into a billion-dollar industry.

There are scores of people grossing $100,000 or more annually by selling their crafts at craft fairs, retail stores, swap meets, and through direct mail. These operators report nets in the 35-to-40-percent range.

Start-up costs can be as low as $1,100. Materials range from fine hardwoods to a little glitter and some glue. We found one man who converted old tin cans, wax, and cotton string into a profitable candle business. Just by selling at swap meets and fairs, one woman was grossing $400,000 every year with her hand-tooled belt business. Then there was the shrewd operator who was importing wooden boxes at a cost of $0.50 each, decorating them with paint, and selling them for $15.

Simple to Make

Though some crafts really do require expert skill, many are surprisingly easy to learn. So what if you're all thumbs? Even the most crudely constructed crafts can sell—just substitute the word "primitive" for crude and you'll get the idea. Anything that's unique, not mass-produced, is a natural in today's market.

Handmade Is In!

No one wants something that looks like everyone else's. That's why factory-made clothing, jewelry, accessories (even furniture) are being frowned upon in favor of handmade items. Witness the recent popularity of southwestern furniture and decorative items. Handmade earrings and necklaces abound in craft shops and jewelry departments across the country. Even personalized clothing is selling—sometimes in the clothing departments of the most expensive department stores.

The market for crafts is almost unlimited, and new outlets open up every day. For starters, there are more than 6,000 craft fairs held each year. Along with this marketing network, there are county fairs, state fairs, gift shops, boutiques, swap meets, and major department stores as potential outlets for your goods. The possibilities are practically endless.

Market Research Reveals Taste

Find out what customers want before you get started. Ask yourself: (1) Is there a need for my particular craft? (2) Can I make this unique, compared to other versions of the craft? (3) Can I possibly sell this craft?

One shrewd operator in Iowa answered yes to all these questions. He decided to make candles because they were popular, but he wanted something to make his different. He thought up the idea of personalized candles that would commemorate some important date: a graduation, a birthday, a wedding anniversary, or a promotion. He got some old lead type forms from a printer, filled them with wax, and glued these onto his standard inventory of candles. He sold the result for $10. His product cost? A mere $2.00.

Build Your Capital As You Build Your Crafts

A big advantage to selling crafts is that this kind of business is often self-amortizing. If you begin with $100 worth of lumber for country pine items and create $1,000 worth of products, you can then buy $700 or $800 and greatly increase your production.

=========== BRIGHT IDEA ===========

A REAL STEP UP

Sometimes thinking creatively just means being literal. Michigan entrepreneur John R. McDowell wanted to give his son a footstool for his 1985 bachelor party, so he nailed a few fake feet onto a seat, laced up a pair of athletic shoes, and called it a gift. His son got such a kick out of the joke that McDowell decided to try it out as a real product.

He made a few stools for the Oakland Hills Country Club in Pontiac, Michigan. When the U.S. Open was held at their golf course, the stool made national television. Sportscaster Jim McKay placed one of the stools at the eighteenth hole. By the end of the match, the pro shop had taken over sixty orders over the phone. And so Foot Stools Unlimited was born.

During 1986, its first full year in business, the firm sold about $150,000 worth of footstools. In 1987, sales escalated to $200,000. Due to licensing agreements with the National Football League, major league baseball, and the National Basketball Association, 1988 sales zoomed to almost $300,000.

=========== BRIGHT IDEA ===========

PAMPERED-PET PRODUCTS

A dog's life used to be simple. He slept in a makeshift doghouse, wore dime-store collars, and—well, smelled like a dog. No more. Every dog has its day, and that day is today. The same goes for cats, birds, and fish. Upscale pet products are selling like hotcakes. Animal lovers spent $3.8 billion on pets and pet accessories in 1988, and at least $8.2 billion on dog and cat food, according to the Western World Pet Supply Association.

In recent years, we've reported on designer dogwear (made from alligator and zebra prints), futuristic domed doghouses, gourmet pet treats, and even designer-inspired pet perfumes. As New Jersey manufacturer Carolyn Parrs, cofounder of Poochi Canine Couture, points out, pet owners are spending hundreds, sometimes thousands, of dollars on pedigreed pets—why spoil the effect with drab accessories and ordinary treats?

At the Doggie Deli in Chicago, pets get more than food—they get service. In addition to being a "complete department store" for pets, Doggie Deli also sports a restaurant, complete with red-checked tablecloths. What's on the menu? All natural foods with no sugar, salt, or preservatives. And for that special birthday boy or girl, there are bone-shaped cakes in chicken and liver flavors.

Until recently, pet supplies and accessories were merely functional. Now that style is a consideration, consider putting your designing talents to work on bird cages, fish tanks, scratching posts for cats. And don't overlook nutrition: pet owners want food that makes their dogs healthier, their cats livelier, their rabbits friskier, and their fish brighter (yes, that's right, brighter). As more and more upscale pet products enter the market each year, there's a whole new meaning to the term "haute dog."

165 Guides to Help You Start Your Own Business

ANIMAL-ORIENTED BUSINESSES

Business Guide No.	Reg. Price/Sub. Disc.
1033. Pet Hotel & Grooming Service	$69.50/59.50
1007. Pet Shop	$69.50/59.50

APPAREL BUSINESSES

Business Guide No.	Reg. Price/Sub. Disc.
1161. Children's Clothing Store	$69.50/59.50
1272. Large-Size Women's Apparel Store	**$29.50**
1152. Lingerie Shop	$69.50/59.50
1290. ``Sweats''-Only Retailing	$69.50/59.50
1043. T-Shirt Shop	$69.50/59.50
1229. Used/Consigned Clothing	$69.50/59.50
1333. Women's Accessories Store	$69.50/59.50
1107. Women's Apparel Shop	$69.50/59.50

AUTOMOTIVE BUSINESSES

Business Guide No.	Reg. Price/Sub. Disc.
1076. Car Wash	$69.50/59.50
1268. Cellular Phone Service	$69.50/59.50
1146. Detailing, Automobile	$69.50/59.50 †
1224. Limousine Service	$69.50/59.50
1054. Oil-Change, 10-Minute	$69.50/59.50
1197. Parts Store, Auto	$69.50/59.50
1018. Sales, Consignment	**$29.50**
1108. Used-Car Rental Agency	$69.50/59.50
2330. Used Car Sales	$69.50/59.50 ‡
2329. Vehicle Leasing	$69.50/59.50 ‡

What's inside an Entrepreneur How-to Business Guide:

Imagine having a group of business owners unselfishly confide the details of their success in the kind of business you want to start. They reveal profits and operating costs. They share their solutions to typical problems. They give you their own secrets for making the business "hum".

That's what it's like inside an Entrepreneur Business Guide. You get inside information compiled, analyzed and categorized by our staff and put in a form that's easy to read and understand. It gives you the equivalent knowledge of many years of experience in your new business even though you're just starting out.

Each Guide is approx. 200 pages in length, and comes full tabbed for easy reference in its own handsome, vinyl-covered loose leaf binder.

YOU LEARN–

■ The profit potential for this business ■ The specific start-up costs ■ The size and scope of the market ■ How many hours a week it will take ■ How to easily manage this type of business ■ Site selection and lease negotiation ■ What kind of equipment you may need ■ Anticipated sales volume ■ Sample floor layout of your operation ■ How and where to buy supplies ■ How to set prices ■ How to set up an accounting system ■ Licenses and permits you may need and where to get them ■ How to hire and set up payroll when you're ready ■ How to advertise and promote your type of business.

Each guide comes with an unconditional 90-day money back guarantee (from date of purchase, less shipping and handling).

CALL TOLL FREE 1-(800) 421-2300
in California 1-(800) 352-7449

COMPUTER-ORIENTED BUSINESSES

Business Guide No.	Reg. Price/Sub. Disc.
2335. Bookkeeping Service	$69.50/59.50
1221. Consulting & Temporary-Help Service,	$69.50/59.50
1288. Desktop Publishing	$69.50/59.50
2333. Diet & Meal Planning	$69.50/59.50
1084. Hardware Store, Computer	$69.50/59.50
1265. Home Computer, Making Money With a	$69.50/59.50
1237. Information Broker	$69.50/59.50
1256. Repair Service, Computer	$69.50/59.50
1253. Software Locator Service	$69.50/59.50
1261. Software Store	$69.50/59.50
2332. Tax Preparation Service	$69.50/59.50

CRAFT & MANUFACTURING BUSINESSES

Business Guide No.	Reg. Price/Sub. Disc.
1304. Craft Businesses	$64.50/54.50
1262. PVC Furniture Mfg	$64.50/54.50

EMPLOYMENT SERVICES

Business Guide No.	Reg. Price/Sub. Disc.
1051. Employment Agency	$69.50/59.50
1228. Executive Recruiting Service	$69.50/59.50
1260. Resume Writing & Career Counseling	$69.50/59.50
1189. Temporary-Help Service	$69.50/59.50

FAST-FOOD BUSINESSES

Business Guide No.	Reg. Price/Sub. Disc.
1270. Chicken, Flame-Broiled	**$29.50**
1083. Cookie Shop	$69.50/59.50
1126. Donut Shop	$69.50/59.50
1073. Hamburger/Hot Dog Stand	$69.50/59.50
1187. Ice Cream Store	$69.50/59.50
1056. Mobile Restaurant/ Sandwich Truck	**$29.50**
1006. Pizzeria	$69.50/59.50
1279. Restaurant Start-Up	$69.50/59.50
1079. Yogurt (Frozen) Shop	$69.50/59.50

FOOD & SPIRITS, RETAIL

Business Guide No.	Reg. Price/Sub. Disc.
1158. Bakery	$69.50/59.50
1202. Coffee & Tea Store	$69.50/59.50
1173. Convenience Food Store	$69.50/59.50
1296. Health-Food/Vitamin Store	$69.50/59.50
1024. Liquor Store	$69.50/59.50
1295. Muffin Shop	**$29.50**

HOMEBASED BUSINESSES

Business Guide No.	Reg. Price/Sub. Disc.
1278. Bed & Breakfast Inn	$69.50/59.50
1288. Desktop Publishing	$69.50/59.50
1258. Freelance Writing	$69.50/59.50
1306. Gift Basket Service	$69.50/$59.50
1265. Home Computer, Making Money With	$69.50/59.50
1092. Import & Export	$69.50/59.50
1015. Mail-Order Business	$69.50/59.50
1308. Silk Plants	$67.50/59.50 †

HOME FURNISHINGS

Business Guide No.	Reg. Price/Sub. Disc.
1212. Used/Consignment Furniture Store	$69.50/59.50

PERSONAL SERVICES

Business Guide No.	Reg. Price/Sub. Disc.
1194. Dating Service	$69.50/59.50
1170. Hair Salon, Family	$69.50/59.50
1264. Image Consulting	$69.50/59.50
1274. Nail Salon	$69.50/59.50
1239. Tutoring Service	**$29.50**
1330. Wedding Planning Service	$69.50/59.50

PHOTO-RELATED BUSINESSES

Business Guide No.	Reg. Price/Sub. Disc.
1209. One-Hour Photo Processing Lab	$69.50/59.50
1204. Videotaping Service	$69.50/59.50

PUBLISHING BUSINESSES

Business Guide No.	Reg. Price/Sub. Disc.
1067. Newsletter Publishing	$69.50/59.50

RECREATION & ENTERTAINMENT BUSINESSES

Business Guide No.	Reg. Price/Sub. Disc.
1242. Balloon Delivery Service	$69.50/59.50
1186. Bar/Tavern	$69.50/59.50
1269. Bowling Center	$69.50/59.50
1308. Compact Disc-Only Store	$69.50/59.50
1132. Hobby Shop	$69.50/59.50

**CALL TOLL FREE 1-(800) 421-2300
in California 1-(800) 352-7449**

1342	Mobile DJ	$69.50/59.50
1124	No-Alcohol Bar	$69.50/59.50
1100	Pinball & Electronic Game Arcade	$69.50/59.50
1226	TV & Movie Production	$69.50/59.50
1192	Videocassette Rental Store	$69.50/59.50

RESTAURANTS, SIT-DOWN

Business Guide No. ....Reg. Price/Sub. Disc.

1289	Diner	$69.50/59.50
1279	Restaurant Start-Up	$69.50/59.50
1156	Sandwich Shop/Deli	$69.50/59.50

RETAIL BUSINESSES, MISC.

Business Guide No. ....Reg. Price/Sub. Disc.

1318	Baby Store	$69.50/59.50
1277	Beauty Supply Store	$69.50/59.50
1293	Bookstore, Children's	$69.50/59.50
1331	**Character Merchandise Store**	**$29.50**
1135	Cosmetics Shop	$69.50/59.50
3361	Buying Products From Other Countries	$59.50/49.50
1143	Flower Shop	$69.50/59.50
1144	Framing Shop, Do-It-Yourself	$69.50/59.50
1306	Gift Basket Service	$69.50/59.50 †
1218	Gift, Specialty Store	$69.50/59.50
1323	Kiosks & Cart Business Opportunities	$69.50/59.50
1222	Multilevel Marketing Sales, How to Develop	$69.50/59.50
1316	**Off-Price Retailing**	**$29.50**
1283	Party Goods/Gift Store	$69.50/59.50
1325	Print/Poster Store	$69.50/59.50
1214	Religious-Gift/Book Store	$69.50/59.50
1340	Sock Shops	$69.50/59.50
1337	Silk Plants Shop	$69.50/59.50 †
1322	Sports Memorabilia Store	$69.50/59.50
1117	Used-Book Store	$69.50/59.50
1182	Wedding Shop	$69.50/59.50

SELF-IMPROVEMENT BUSINESSES

Business Guide No. ....Reg. Price/Sub. Disc.

1172	Physical-Fitness Center	$69.50/59.50
1046	Self-Improvement/Insight-Awareness Seminars	$69.50/59.50

SERVICES TO BUSINESS

Business Guide No. ....Reg. Price/Sub. Disc.

1223	Advertising Agency	$69.50/59.50
1292	Advertising, Specialty	$69.50/59.50
1236	Apartment Preparation Service	$69.50/59.50
1317	Business Brokerage	$69.50/59.50
1307	Business Development Center	$69.50/59.50
1207	Collection Agency	$69.50/59.50
2328	Construction Cleanup	$69.50/59.50 ‡
1329	Construction Interior Cleaning, New	$69.50/59.50
1151	Consulting Business	$69.50/59.50
1232	Coupon Mailer Service	$69.50/59.50
1328	Freight Brokerage	$69.50/59.50
1237	Information Broker	$69.50/59.50
1336	Instant Sign Store	$69.50/59.50
1034	Janitorial Service	$69.50/59.50
1098	Liquidator Selling Distressed Merchandise	$69.50/59.50
1332	Mobile Bookkeeping Service	$69.50/59.50
1962	Money Broker	$84.50/74.50
1031	Parking Lot Striping & Maintenance Srvc	$69.50/59.50
1280	Pest Control	$69.50/59.50
1324	Public Relations Agency	$69.50/59.50
1339	Referral Services	$69.50/59.50
1136	Secretarial/Word-Processing Service	$69.50/59.50
1150	Surface Cleaning, Mobile	$69.50/59.50
1148	Telephone-Answering Service	$69.50/59.50
1157	Trucking, Cross-Country	$69.50/59.50
1012	Window-Washing Service	$69.50/59.50

SERVICES TO THE HOME

Business Guide No. ....Reg. Price/Sub. Disc.

1053	Carpet-Cleaning Service	$69.50/59.50
1215	Catering Service	$69.50/59.50
1291	Closet Customizing	$69.50/59.50
1334	Home Inspection Service	$69.50/59.50
1275	**House Sitting/In-Home Care**	**$29.50**
1314	Interior Designer	$69.50/59.50
1105	Kitchen Remodeling	$69.50/59.50
1198	Lawn-Care Service	$69.50/59.50
1343	Mini-Blind Cleaning	$69.50/59.50
1160	Maid Service	$69.50/59.50
1249	Painting, House	$69.50/59.50

CALL TOLL FREE 1-(800) 421-2300
in California 1-(800) 352-7449

1285. Pool Cleaning & Repair	$69.50/59.50
1012. Window-Washing Service	$69.50/59.50

SERVICE BUSINESSES, MISC.

Business Guide No.	Reg. Price/Sub. Disc.
1309. Check Cashing Service	$69.50/59.50
1058. Child-Care Service	$69.50/59.50
1037. Dry-Cleaning Shop	$69.50/59.50
1313. Event Planning Service	$69.50/59.50
1306. Gift Basket Service	$69.50/59.50
1298. Instant Print/Copy Shop	$69.50/59.50
1326. Instant Shoe Repair Shop	**$29.50**
1162. Laundromat	$69.50/59.50
1042. Mini-Storage Facility	$69.50/59.50
1287. Packaging & Shipping Service	$69.50/59.50
1310. Personal Shopping Service	$69.50/59.50
1341. Pet Sitting	$69.50/59.50
1320. Private Investigator	$69.50/59.50
1147. Private Mailbox Service	$69.50/59.50
1335. Senior Day Care	$69.50/59.50
1150. Surface Cleaning, Mobile	$69.50/59.50
1154. Travel Agency	$69.50/59.50
1077. Vinyl-Repair Service	**$29.50**

SPORTS BUSINESSES

Business Guide No.	Reg. Price/Sub. Disc.
1022. Bicycle/Moped Shop	**$29.50**
1286. Sporting-Goods Store	$69.50/59.50
1322. Sports Memorabilia Store	$69.50/59.50

STREET-VENDING BUSINESSES

Business Guide No.	Reg. Price/Sub. Disc.
3360. Sourcebook of Products for Flea Markets	$59.50/49.50
1127. Shrimp Peddling	$64.50/54.50
1299. Vending Businesses	$69.50/59.50

MISCELLANEOUS BUSINESSES

Business Guide No.	Reg. Price/Sub. Disc.
1091. Burglar Alarm Sales/ Installation	$69.50/59.50
2327. Buying Foreclosures	$69.50/59.50 ‡
1227. Government Contracts, How to Obtain	$69.50/59.50
1282. Herb Farming	$69.50/59.50
1222. Multilevel Marketing Sales, How to Develop	$69.50/59.50
1153. Real Estate Company, Flat-Fee	$69.50/59.50
1284. Real Estate, Complete Investment Guide	$69.50/59.50
1071. Seminar Promoting	$69.50/59.50

IMPROVING YOUR BUSINESS ABILITY

Business Guide No.	Reg. Price/Sub. Disc.
3402. Business Plan, Developing A	$59.50/49.50
7205. Calif. Business Start-Up	$64.50/54.50
3370. Complete Government Resource Guide Complete Set	$99.50/89.50
3371. Western Region	$49.50/39.50
3372. Midwestern Region	$49.50/39.50
3373. Southern Region	$49.50/39.50
3374. Eastern Region	$49.50/39.50
1321. Credit Consulting	$69.50/59.50
7000. Incorporation Kits for Any State (Specify State)	$59.50/49.50
1327. Lessons From America's Successful Entrepreneurs	$54.50/44.50
1312. Personal Financial Planner	$84.50/74.50
1111. Promotional Gimmicks	$69.50/59.50
1999. Complete Library of All Business Guides	$5,450/$4,450
1315. SBA Loan Guide	$74.50/64.50
1319. Standard Business Forms for the Entrepreneur	$59.50/49.50

‡ Audio Cassettes Plus Reference Book

† Supplemental Video available

Satisfaction Guaranteed

You have nothing to lose. If you follow the instructions and they do not work for you, return the business guide within 90 days with a simple note, telling us where we went wrong. Yes, return the business guide within 90 days and we'll return the purchase price, less shipping and handling.

Place your order by mail or phone.

To order by phone:
Call TOLL FREE: 1(800)421-2300
CA residents call: 1(800)352-7449

For rush shipments:
Please call our toll free number:
6a.m.-8:30p.m. Monday-Friday
7a.m.-3p.m. Saturday Pacific Coast time.

For customer service or billing inquiries call:
1(800)345-8614
In CA call: (714)261-2325 • 8a.m.-5p.m. • Monday-Friday

To Order by phone: ☎

In order to save you time when ordering, please have the following information ready:

1. Completed order form.
2. Credit card number and expiration date.
3. Customer code number: **9N184**
4. Please note: We do not take C.O.D. orders.

To Order by Mail: ✉

1. Be sure to fill out the order form completely.
2. Please check all your entries for legibility.
3. Please include a home <u>and</u> work phone number in case we have a question about your order.
4. Be sure to include your complete street address for parcel deliveries. U.P.S. will not deliver to P.O. boxes.

CALL TOLL FREE 1-(800)421-2300
in California 1-(800)352-7449

ORDER FORM

Entrepreneur Business Guides

Save up to 20% on Entrepreneur Guides when you subscribe to *Entrepreneur Magazine*

Guide #	Guide Title	Price

California Residents add 6.25% sales tax	
Add $6.75 for shipping and handling	
Add $2.00 shipping and handling for each additional business guide	
Entrepreneur subscription fee	
Canadian orders add $15.50 shipping and handling for first guide, $5.00 for each additional guide	
Total	

Worldwide orders accepted with U.S. funds. Add $35.00 per business guide for shipping. To ensure delivery we mail air parcel post only. Prices subject to change without notice. Allow 3-4 weeks for delivery. **No C.O.D.s.**

SUBSCRIBE NOW!

To qualify for lower prices, see below for information on subscribing to *Entrepreneur Magazine*. If you are already a subscriber, write your subscription number from the label of a recent magazine here: _____

Yes! I want the subscriber discount that comes with my subscription to *Entrepreneur*. I understand I will receive a $10.00 discount on any Entrepreneur guide, **except guides priced at $29.50.** (In Canada add $10 per year. Overseas orders add $20 per year.)

Start my subscription at the basic rate checked:
- ❏ 3 years (save 57% off cover price) $47.97
- ❏ 2 years (save 50% off cover price) $37.97
- ❏ 1 year (save 46% off cover price) $19.97

Payment by:
❏ Check or money order enclosed

Charge my: ❏ VISA   ❏ MasterCard   ❏ Discover   ❏ Am Exp

Credit Card # _____ Expiration Date _____

Sign Here _____ (No orders shipped without exp. date & signature)

Name _____

Address _____

City _____ State _____ Zip _____

May we have your phone # in case we have questions regarding your order?

Work Phone (____) _____ Home Phone (____) _____

Mail to: 2392 Morse Avenue • P.O. Box 19787 • Irvine, CA 92713-9438   **9N184**
Call toll free: 1-(800) 421-2300 • in California 1-(800) 352-7449

CALL TOLL FREE 1-(800) 421-2300
in California 1-(800) 352-7449